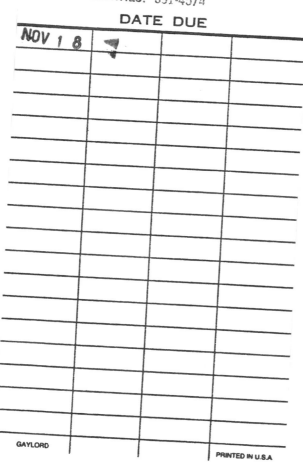

RENEWALS: 691-4574

DATE DUE

NOV 18			
GAYLORD			PRINTED IN U.S.A

Rebel Without a Cause

Rebel Without a Cause... THE HYPNOANALYSIS OF A CRIMINAL PSYCHOPATH

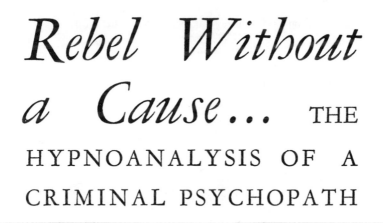

BY
ROBERT M. LINDNER, Ph.D.

INTRODUCTION BY
SHELDON GLUECK, LL.B., Ph.D.
Professor of Criminal Law and Criminology
Law School, Harvard University

AND

ELEANOR T. GLUECK, Ed.D.
Research Criminologist
Law School, Harvard University

GRUNE & STRATTON
NEW YORK
1944

Library of Congress Catalog Card No. SG 44-211

Printed in the United States of America
(E-B)

CONTENTS

INTRODUCTION

Theodore Roosevelt, on his first inspection of prisons, is said to have remarked that those fortresses of steel and stone were built to guard against the escape of but a small percentage of the inmates; and that it is absurd, cruel and wasteful to compel perhaps 80 or 90 per cent of the prison group to suffer the robotizing influences of prison incarceration because of the fear that 10 or 20 per cent might escape.

Among those likely to escape are the most puzzling and recalcitrant criminals, the group known as the "psychopathic personalities" or "constitutional psychopathic inferiors." Studies in various prisons, reformatories and jails usually disclose that this class comprises some 15 to 20 per cent of the inmate population. They bedevil the administration for other prisoners and the directive personnel. They are among the ring-leaders in planning escapades. They resort to assaults upon guards and fellow-prisoners. They are, in a nutshell, the truly dangerous, "hard-boiled," "wise guy" and least reformable offenders.

While the indicia of the psychopathic personality frequently overlap various "borderline" conditions of true psychotic and psychoneurotic groups, the psychopath, as a composite "type," can be distinguished from the person sliding into or clambering out of a "true psychotic" state by the long and tough persistence of his anti-social attitude and behavior and the absence of hallucinations, delusions, manic flight of ideas, confusion, disorientation and other dramatic signs of psychoses.*

Penologists and prison psychiatrists usually content themselves with demanding that psychopaths be "segregated" so that the program for the rest of the inmates may proceed more smoothly. Dr. Robert Lindner, the author of this book, is one of the first prison workers in the world to go beyond such a program of temporary convenience and probe skillfully and with illuminative insight into the psyche of the most recalcitrant among criminals.

Although we are not competent to pass a technical judgment upon the method of "hypnoanalysis," so vividly illustrated in this book (a telescoped psychoanalytic technique employed by the author in analyzing and reconstructing the mental life of a psychopath), we

---

* The psychopathic personality most nearly approaches the "born criminal type" described so minutely by Lombroso.

ix

nevertheless venture to suggest that his work marks a significant milestone on the rough and failure-strewn road of Criminology; for it indicates that it is possible to bridge the crucial gap between the outer and inner life of offenders and trace the intricate process whereby the stuff of environment is selected and "introjected," psychologically masticated and digested, and absorbed into the pre-existing dynamic system of the mind to influence future attitude and propel subsequent behavior.

Long ago, Samuel Butler wisely observed that "a life will be successful or not, according as the power of accomodation is equal or unequal to the strain of fusing and adjusting internal and external changes." It is this delicate yet crucial process that Dr. Lindner has so convincingly delineated. In this respect he has taken a step well ahead of the great majority of contemporary criminologists. Whether attributing major causal force to environmental factors or placing most stress on hereditary disposition, or (as in the case of Lombroso) on hereditary predestination to a life of crime, they fail to describe the subtle and deep-stirring interplay of emotion and experience involved in generating antisocial attitude and behavior.

We do not know whether hypnoanalysis will develop sufficiently to take its place on an equal plane with the now scientifically "respectable," but until recently much-maligned, technique of psychoanalysis. If it does, it will be a great boon in reducing the time and expense required for the exploration of the tangled webs of the psyche and the hygienic reorientation of the personality. Nor do we know whether, in the majority of the cases in which it is applied, it will go beyond diagnostic dissection to permanent reconstruction of the personality. But we cannot help being impressed with the rich potentialities of the technique so graphically described by Dr. Lindner, as an instrument for getting below the surface of much puzzling criminalistic behavior.

Starting as a pioneer scientific experiment subject to the critical scrutiny of other investigators, Dr. Lindner's work will, we hope, stimulate further and more varied experimentation; so that in the years to come, Penology may have the same creative spurt that Psychiatry has only recently experienced through the vitalizing infiltration of Psychoanalysis, the shock therapies, and psychosomatic medicine. Assuredly, any process of diagnosing and treating offenders that is more promising than the almost bankrupt procedures now employed by society is to be given full encouragement.

If hypnoanalysis should be applied more generally in the study and treatment of offenders, it might make an even more significant contribution to the philosophy and techniques of the Criminal Law than to the rehabilitation of numbers of offenders. For it discloses with dramatic clarity the superficiality of an ancient system of symbols and rituals based upon such outworn notions as "guilt," "criminal intent," "knowledge of right and wrong," and the other paraphernalia developed long before the dawn of Biology, Psychiatry and Psychology and but little in advance of primitive law.

The history book of Criminology and Penology is blotted with wreckage of oversimplified conceptions of criminalistic behavior and "cures" for crime. Perhaps Dr. Lindner's work will turn up a brighter page. At all events, he is to be congratulated upon a courageous and ingenious pioneer endeavor.

His book is not intended for the layman. The psychiatrist and psychologist of any school of thought or therapy, the alert judge of a juvenile or adult criminal court, the thoughtful clergyman, the criminologist of inquiring mind, the penologist who conceives his job in higher terms than as keeper of a zoo for human derelicts, and the educator of vision should find this work instructive and provocative. It is especially to be prescribed as sobering medicine for both the physical anthropologist and the sociologist concerned with criminals.

SHELDON AND ELEANOR GLUECK

Cambridge, Mass.
February, 1944

AUTHOR'S PREFACE

This writer's concern both with hypnoanalysis and psychopathic personality goes back at least five years to the time when he was first called upon to learn about—and do something about—psychopaths and psychopathic personality. It was in this effort to understand that peculiar variety of behavior that the first experiments with hypnoanalysis were undertaken. Therefore it is fitting that this puzzling disorder should form the vehicle to expound and illustrate a technique which seems to offer certain advantages in the exploration and treatment of psychogenic and behavior disorders.

In preparing the material for publication, the writer was torn between two desires which apparently exerted almost equal weight. He was anxious to offer for discussion and experiment a psychotherapeutic technique of promise especially at a time when it could be used to such advantage in the armed services and on the home front where the strains of living in a period of chaos are reflected in mental casualties. At the same time, he earnestly desired to present the findings of research with a type of personality disorder that is responsible for much of crime and has broad social and even political implications. If this book does both, it will have realized such intentions.

The dedication acknowledges only a fraction of the author's indebtedness. Many of those persons who worked long and hard to bring to fruition what lies between these covers must remain nameless, although some have borne and bear now identifying numbers. Foremost among those who can be named are Prof. Sheldon Glueck and Dr. Eleanor Glueck, Dr. Bernard Glueck, Dr. Hervey Cleckley, Dr. Milton H. Erickson and Professor Philip L. Harriman—all of whom have been sources of inspiration and encouragement. To the United States Public Health Service which has the vision and daring to encourage research in human behavior is due an obligation that can never be repaid.

Finally, the reader is reminded that all opinions expressed herein are the responsibility of the author alone and do not necessarily reflect the views of the Service to which he is attached.

ROBERT M. LINDNER

Lewisburg, Pa.
January 1944

THE PROBLEM: CRIMINAL PSYCHOPATHY

I

Man has always sought to understand himself and his universe by the simple mechanics of sorting. The nicety of this operation, its precision and incisiveness, its sterility and keenness, is best understood by modern man who, even in his confusion about himself and his destiny, has invented a myriad of categories, rubrics, classification schemes, statistical techniques and pigeonholes to lend order to the chaos about him. This modern proclivity for sorting is nowhere better demonstrated than in those sciences in which man deals with man—psychology, psychiatry, sociology—where with consummate artistry stiffly parading as diagnostics, the species is dissected and labelled, named and branded, tagged and stamped.

Among those categories by which man describes his fellow-man is one that has served as a miscellany for many decades. It is only half-understood and less than half-appreciated. It is a Pandora's box, brimful with the makings for a malignant social and political scourge. The name of this category is *psychopathic personality*. Its half-understood nature, evidenced by the multitude of terms by which it has been and is called—constitutional psychopathic inferiority, moral imbecility, semantic dementia, moral insanity, sociopathy, anethopathy, moral mania, egopathy, tropopathy, etc.—is further attested to by the contradictory multiplicity of its signs and symptoms. All those characteristics which, by any count, may be considered the negative of qualities suitable for current civilized communal living, have at one time or another been assigned to the individual called 'psychopath.' And, in truth, there is no other way in which he can be described except by reference to the social order in which he happens to exist. Those searchers of the soul—psychiatrists and psychologists—have wasted much fine paper in vain attempts to attach a single group of signs to the disorder, unfortunately neglecting to extend their scientific objectivity to the proposition that psychopathic behavior is relative to the culture in which it flourishes and can be measured by no other rule than that of the prevailing ethic and morality. So in a society where total abstinence is mandatory— as among the Brahmins of India—a sign of psychopathy would be inebriation: and, among the prostitute priestesses of Astarte, the persistent continence of a beauteous devotee consecrated to the distribution of erotic favors would indicate a psychopathic trend. In short, psychopathy is a disorder of behavior which affects the relationship of an individual to the social setting.

Symptomatologically, then, the description of psychopathy derives from the consideration of the culture in which it appears and to which it is relative. Considered in this light, the psychopath, like Johnstone's rogue-elephant, is a rebel, a religious dis-obeyer of prevailing codes and standards. Moreover, clinical experience with such individuals makes it appear that the psychopath is a rebel without a cause, an agitator without a slogan, a revolutionary without a program: in other words, his rebelliousness is aimed to achieve goals satisfactory to himself alone; he is incapable of exertions for the sake of others. All his efforts, hidden under no matter what guise, represent investments designed to satisfy his immediate wishes and desires.

Now the wish for immediate satisfaction is an infantile characteristic. Unlike more or less matured adults, the child cannot wait upon suitable circumstances for the fulfillment of its needs. Where the adult can postpone luncheon for a few hours, the infant expresses hunger-frustration by crying or other perhaps more aggressive techniques. In the early stages of development, when a need of the organism is apprehended it is followed instantly by the type of behavior expressive of the need. The psychopath, like the child, cannot delay the pleasures of gratification; and this trait is one of his underlying, universal characteristics. He cannot wait upon erotic gratification which convention demands should be preceded by the chase before the kill: he must rape. He cannot wait upon the development of prestige in society: his egoistic ambitions lead him to leap into headlines by daring performances. Like a red thread the predominance of this mechanism for immediate satisfaction runs through the history of every psychopath. It explains not only his behavior but also the violent nature of his acts.

Beyond the wish for instantaneous gratification, psychopathic behavior may be compared with infancy in other ways. As a matter of fact, psychopathy is, in essence, a prolongation of infantile patterns and habits into the stage of physiological adultism. The random behavior betrayed in typically psychopathic nomadism, the inability to marshal the requisite determination for the achievement of specific goals of a socially acceptable order—these reflect to a startling degree the loose, undetermined, easily-detoured and almost purposeless conduct of the very young child.

One of the foundation-stones of living rests upon the ability of the psychologically balanced adult to point his behavior toward an object or event and then to attain to this 'goal' by regulated, planned, orderly, logical procedures. No matter what the attractions on display in the peep-shows off the midway; no matter what the barriers to be side-stepped, a sequential, sometimes unclear but always relatively pertinent path marks the average adult's progress toward an accepted goal. Some investigators have, indeed, given this phenomenon prominence in the hierarchy of psychological activities. The fact that the dynamics are often interfered with by influences not under the control of the performing organism, or that the goal changes and surrogates are found to be equally acceptable, alters not one whit the importance of this deterministic attribute of adult life. Actually, this peculiar glue-like perseveration is one of the most amazing of all human capabilities. Into its functional channel flow the streams of memory and thinking, of- anticipating and doing. Is it no less remarkable because it is so common that, when I have a letter to mail, I may stop to chat with friends on the way to the post-office, notice an interesting bill-board and decide to attend the evening's performance, purchase a newspaper and discuss the weather with the newsvendor, window-shop, and then all unconcernedly and without effort deposit my letter in the post-box on my way home? But with the psychopath as with the infant, determined progress toward a goal—unless it is a selfish one capable of immediate realization by a sharply accented spurt of activity—, the dynamic binding together of actional strands, is lacking. As a consequence he is characteristically aimless, choosing ambitions only within the range of the horizon or impossible of attainment, assuming one task merely to put it aside for another, mistaking each attractive by-path for the promised land. He does not develop skills suited to the farm or office or factory although he may, by nature, be endowed amply with manipulative abilities. In this, again, there is a strong suggestion of the child. Like the play-pattern of the very young, he shows an intensiveness, even a brilliance, at the outset of work; but the performance rapidly falls apart into a fitful type of behavior; and what was once interesting and fascinating now disintegrates into repetitious drabness. The limen of satiety is low with the psychopath as with the playing child, and boredom follows rapidly after but a few possibilities of the task or job have been exhausted. A perpetual need for the renewal of energy-outlets is a hall-mark of the disorder.

It follows naturally that those goals which are realized by the psychopath—if they are not such as are directed upon the immediate satisfaction of infantile needs—are initially anti-social in the sense that 'normal' objectives, requiring as they do the preliminaries demanded by conventional community life, *i.e.* gradualness, persever-ation, and the flavoring of increasing anticipation, cannot be abided because they must so long be prepared for and awaited. The psycho-path, however, must live in a world and in a society where those very qualities are held as desirable virtues. For this reason the common consequence is frustration, sharply apprehended and deeply nourished; so that the psychopathic way of life is characterized by its effects— aggressive behavior, the expression and actional counterpart of a belligerent social attitude, the forceful surmounting of frustration-provoking barriers by acts of voluntary wilfulness, as well as by techniques of escape and avoidance the exercise of which removes the psychopath from the frustrating situation. He becomes, then, a wanderer and a nomad, always frantically searching out an avenue of escape: or, if he cannot so easily manipulate his physical presence to quit the scene of his frustration, he resorts to those psychological highways frequently bordering on, if not actually, madness—patho-logical lying, ideas of reference, delusional systematization of thought into grandiose or persecutory patterns. Where any variety of escape is not ready to hand, aggressiveness remains the keynote, providing as it does not only relief from and an outlet for frustration, but an ever-renewing source of infantile sadistic satisfaction.

Coexistent with the patterning already described is a variety of intelligence that, at least to this writer, seems both unique and specific for psychopathy. In the literature on the subject frequent mention is made of the 'high' intelligence of psychopaths. Sometimes these statements are based on evidence from supposedly dependable psycho-metric examinations; sometimes they rest with the casual observations of clinicians. However derived, these notions are misleading or at least insufficient to serve either as diagnostic aids or explanatory propositions. In the first place, our present day concept of intelligence is, at best, ill-defined and crudely instrumented: in the second place, there is no logic in ascribing symptomatic significance to such an all-inclusive and panoramic item.

So far as intelligence *per se* is concerned, however, what is outstanding about psychopathy is not its arithmetic proportions but its peculiar variety and design. The frozen statistics, accumulated ream upon ream in endless filing cabinets, reflect not at all the particular features of the psychopathic intelligence; and numbers, for all their imposing array in graphs supplemented by mathematical hieroglyphs, are unsuited to its portrayal.

The intelligence of the psychopath can be described only adjectivally and in terms of the whole personality. Perfectly adapted to his needs in the same way as protective coloring is suited to the preservation of the life of an animal, all those psychological functions (thinking, understanding, imagining, remembering, etc.) which are held to be components of 'intelligence' have in the psychopath superimposed on them an aura of shrewdness and secretive cunning, of calculating canniness. These elements not only serve psychopathic ends but effectively distort and divert all known measuring instruments, the rigid designs of which prevent their divinatory use with such individuals.

In the widely accepted sense it is held to be a social as well as a scientific truism that intelligence acts generally in the manner of a regulatory device for action, as a 'brake' upon behavior, as a guide-rule for adjustment. The psychopath, literally an excommunicant in the matter of socially acceptable goals, and fettered with this specialized and peculiar quality of intelligence, cannot avail himself of the restraining tools of so-called normal living. Consequently all his activities, in addition to the other psychopathic trade-marks they bear, are restraint-free, sometimes strikingly bizarre, always unappreciative of consequences. For this reason, even when absolute measurements disclose a 'high' intelligence, so far as its applicability to the routine tasks of life and the special activities of the moment are concerned, its function as mediator and regulator is absent.

A further striking feature of the intelligence of the psychopath, and one which appears only after long-time acquaintance with such individuals, is concerned with the amazing excess-cargo of uncoordinated and useless information they possess. Frequently one is misled by their typically encyclopaedic range into considering them persons of high intellect, even of culture. Penetration with time, however, discloses that like the veneer of mahogany applied to inferior wood, this mass of 'knowledge' is superficial and undigested; that it is free-floating, lacking the requisite elements of cohesiveness and relativity. The design of psychometric examinations is unsuited to plumb such depths.

Much of the literature on the disorder so unfortunately called psychopathic state or personality treats of the immaturity of such individuals in the sexual sphere. It is undeniable that the universal sexual aims regarded as normal have little place in their style of life. Where there is a sympathetic attachment toward another human it is frequently homoerotic or perverse in some other sense. It is, as well, neither lasting nor firmly set upon a community of desires. Finally, it is always self-aggrandizing. This fact has been ascribed to various conditions of psychopathic life. Basically, it would appear to be initiated and maintained as a result of the fixation of sexuality (libido) at an infantile level of development: the overlay of convention and its rigid rules and commands are as yet unapprehended, and the dynamic concentration is upon the self as the sole recipient of all kinds of gratification. It is a thesis of the present work that the psychopath has never got beyond the pre-genital level of sexual development to the stage of object-love; that the socialized mode of sex, the reaching out and sharing, is wholly absent. As will be shown in a later section, the mechanics involved are analytic: precipitation by environmental factors causing an abrupt cessation of psychosexual development *before* the successful resolution of the Oedipus situation. The fixation of libido or sexual energy at or before the genital level, coupled with the need for instant satisfaction, leads to the chaos and immaturity of the psychopath's sexual life. It accounts for his numerous offenses of bastardy and fornication wherein the partner, haphazardly chosen, is immediately deserted, and for the primitive and frequently violent methods by which his ends are sought.

That the psychopathic super-ego is weak has been mentioned by authors who have regarded such a statement as self-explanatory.

They have, however, failed to set forth the reasons for this enfeeble-
ment of the mechanism which includes such precepts as authority and
morality, and which holds the organism within traditional bounds.
While a deficiency in the deterministic aspect of functioning, an intelligence of a peculiar quality, a fixation of libido at an early stage and
other factors account for the style of life of psychopaths, yet our
explanation would be inadequate were we to disregard the uncom-
promising fact of super-ego stunting.   There seems to be little doubt
that the special features of psychopathic behavior derive from a
profound hatred of the father, analytically determined by way of the
inadequate resolution of the Oedipus conflict and strengthened
through fears of castration.   Now since the father (or his surrogate)
is the channel through which society—construed in its broadest sense
and including all precepts, commands and conditions for satisfactory
social living—is introjected, and since the father is hated and resented,
the super-ego is correspondingly under-developed.   If, as Devereux
has held, the formula Father = Society should be reversed as Society
= Father (or whoever it is who interferes with the child's energetic
attempts to obtain the attention and affection of the mother), the
end-result, the effect upon the development of a satisfactory social
attitude, is unaltered.   Allers' *Wille zur Gemeinschaft*, (hopelessly
translated to "will to community") if it could be freed from its
mystical implications, would be a highly useful explanatory concept,
based as it is upon the notion that in the course of development this
'feel' for communal living is dwarfed (or missing) and the psychopath
subsequently maintains his life on a zoological plane which expresses
his complete independence of social demands.   It may well be that
somewhere in all this speculation the differential factor among the
patterns of psychopathy, psychoneurosis and psychosis is to be found.
Perhaps here is also to be found the reason why the psychopath shows,
as Cleckley suggests, a complete semantic incomprehension of the
rights of others, which is one of the most important features in the
psychopathic syndrome. Psychopaths invariably show a naive
inability to understand or appreciate that other individuals as well
have rights: they also are inaccessible to and intolerant of the demands
and pleas of the community, scornful of communal enterprise and
spirit, suspicious of the motives of community-minded people or their
representatives in public service.   That the super-ego—for it is to
this term all other concepts and suggestions resolve—is stunted and

not merely crippled in certain directional aspects, is shown by the psychopath's *unselected exploitation of everyone and everything*. Just like the infant the psychopath will trade upon the good-will and sympathy of all without distinction, without plan, system, program or choice. He victimizes and exploits randomly and not for profit but instant gratification, his aggressiveness pointed at society-as-a-whole, while he is patently indifferent to individuals. So with a labile, unformed, literally sickly superego; and with a libidinous component fixed at a stage of immaturity, the constraint and caution so necessary for freedom from conflict is missing; and the rampant, unreined conduct typical of psychopathy results.

Modern analytic theory predicates criminality and all other activities of an aggressive or debasing order upon the prepotency of the *Death Instinct*, which is believed to exert an influence sufficient to catapult an individual toward self-destruction. It has become fashionable for our topic to be considered in this light: the psychopath is thought by some to suffer from the result of the ascendancy of death desires (Thanatos, Fatum) over his instincts to live (Eros). This explanation is eminently facile, appealing especially to those who are metaphysically disposed. But in the psychopath we are presented with the curious fact of his intense egoism as the natural outgrowth of a powerful ego-component which, in collusion with energetic and primitive libido demands, avidly engorges experience for selfish ends. How the 'Death Instinct' could operate in the face of such performing is unclear to this writer. Cleckley has pointed out that no psychopath ever commits suicide. In an Adlerian sense it is of course possible to see in this egoism an over-compensated denial of forceful impulsions to die; but the present writer can find no evidence to support this view, although he readily cedes to the dialectical notion of opposition in all natural processes. He does, however, recognise in psychopathic behavior the expression of the need for punishment, for atonement, for expiation of guilt, of which the ultimate consequence may well be death.

That the psychopath is burdened with guilt and literally seeks punishment has been observed by the author in countless cases. The clue to this strange situation lies, as one would suspect, in the Oedipus situation. Deprived of an avenue to satisfactory post-Oedipal adjustment and continuously beset by consequent incest and parricidal phantasies, the emergent guilt can be assuaged only through expiation. "I have sinned against my father and I must be punished" is the unverbalized theme of psychopathic conduct: and for this reason they very often commit crimes free from acquisitional motives, marry prostitutes or, in the case of women, apportion their charms occupationally in an attempt at self-castigation. That such activities constitute a species of 'neurotic gain' is also to be considered. The fact of punishment sought, received and accepted does not complete the tale: there is in addition a narcissistic 'yield' which derives directly from the punitive act and mediates the original need. This is naturally on a subliminal level of apprehension, unreportable directly but always noticeable.

II

No accounting of the psychopathic syndrome—or for that matter any other facet of psychopathology—can be considered even relatively complete if it confines itself solely to the precipitating mechanisms. Man is a creature united in all respects; his organism psychologically and physiologically interdependent. He is a being constantly modified; a creature of the predisposing, unalterable facts of heredity and endowment, and the moderating, sometimes traumatic precipitating experiences of a social environment viewed in its broadest sense. Behavior as we know it on Market Street or as we view it microscopically in the clinician's office is the mathematical (possibly geometrical) resultant of these precipitants and predisposants—the hammer of environment shaping the individual against the anvil of heredity. The factors already outlined are conceived of by the author as precipitants, as crucial and dramatic events effecting changes in the organism. Such changes, however, must produce the psychopathic personality only when they occur in an organism already prepared or predisposed for the psychopathic role. They act very much as catalytic agents in the chemist's experiments.

The paucity of work on the physiology and biology of the psychopath is appalling. It would seem that in all but a few instances researchers have thrown up their hands; and yet there is scarcely another investigative field that is so important when it is considered that the social ravishment directly attributable to psychopathy staggers imagination.

We can, at present, only speculate as to the nature of the substructure of psychopathy. Such speculation derives from the tentative proposals of latter-day research. The fact that the behavior of the psychopath appears to be a type of reaction that expresses itself through primitive responses awakens suspicion of malfunctioning in the higher cortical regions which are presumed to exercise restraint and control over those lower 'centers' through which basic drives and motives are mediated. It is not too far-fetched to suggest that since these higher centers are phylogenetically more recent, a specific *anlage* of psychopathy may be a structurally defective brain. Certainly the empirical evidence is sufficient; psychopaths behave in the restraint-free manner clinically described as lacking in judgment; they are swayed by few considerations other than the immediate satisfaction of infantile wishes and whims of the moment; their 'sense' of community responsibility is absent, and they lack such inhibitions as more social individuals express.

While autopsy findings have not yet indicated a quantitative difference between the neural structuralization of such persons and individuals of different personality organization, there are some grounds for suspicion that qualitatively (especially from the side of function) differences exist. Silverman has shown that the 'brain-wave' patterning of criminal psychopaths is recognizably of a different order than similar tracings from other groups. At the same time the striking resemblance of psychopathic behavior manifestations to the sudden, marked, crucial and permanent defects of character and temperament which follow upon such diseases as some of the encephalitides, epilepsies, head injuries, choreas and brain lesions of various kinds bespeak neuroanatomical aberrance of function or organization.

The responses obtained from the randomly-selected adult when his great bodily systems, *i.e.* respiratory, circulatory, etc. are tapped and measured, are rhythmical and repetitious, following a circumscribed pattern that is easily detected. The pattern from the psychopath—as recent research has shown—is different and (if the former is conveniently accepted as the normative) arrhythmic. This arrhythmicity, then, is characteristic of the psychopath in the physiological as well as the psychological sphere, and lends physical substance to the hitherto meaningless concept of 'instability.' Since these bodily processes accompany, support and presumably govern psychological activities, it is conceivable that psychopathic behavior is maintained by this aberrant variety of functioning once it has been evoked by analytic precipitants.

Another provocative research conclusion refers to the more sensitive organization of physiological preparatory devices for action which the psychopath seems to possess.   In a word, he appears to be more *delicately-poised* than his fellows; and he is provided with a curious animal ability to marshal support for hair-trigger movement.   This physiological finding as it appears in studies of emotion causes consideration of the challenging proposition that anticipatory functioning is more highly developed among psychopaths than other individuals; a statement made more tenable when one recalls that the earliest psychological activity of man is somatic expectancy, the reaching forward of the infant to the next stage in the digestive cycle.   That this should persist into adult life; that it should appear in a measurable group of organic processes, lends testimony to the view of psychopathy as a prolongation of infantile habits and patterns.

Some of the symptoms of psychopathic personality appear to succumb to a physiological explanation.   Much of the mystery of the psychopathic reaction, especially of its eruptive, episodic character, is explicable by resort to an hypothesis based upon Cannon's notion of *homeostasis*, a cornerstone of modern physiology.   It may well be that the protest, aggression and hostility of the psychopath are merely homeostatic adjustments operating to restore a disturbed organismic balance.   In other words, it is quite likely that the overt destructiveness of the psychopath is designed to fulfill a need for return to that state of dynamic equilibrium which characterizes the normal condition of man.   The titanic internecine strife between analytically determined drives or needs and social or superego prohibitions perhaps engenders an amount of tension beyond the bounds of tolerance, to the point where unless it is relieved the organism is threatened with disintegration and destruction.   So, in order to restore a balance and achieve a relative quiescence, the personal or social aggression is released with such explosive force that it expresses itself as an attack, a burglary, a murder.

It is within the realm of possibility that the intention of the overt psychopathic symptom, as we see it on the ward, in the street, the courtroom or the consulting room is to relieve the tension produced by underlying conflicts and restore the internal balance. If such is the case, some of the specific signs of the disorder no longer need puzzle us. As an instance, it has been noted that the emotional response of the psychopath to his depredations or other acts is lacking; and this (it follows) is to be expected since a state of dynamic equilibrium, of inner physiological and psychological peace, has been obtained through the release which produced the aggression, the asociality. Furthermore, if the homeostatic interpretation of the disorder is sufficient to the case we may have hold of a reason for diagnostic distinction between psychopathy and other conditions. For example, when the drainage is incomplete and inadequate, leaving a residue of tension and distress, guilt and remorse arise to form the symptoms manifest as in neuroses.

III

We have so far sketched the individual precipitating mechanisms which touch off the psychopathic personality patterning; and we have touched upon the possible predisposants of the condition. Since, however, behavior does not take place in a vacuum nor is it ever independent of the peculiar setting against which it is staged, we have yet to remark concerning the social milieu which acts to awaken latent psychopathy in the same manner as any one or group of psychological factors already discussed.

It is a thoroughly unoriginal contention of the writer that modern society provides amply for those conditions which make for traumatization of the personality along the specific lines which lead to the evolution of the psychopathic type. These conditions flourish, for the most part, in cities or densely-populated areas resembling cities where personal and familial privacy (among other factors) are absent, and where infancy and early childhood are more than normally hazardous periods. They do not have to be stressed here, since only the conveniently deaf have failed to hear the sociologist's condemnation of the manner in which we permit a broad segment of our population to live, and the psychologist's monotonous belaboring of the unwholesome effects of pernicious environmental factors.

Together with the abomination of unplanned cities and mushroom industrial centers, modern American society errs in failing to provide the kind of substitute for self-expression which in other times and in other cultures drained off a considerable portion of behavior opposed to the best interests of the most people and helped combat the sociogenic psychopathic virus.

Concentration in cities coincident with the disappearance of frontiers—both physical and psychological—is the responsible social factor in the genesis of the psychopathic pattern. Behaviorally regarded, the psychopath's performance is of the frontier type.

Now it is both a psychological and sociological fact amply demonstrated in literature and history that frontiers and outposts are scenes of behavior that is typically unsocial and psychopathic. Our own West has won world renown as the theatre of crime and vice, outlawry and drunkenness, and every other type of conduct opposed to the standards of the rest of the country. There seems, in fact, to be a variety of community activity which is best expressed by the word 'centrifugal,' in which the community functions as a giant centrifuge in throwing off behavior contrary to the best interests of the group. It is to be noted in the saga of every great city how, in the early life of a community, the habitation of vice and crime is invariably established on the outskirts and borders. The modern roadhouse is an apt illustration of this principle. After a time the expanding city encloses these places and encysts the evil within itself. Frontiers and borders are, however, admirably suited to the working off of compulsive antisocial behavior; they sparkle with the glitter of personal freedom; the checks and reins of the community are absent and there are no limits either in a physical or in a psychological sense. So when the geography of a nation or a community or even a civilization becomes fixed, behavior of an unsocial variety which has been flung there by centrifugal action, now works itself out in a harmful manner in the culture itself. Especially is this true where the psychological horizon is similarly limited by economic underprivilege, lack of educational opportunities, the immediacy of poignant social contrasts and repetitious occupational activity; in a word, by social disinheritance.

IV

It seems to this writer that it is of paramount importance that we know more about psychopathic personalities than the tentative conclusions we have thus far outlined. While the present status of psychopathy is that of an irritant to the clinician (who despairs of doing anything more than diagnosing a case), a local annoyance to prison and hospital officials, a source of problems to police and service officers, and a slough of shame and hopelessness to sorely-tried parents and relatives, the essence of the problem of psychopathy is that it represents a social and even political problem of the first magnitude. It is the contention of this investigator that psychopathy is more wide-spread today than ever before in the history of our civilization; that it is assuming more and more the proportions of a plague; that it is today ravishing the world with far greater ill effect than the most malignant of organic diseases; that it represents a terrible force whose destructive potentialities are criminally underestimated.

That the incidence of psychopathy is increasing is evident not from the neat statistical studies originating in the basement laboratories of our universities or the brightly-lighted halls of government bureaus but from a glance at the current world situation.   The last few years have witnessed the triumphal heavy-booted march of psychopathy not only over an entire continent but over every painfully won tenet of what we call our civilization.   And as when a stone is cast on still waters, the mononuclear psychopathic center has communicated its convulsive impulses outwardly to awaken latent psychopathy many times removed from the volcanic core.

This is the menace of psychopathy: The psychopath is not only a criminal; he is the embryonic Storm-Trooper; he is the disinherited, betrayed antagonist whose aggressions can be mobilized on the instant at which the properly-aimed and frustration-evoking formula is communicated by that Leader under whose tinseled aegis license becomes law, secret and primitive desires become virtuous ambitions readily attained, and compulsive behavior formerly deemed punishable becomes the order of the day.

History has assigned to this country and her allies the task of cleansing civilization of the predatory creature whose typical history is presented in this volume.   Psychological science has provided us with an instrument to study him closely and at first hand; to examine him thoroughly as we would a virulent bacillus; to dissect him and obtain his measure; perhaps even—assisted by those great social forces which are beginning to clear the slime and muck of under-privilege and economic expediency—to make of him a good citizen in a new world . . .

THE METHOD: HYPNOANALYSIS

I

Since the cavalier abandonment of cathartic hypnosis by the founding fathers of psychoanalysis instituted a tradition of disrepute for hypnosis in particular and suggestive therapy in general, psychiatrists and psychologists have been wary of identifying themselves with treatment procedures reminiscent of these methods. However, informal use has undoubtedly been made of the investigative and therapeutic technique herein to be described and illustrated as *hypnoanalysis*. In no place and at no time, though, has it been subjected to careful scrutiny as a respectable procedure warranting the serious and unprejudiced consideration of clinicians engaged in the study and treatment of mental or behavior disorders.

The variety of hypnoanalysis to be dealt with in the following discussion literally grew under the hand of the writer from the first tentative experiments in 1939 through to what at this writing is a respectable list of differing diagnostic categories. At no time did it spring forth full-blown and armored: its growth was independent, painful; its application cautious and, in truth, hesitant. It is as yet in a formative stage, and not all of its principles and precepts can be expounded. But, so far as it has matured in practice, it would seem to be at least a technique that merits, if nothing more, the critical appraisal of co-practitioners.

Hypnoanalysis is primarily an instrument, a method, a way of approach to the riddles of behavior posed by maladjustment, crime and psychopathology. As its name proclaims, it is a technique compounded of psychoanalysis and hypnosis. From psychoanalysis it has extracted certain procedural modes and the interpretative core. In return it acts to validate beyond question the data of analysis and to provide a fixative means for the therapy without which analysis is no more than an exercise in diagnosis. From hypnosis it has drawn a probe for penetration into the darkest recesses of human performing. In return it increases the scope and function of an ancient and honorable art, removes from it the stigmata of mystery, charlatanry and ill-fame, and recalls it from the limbo where it was so hastily consigned at the turn of the present century. But while it acknowledges a sizable debt to both techniques, the very fact that it should have been necessary to call hypnoanalysis into existence is a proof of the inadequacy of each.

Suggestive or hypnotic therapy has been concerned almost solely with the alleviation of *symptoms*. Very likely this has been because its practice was confined almost exclusively to physicians, who notoriously subscribe to a faith that immediate 'relief' is everything. A course of hypnosis aimed specifically at amelioration may for a time obviate pain or discomfort. Symptoms disappear; the organism resumes its accustomed pattern of functioning. But the tragedy is that symptoms return, often under a different guise. In the enthusiasm for 'cure' the obligation to discover and deal with *causes* has been studiously and conveniently ignored by all except such flinty pioneers as Janet and the French school, and in this country Erickson and Kubie as well as various assorted daring souls at Bellevue and in Topeka.

Beyond this, hypnosis has been the victim of a series of malicious fictions that do not bear the light of investigation, yet have been propagated in the manner of tribal taboos on the basis of pontifical injunctions from the higher councils of Vienna, New York, Chicago and Boston. We shall weigh some of the evidence later.

As for psychoanalysis, it stands indicted for what Devereux has rightly called its "ritualistic" character; its insistence upon punctilious cant and unrelaxed ceremony. From it has arisen a virtual mandarinism that appears to be not only inflexible but also opposed to the public interest. The activities of psychoanalysts have by and large remained hidden from the public eye, since the bulk of humanity is excluded from the quiet of the analytic chamber; and consequently there has been developed about it and its devotees a lush, effete, decadent, even (in the public mind) an obscene repute. Thus its virility, the essential wholesomeness idealized for it by its founders, has been denied it by its own champions. And beyond its economic inexpediency and cultism of orthodoxy, its endlessness in point of time constitutes a barrier to practicability, especially when it is compared by the laity with the relative swiftness of modern medical practice.

The relinquishment of hypnosis as an agent in analysis was encouraged by the early analysts. They urged, in the first place, that its use was limited since (they claimed) not all patients could be hypnotized. Now it seems that this criticism is not only unjustified but, in a sense, ludicrous when it originates with practitioners of a method which is confined to individuals under a certain age, possessed of a certain level of intelligence and generally obliged to fulfill other conditions. And what is more, it is not conclusive that all individuals cannot enter the hypnotic state. While this writer has encountered persons whom he could not immediately hypnotize, he has found that failure was usually due to (1) the fact that in the eyes of his subject he lacked prestige; or (2) that he too soon abandoned his efforts. It is now his belief that there is no other reason for the inability of some persons to enter a hypnotic trance than the fact that in such cases the transference—depending as it does upon the neat balance of prestige, flow of energy toward the analyst and the analyst's own attitude—is inadequate. Where the transference is complete and adequate, hypnosis can be accomplished. Positive transference in a very real sense is actually the end-product of disintegrated resistance. Hypnoanalysis offers a means to the dissolution of the resistance normally present when treatment begins, and for the continual control of the transference as treatment proceeds. Moreover, with such a method Stekel's objection that the patient "is never freed from the transference" is meaningless, since its dissipation becomes, through hypnosis, a relatively simple matter.

In the past hypnosis was likewise regarded unfavorably since it was said that although a specific symptom could be 'cured' through the emotional catharsis during the trance, the 'cure' was temporary. Anna Freud has even stated that in hypnosis the ego could take no part in the therapeutic procedure, implying that the patient was robbed of the cathartic working-through of the precipitating events. But the hypnoanalytic method—as will be explained and demonstrated subsequently—guarantees the full effect of the cathartic action by providing not only that the emotion these events evoke *sich auswirken* in the trance state but in the waking state as well. It is a sort of 'double-action,' certifying the reliability and validity of what transpires, enabling the clinician to measure accurately the depth and color of feeling involved and, above all, is one in which the *whole* personality shares. The further objection to hypnosis on the score that it influences those 'unconscious' factors which have been striving for expression and does not effect the prohibiting 'forces' responsible for their exclusion is correspondingly obviated by the peculiar hypnoanalytic concern with resistances and their dynamic treatment.

Through the use of hypnoanalysis the period of treatment for most if not all psychopathological conditions can be shortened effectively without loss to the patient, for the cathartic and abreactive processes are just as complete and the therapeutic yield as rich as that claimed for any other given psychotherapeutic tool. In this respect the method may be viewed as an heroic one, assaulting the organism somewhat in the manner of metrazol or electric-shock therapy, literally tearing aside the veil. Hypnoanalysis should last no more than three or four months, the final month being devoted to reorientation, exposition and re-education. With Stekel, the writer holds that the orthodox analysts betray a lack of psychological acumen in their naive dependence upon patients to disclose their secrets voluntarily. It is always to be reckoned with that there is in any psychological condition of mal- or dysfunction a gain to the patient that bids him cling to his symptoms or ways of behavior. It is in the establishment of satisfactory transference relationships, in the overcoming of resistances and natural reluctances and, finally, in the attempt to promote relinquishment of these "rewards-of-illness" that time is consumed in the passive way of analysis. With hypnoanalysis it is as if surgical removal of such barriers and hazards has been accomplished. Moreover, each disclosure is subject to test; and so the presence of screen-memories which so frequently blur and obscure true but latent memories of utmost importance—and so often lead astray—do not interfere with the progress of the analysis.

The peculiar conditions of hypnoanalysis make insignificant the question regarding the validity of hypnotic data, since the core of the method is a perpetual checking of material obtained in both the waking and the hypnoid states. Because of this, the position that the hypnotic reaction is an hysterical one is demonstrably untenable.

II

Hypnoanalysis functions both as a research and a therapeutic instrument. In its investigative capacity it operates to pierce to the psychic substrata in the most direct fashion and thence to raise to the level of awareness the repressed, often emotionally surcharged material. It seeks also to validate beyond doubt the contents of that segment of 'consciousness' which is not immediately available to ordinary recall. As a therapeutic tool it provides for the development of self-knowledge based upon a reconstructed approach to individual history. It further aids in the implantation of healthy attitudes and approaches to life by imbedding firmly, as novel accretions to the personality, the analytic interpretations arrived at through the mutual efforts of analyst and patient.

A hypnoanalytic course of investigation or therapy is initiated by training in hypnosis. The writer's method is first to instruct patients or subjects in the technique of achieving the trance state with a minimum of effort on the part of either participant. In a series of daily sessions wherein the aim is to enable a rapid passage from the waking state to sleep, patients are familiarized with hypnosis and its functions. The usual response—no matter what the condition of the patient or his problem—is a rapid mobilization of all those factors which comprehend a workable and manipulable transference. By the end of this preliminary period (to which no more than a week is given) that unique relationship is in a state of readiness for exploitation.

The close of the first week then finds the patient adept at passing confidently from a waking to a sleeping state almost on the merest suggestion of the clinician. If progress has not been unusually difficult during this time, the trance state will also have been explored and examined both for any special characteristics it may contain as such, or for any sequelae to which it might lead. In a statistically insignificant number of cases special reaction types to trance may be encountered which will enforce a slightly different approach; just as it will be necessary for alternate methods of inducing hypnosis to be utilized from time to time. (In this connection a case is recalled wherein traces of multiple personality were discovered during exploration of the trance. This caused a redirection and re-emphasis to be given to the entire problem.) So far as exceptional sequelae to trance are concerned, none have been observed in the experience of this reporter; but the caution would seem to be in order in view of the paucity of knowledge on this score.

Energy should also be devoted to 'depth levels' of trance and to the problem of post-hypnotic suggestion. Testing for depth of trance is simple but most important. As will be shown, in distinguishing real from screen memories it is often necessary to achieve a decisive penetration (viewing the trance state as a vertical phenomenon) through progressive removal of the patient's 'conscious' control over his utterances. Finally, the "training-in-hypnosis" period should not be abandoned until it has been established that post-hypnotic suggestions are carried through in a fashion that leaves no doubt of the mastery of the situation by the operator. It is necessary that amnesia and recall be emphasized in this connection. Patients should be brought to the point where, on the suggestion of the clinician, they are able either to recall accurately or forget completely what has transpired during a session.

The second phase of the work deals with recall under hypnosis. The aim is to develop the facility of a patient in reverting (Cf. below) to earlier times and places, at the same time presenting them for consideration in as explicit a fashion as possible.

It is best that encouragement in recall under hypnosis proceed cautiously and by easy stages. Experience shows that the method of choice is one in which the patient is requested to remember and report events of the instant day, then of immediately preceding days, finally of preceding weeks. Often this requires some 'scene-setting' on the part of the hypnoanalyst: and he should be prepared for such tasks by an acquaintance with at least the formal history of the patient.

Toward the close of the second week a patient or subject should possess a number of accomplishments which are prerequisites for successful therapy or research. He should be able to enter a deep trance almost as soon as he is instructed to do so; he should be able to revert memorially to earlier periods of his life: he should be able to verbalize while in the trance state: he should be able to carry out suggestions for post-hypnotic behavior especially as these apply to recall or amnesia. By this time, moreover, he will have entered into a reciprocal rapport with the hypnoanalyst that will bear fruit in the work on which they will presently become engaged.

During the approximately two weeks of preparation, that which led the patient to seek out the clinician is not touched upon formally. It has been found that one runs the danger of precipitating a change in a patient's attitude if, during the training phases, symptoms, complaints, characterological problems or conflicts are discussed. He is likely to feel—with some justification—that his difficulties are not being given the attention they deserve. In general, it is feasible either to explain or to state categorically that the initial period of treatment is to be devoted solely to mastering a special technique.

Following the sessions devoted to training, the actual hypnoanalysis is entered upon. As in other forms of psychotherapy, the patient is seen daily. He is instructed to utilize the method of free-association; to begin each session with whatever topic he brings to the hour, or whatever occurs to him at the time. Alternate procedures are available for the clinician in the matter of deciding upon the point at which free-association should be abandoned and the analysis aided by hypnosis. In the case which is presented in this volume—the first of a long series to be handled hypnoanalytically throughout by this writer—hypnotic recall was delayed until it became apparent that the resistance to disclosing crucial material was of serious proportions. Latterly, however, it has been found efficacious to hypnotize *immediately upon striking the variety of resistance which does not originate from the transference*. That is, where resistances are encountered, and where they arise naturally rather than from a shift in *entente* between the participants, hypnosis should be resorted to at once; and under its influence the patient encouraged to reveal what he had been withholding so reluctantly. Such revelations can be expedited merely by repeating to the patient the last few associations and recollections he had produced prior to the hypnoidal sleep. Following the subsequent disclosures during hypnosis, it is necessary to give the patient complete amnesia for the events that transpired *after* he had been placed in the trance. At the following session, however, the key associations, *i.e.* those which had been given by the patient immediately before he was made to sleep, are again presented.

Now it is a constant and unvarying phenomenon that patients repeat, soon after such an hypnoidal session, the material which they had already presented *if it is memorially valid and not a screen-memory*. The importance of this fact cannot be over-estimated. It provides us, first of all, with an objective tool for estimating the validity of analytical material and, secondly, with a prepotent weapon for the literal disintegration of resistances. Apparently the mechanism involved is that of a subliminal appreciation by the organism of diminished 'need' for preserving secrets. In spite of the complete induced amnesia—which can be proved beyond question—the material which resisted disclosure actually flows as smoothly post-hypnotically as if no reluctance against its production had ever been present. This single benefit of hypnoanalysis is perhaps responsible for the saving of more than half of the total treatment-time. It effectively counters the already-noted objection that the total personality rarely if ever participates in the disclosures made under hypnosis, and removes what was perhaps the only objection to the employment of hypnosis in the treatment of psychogenic disorders that ever counted for very much in an academic or practical sense.

As to the memories which in the course of hypnoanalysis are called forth by hypnosis, Erickson has best described the two forms in which they appear. He distinguished—as the reader will undoubtedly do during his review of the material presented—the *regressive* and the *revivified*. With the regressive, memories appear in terms of the patient's or subject's present regard of his past. That is to say, his attitude toward what has happened to him is predicated on his present understanding of his recollections and colored by the sum of his experiences since the events he reports. Such memories, as they come to the surface, reveal themselves as regressive by the fact that they are more frequently than not accompanied by expressions of value or attitudes of judgement. In the revivified form, the patient actually lives again the time of which he is telling; and it exists *now*, uninfluenced by the accumulations of life since the event. The revivified form of recall discloses itself, for the most part, behaviorally. In other words, the hypnoanalyst by observing the motor performing of the patient during the recital under hypnosis of a crucial historic episode can not only distinguish it as revivified, but he can also determine (often more accurately than by any other method) the exact period of life when it transpired. Scrutiny of the motor apparatus in terms of skill and coordination, and comparison with known developmental standards (*e.g.* Gesell's) provides a useful time-line.

The types of recall which appear under hypnosis furnish handy manipulative machinery for the hypnoanalyst, who can so control them as to substantiate his material, fill in detail, make his data vivid and alive. It has been found that although these memorial varieties appear spontaneously, apparently in no set sequence and responsive to no set laws, they can be invoked by a simple formulation under hypnosis. This increases their value many times, for in practice one can observe and record exactly the effect of an event on the patient at the time of its occurrence, as well as the attitude toward it that is maintained at the time of treatment.

Hypnoanalysis takes its place among the active forms of psychotherapy in contrast to those genera which require patients to find their way alone through the psychologic maze. It therefore requires the constant direction of the clinician, who must decide when to employ hypnosis, when to encourage free-association, when to employ revivification or regression, when to demand abreaction in the waking state, when to engraft the interpretations and significances directly onto the personality. The last is probably the most delicate and skill-demanding of all the hypnoanalyst's tasks. In orthodox analysis the acquiescence of the patient in the new attitudes and ways of behavior is demonstrated by verbalization as well as by action. Apart from utilizing the transference to insure acceptance and comprehension, other means are not available. Hypnoanalysis, on the other hand, has at its command not only the transference but also the prepotent post-hypnotic suggestive method to enforce comprehension and acceptance of those necessary but novel ways of regarding the past, new attitudes, ambitions and patterns of behavior. Through this means the benefits of treatment are assured. And through this means as well is the transference at last dissolved by the displacement and redirection of its energies into the paths prescribed by the recently acquired and developed insights. In all essentials, this is the re-educative process.

The pith and purport of the method of hypnoanalysis as it has been employed in the case to be reviewed and with other patients and conditions as well are contained in the foregoing. It is, like other ways of approach to the functioning organism, an art requiring a blend of technological skill and judgement and knowledge. In the author's opinion, it is an approach that offers a rapid, sure and valid way to the understanding and treatment of psychogenic disorders and aberrations of behavior. Its applicability seems limited only by the professional equipment and deftness of the hypnoanalyst. Thus far it has been applied in a wide range of diagnostic entities with a degree of success and a range of usefulness that promises brilliantly for the time when its principles are more fully comprehended.

Beyond everything, however, the success of hypnoanalysis in penetrating to the core of psychopathic personality for the first time in the long history of psychological concern with this puzzling classification, warrants the direction upon it and its tenets of experimental and clinical regard. . . .

THE RESULTS

The history of Harold, our subject, has been made available to the writer in many forms. Each of his delinquent acts when subject to court review was supplemented with detailed social service investigations according to the admirable latter-day judicial routine; and on the occasions of his incarcerations further study was made of the essential features of his home, family and personal life. Rarely has a clinician been provided with a more complete and documented anamnesis. This material proved eminently useful as a constant check and source during the hypnoanalysis, and provided a frame of reference, almost a topography, for the incidents and events elicited from the patient.

Harold's father, an unnaturalized Pole and a machinist by trade, came to the United States during the great exodus from Europe at the turn of the century. He was a big, bluff, hearty peasant of excellent work habits. Within a short time he met and married the native-born girl who became Harold's mother; and having settled in an industrial suburb of a large city in the East the couple soon became the parents of our subject and in time of two daughters. The father contracted an occupational disease early in his career, and the medical regimen imposed on him forced his abandonment of factory employment but permitted his occupation in a free-lance manner. His average earnings, computed over many years by social workers, were twenty-five dollars a week. Investigators described him as a hasty disciplinarian who is more ready with curses and unkind words than blows. He does not smoke or use intoxicants, is cut off from his family by reason of his unfamiliarity with English and his illiteracy (despite his long residence in this country); and the fact that his standards are, on the whole, old-world and markedly unprogressive. His reputation in the community is excellent and his affiliations with Polish-American organizations have resulted in firm if taciturn and blunt friendships with men of his own temper and kind. Now, at fifty-three, he is still pursuing his trade, more frequently, however, eyeing pastures he should have cultivated twenty years ago. He claims even at this date an interest in Harold, but investigators note his lack of patience toward his son's problems.

Harold's mother is today as she seems always to have been a symbol of patient and unrequited motherhood, a person who invites sentiment.   A beautiful and buxom girl when she married at an early age, she is now a worn and tired woman, a product of housewifely routine and the monotonous drudgery of feeding, caring and worrying for a family in slightly above marginal economic circumstances.   Her loyalty to her children and especially to Harold is famous among her acquaintances, and social workers note her over-solicitous, over-protective nature.   This she has rationalized by pointing out the social limitations and barriers faced by Harold because of his peculiar physical defect.   She is lavish in her statements of affection for the boy and admits to having saved him from pitfalls on many occasions. By all accounts, she is a sensible, intelligent and industrious woman in all affairs but those dealing with her son.   She is a voracious reader of cheap romances and an ardent movie-goer, readily moved to tears and easily imposed upon.   Her attention has for so long been fixed solely upon her family that she has but few friends; these she visits and entertains regularly with coffee and gossip.   Her own family, including her mother, two married sisters and a brother, is bound by ties of mutual dependence in their unrelenting borderland of impoverishment.

Two younger sisters complete the family group.   The elder of these is a pert, vivacious girl of nineteen who works steadily at a factory job and who contributes her entire wages to the parents: the youngest is a schoolgirl, bright and lively, the pet and joy of the old folks.

The whole family, with the exception of Harold is well regarded by neighbors and friends.   They practice the Roman-Catholic faith, own a car and are considered respectable additions to the neighborhood.   The section in which they live is a crowded district of foreign-laborer families.   They maintain a four-room apartment above a saloon in an old building with a few modern conveniences: rent is twelve dollars a month.   The home is clean, modestly furnished in a comfortable if somewhat worn style.   Beyond the youngest daughter's school-books, the mother's rental library romances, the eldest daughter's movie-fan pulps, and the Polish language newspaper, there are no books or periodicals in the apartment.   A radio and some religious chromos complete the cultural scene.

Those relatives visited by investigators were cut from the same pattern and along the same lines as Harold's parents. The family history, so far as it can be traced, is negative for feeblemindedness or mental disorder of any variety, except for traces of alcoholism in the male members of the distaff branch.

The mother reports that Harold's birth, assisted by a midwife, was entirely normal following a labor of six hours duration. The child was healthy and there were no abnormal pre- or post-natal circumstances. At the age of one or two, Harold suffered measles, and between two and six other childhood exanthems were experienced. Tonsillectomy and adenoidectomy were performed when he was twelve. Except for these and his eye condition, his health was normal.

As to the optic disorder, it was the recorded opinion of two physicians whom his mother consulted that the diagnosis was *Nystagmus Amblyopia* resulting from the measles: another consultant diagnosed *congenital defective retinae* incorrectable, with ten per cent normal vision in the right eye and fifteen per cent in the left. The mother reports visits to numerous specialists in order to obtain some kind of favorable treatment. In all cases, however, results were unsatisfactory.

Harold attended public school from the first to the fourth grades in the city to which the family moved soon after his birth. Records from these years cannot be located, but his mother reports regular attendance and satisfactory performance. The fourth to the seventh grades were spent at a parochial school. The nuns who were his teachers have stated that he was a fair student and conducted himself passably well. He left parochial school to become a pupil in a special class for students with defective vision. At fifteen he graduated to High School, which he quit after one year. Officials and High School instructors considered his conduct fair but regretted that he did not produce to the level of his capabilities. At sixteen he renounced all scholastic pursuits and from that time forward worked fitfully on a relative's farm.

Harold's recorded criminal history began at the age of twelve when in the company of other small boys he broke into a grocery store and made off with almost seventy-five dollars worth of candy and tobacco. He was apprehended and sent to a juvenile institution for examination by specialists; but while awaiting his turn he escaped custody by leaping through a window. Again apprehended, he was placed on two year's probation. At thirteen he was arrested for a trespassing offense and the Juvenile Court extended the probationary period.

After a two year respite Harold once more came into conflict with the law when he stole a sizable sum from a storekeeper. Probation was renewed. One month later, having made off with money from his mother's purse, he purchased a rifle and with it attempted to rob a couple in an automobile on a deserted city street. Tricked by his clever victim, he was held for the police who hailed him into Juvenile Court, where he was again probated for five years. Minor charges for trespassing, breaking and entering and vandalism were lodged during the following year. On one occasion he received a short sentence to a correctional institution; on another, a light jail term. Several similar charges and warrants were pending when he was arrested for the offense for which he is now serving. The details of this offense cannot, unfortunately, be revealed here, but it was a crime serious enough to carry a heavy penalty.

Many psychologists and psychiatrists have interviewed, examined and tested Harold. While they disagree on the causative factors in his case, all are in accord on the diagnosis of psychopathic personality complicated by social difficulties arising from the condition of the boy's eyes. One psychiatrist stressed the avoidance by other children which Harold probably experienced, stating that they undoubtedly considered him a freak and this, as a consequence, forced his mother's indulgence. Another specialist reported a need for productive occupation, and asociality and egocentricity as the leading factors in the clinical picture. Still another stated that Harold evinced pronounced feelings of inferiority in respect of his place in the family group, adding that he found the boy to be cowardly, unreliable and a schemer. This specialist also reported the presence of "subconscious jealousy of the father and a mother fixation." The last examiner's report closes with the statement: " . . . unless someone is able to psychoanalyze and reconstruct his personality from about three years of age on, the boy will continue on his career of crime and, because of his violent impulses, will become a more and more dangerous criminal." A final expert found Harold honest in his statements and fairly intelligent; and, questioning him closely on his sex habits, obtained an admission of masturbation and sexual relations with girls in the neighborhood.

On his arrival in the institution where the writer made his acquaintance, Harold showed a Mental Age of sixteen years and one month; an Intelligence Quotient of one-hundred and seven. He was found to be free of disease; serology was negative; weight 150 lb.; height 5 ft. 8 in.; ophthalmological diagnosis was *Nystagmus, Strabismus, Ptosis;* psychiatric diagnosis was *Psychopathic Personality.* The psychiatric initial summary revealed: " . . . a recidivist whose attitude toward officials and fellows is poor. . . . Since childhood he has had practically no respectable occupation or regular employment and it is evident he has matured without benefit of proper parental discipline. . . . During interview he presents the picture of a sullen, resentful, weak-willed, gullible, fidgety youth . . . lacks insight and judgment . . . enjoys using the language of the underworld and frequently lapses into gangland lingo when describing his escapades. . . . Prognosis for institutional adjustment and rehabilitation is guarded."

On a spring morning some time ago a prisoner sat apprehensively on a chair in the anteroom of the writer's office. He had been sent for at the urging of a clinical assistant who felt that at least some of the symptoms which the young man showed should be studied and treated. Since the inmate had no inkling of the reason for his call, he was filled with that nervous anticipation and foreboding of personal danger that only petitioners and clients of professional people can know. Several times he rose from his chair and paced the room with the curious litheness and agility common among psychopaths.

He was a moderately tall, sparingly built boy, wide-shouldered and narrow-hipped. The cast of his face would have evoked an impression of 'intelligent' from the layman; and there was a suggestion of competence in his large-knuckled hands. The one feature that attracted immediate attention was his heavy-lidded, continually fluttering eyes. These lent his appearance the almost mask-like quality of the totally blind, until the observer noted the restless, shifting play of the pupils and the quick winking of the lids.

During the interview and examination, Harold maintained a sneering sullenness modified by the abject disinterest such individuals often demonstrate in the presence of prison or hospital officials. He stated apathetically that he could foresee no benefits from any kind of treatment; that he had been dancing attendance on all varieties of medical specialists without reward; but that he would be willing to allow an examination and experiment with a new therapy. Accordingly, he was subjected to a complete physical check and another examination by a competent ophthalmologist. There was no change from his admission status.

A chance remark passed by Harold during the initial examination determined the writer first upon a therapeutic program based on post-hypnotic suggestion. In response to the question, "Would you rather be blind than get so that you can keep your eyes open for longer periods?" Harold answered, "I'd rather be blind than to see some of the things I have seen." The presence and verbalization of so peculiar a remark, with its undertones suggestive of a pathological solution of conflict, settled the immediate initiation of a course of hypnotic therapy.

Harold entered the trance state rapidly and easily, obeying each instruction as it was issued. Various tests, ranging from hand-levitation to catelepsy to the production of anesthetic areas, were consummated successfully. Then, in response to the suggestion that his lids would open and remain fixed and steady while a strong light from an ophthalmoscope was directed into his eyes, Harold—who had never looked into daylight with open eyes and for whom an electric light was only a stimulus to rapid blinking—opened his eyes and stared directly before him as the sharp shaft played over his eyeballs. This convinced the writer that he had here to do with a condition which, although it was essentially physical, perhaps had been initiated by a traumatic assault on the organism at a crucial stage in its development. A course of treatment was begun and carried out faithfully for about two weeks. Each session concentrated on the lengthening of the post-hypnotic period during which Harold's eyes were to remain widely open and impervious to light. Results were not only highly satisfactory in respect of Harold's ability to control the mobility of his lids, but the writer noted the development of an increasingly favorable rapport.

All this time the author was keenly aware that he was attacking *symptoms* rather than *causes*. This, coupled with the temptation to capitalize on the rare, excellent rapport with a psychopath, (which was not understood at the time) prompted a resolve to attempt an analysis which, it was hoped, would for the first time ferret out the psychological factors responsible for the psychopathic pattern. The nature of the undertaking was described to Harold and he assented to being hypnoanalyzed.

It occurred to the writer that it would be invaluable to have a permanent and complete record of the entire transaction for the light it promised to throw on crime and psychopathy. A microphone was therefore concealed in the couch on which Harold was to lie during the sessions. Connection with a loudspeaker in another room was made, and there a competent stenographer of the writer's staff took down and subsequently transcribed the proceedings verbatim. This material, edited only to eliminate tiresome and meaningless repetitions and redundancies, is herewith made available to the reader.

But before we examine the transcript of the hypnoanalysis, a word needs to be said here concerning the peculiar ethical problems which beset the psychiatrist or psychologist practicing in a penal institution. Because of the fact that he is, to those of the inmates who consult him, someone who is unselfishly interested in their welfare, he is often made privy to information which his duty to the State or Government urges him to communicate to law-enforcement agencies, but which his sense of obligation to his patient and to his professional standards compels him to keep to himself. In the present instance, this insistent dilemma was happily resolved by the patient himself during the period of re-education which followed the hypnoanalysis. Not only did he grant permission to the writer to publish this material, he actually urged its publication: this because he had come to a genuine and sincere realization of the social importance and the dangerous significance of his condition . . .

THE FIRST HOUR

The patient was instructed to choose a starting point and to talk without regard for topic or continuity.*

There is a lot of rain now. Showers all the time. For the last two years we've had no showers. We've had dry summers and drought. There will be plenty of water for showers this year, not like the past two years. It got so hot and dry here even the corn died. Many of the plants were not even growing. It was so hot that they all

---

* Unless otherwise specified, these instructions obtained at the beginning of all subsequent treatment hours.

shriveled up and died. This is a funny country. One year dry, the next year wet.

In the night when I can't sleep because it's so hot I lie on my bed and think.

I don't read much. My eyes are so bad.

I was reading a *Life* magazine this morning. I remember the army maneuvers at Fort Knox. They had pictures of tanks and the men needed to operate them. I hear and read so much about war and politics and economics that there is not time for anything else.

The light that is coming in over the transom reminds me of the light that comes into my cell through the small window. When I lie in bed after 9:30 I watch the light and it makes a complete turn, a complete circle. I see some dark spots in the circle. My eyes probably cause that. The day before yesterday I watched it go completely around. Sometimes when I lie in bed looking at the light I get bright spots before my eyes.

It's hard to sleep at night because of the heat. Usually after the siren blows I get about fifteen minutes sleep until count-time.

The population count thrice daily is an item in prison routine.

Sometimes I get more real sleep in those minutes than I do all night. To get to sleep at night I think about what I am studying or I count. Most of the time I just try to keep everything out of my mind so I can fall asleep.

Right outside my window is the garden. The circular bed with th: flowers bordering the lawn is right in the center. There are big red flowers in the center. They are called Canna. They remind you of Gladiolus. They are an old-fashioned flower, growing from a tuber like Dahlia. A Dahlia tuber reminds one of a carrot, soft, not as hard as a carrot, about three or four inches long and pointed at each end. A Canna tuber is not pointed: it is long and thick and rounded at the ends, and it has eyes like a potato. From these eyes grow the flowers.

When I was at my aunt's farm, I used to help work my friend's place. I used to help digging potatoes. They had a team of horses and a plow. I used to drive ahead and two people would follow behind and pick up potatoes and throw them on the wagon.

Me and Toby palled around together. We had Saturday and Sundays together. Those were the only two days we ever had.

There was no place to go except to a little town a couple of miles away, twenty-five thousand people and a couple of movie houses. But we didn't go to the movies very much. We'd go out in the car to see how fast it would go, how fast uphill and how fast downhill.

Toby was a better driver than I. I only drove it once or twice. Hank, his brother, would drive it a lot. Hank was a Sunday driver, always on the right side of the road and very careful. Toby didn't care and just drove anyway. We used to race cars and sometimes we'd wind up in a ditch. We liked to drive over ramshackle bridges fast and feel the boards rattling underneath us.

There was a little town, Arcia, nearby. It had about fifteen hundred people and a nice little church. My grandmother used to make me go to church. My uncle was just like me. He didn't like to go to church, but when grandmother was there she made him.

My uncle used to drink a lot. After he married my aunt he stopped drinking. I guess they still live on the same level. The farmers don't seem to progress there like they do in other sections. There is a shortage of markets for what they produce.

Farmers in the south don't make as much as those in the north. Transportation facilities are better in the north. And then markets are more easily available. In the south there are not enough cars for them to load their products. Farmers can't make a contract for their products at a certain price. The cotton farmers have a pretty hard time now. I talked with a fellow whose father has a farm and he says it hardly keeps them alive. This fellow used to be interested in electrical appliances. He used to sell all kinds of appliances, like washers, toasters and such things. Many men in this country work and work as hard as they can. There are not ten million unemployed as they say but twenty-five million. One hundred and ten percent more than what the average believes. Of course many of those have part-time jobs. And the WPA.

The WPA is supposed to be a business stimulant; it circulates the money. It is the pet idea of the New Deal, but I think it stimulates mostly the automobile industry. According to some statisticians, families live on ten thousand a year and some on one thousand. It shows that a man living on a certain standard spends as much as he can for pleasures. Money seems to be a substitute for anything in the world. There are many men in this world who don't care much for money.

The question is production and consumption.   Money is just the exchange value.   You buy something with it.   And then the money is still there.   The commodity you bought is destroyed but the exchange value is still there.   This is something I can't understand. When you buy an automobile, as you use it, it is being destroyed. The cash you used to buy it with is moving on to produce more. When I think about things like that I get a headache.   How is it made and how is it destroyed?   Eventually I think I'll be able to understand.

I am not interested in making money.   I am interested much more in understanding and finding out things, and in writing books.   I don't know whether I can write.   At night, when I am in my cell, I have a pencil in my hand to write down what I think.   Anything, poetry or anything else.   And in the morning when I look at it I find it more of a puzzle than the night before.

> *It seems clear that the reference to poor handwriting and the inability to decipher it is an apology for the lack of clarity and cohesion in what he has just produced.*

I have been thinking of how to get money to buy a typewriter. My handwriting is bad.   I scribble something down and one letter is too big and one too small.   When I think of something and I want to write it down I scribble so hard I can hardly read it.   Other times when I am not thinking about it I can write pretty well. . . .

THE SECOND HOUR

We went to a factory, my cousin Pete and I.   We went there and neither of us got the job.   I was rejected and they put him on the list.   I don't know if he is working there now, but I believe he is. My other cousin, John, (he's Pete's brother) is getting married soon. I think when a man gets married he settles down and lets the world go by and pays no attention to anything after that.   He goes to work and settles down and the world slides by.   The same thing, day after day.   I think when a man gets married he has a big obstacle in his way.   No great man in history ever aspired to get married.

I don't think I am going to get married.

> *A standard sign of Psychopathy, indicative of an inability to accept social responsibility.*

At least I'm not going to get married right away. I want to write
some books on politics and economics. I think I want to get up to
my aunt's place, away from everything and everyone and write.

It gets just as hot up there as it does here. Only up there it is
cooler at night and in the morning because of the mountains. My
aunt has a home at Mount Abel. There is a little school there, two
rooms and a teacher or so.

It's very hard for most of the kids in that part of the country.
Most of them are of foreign parentage, Polish and German. It's very
hard for them to concentrate on English grammar and mathematics.
To them it is something entirely new. In their homes the language
the parents speak is the only one they hear.

I was out there several years in the summertime. There was a
Polish girl I used to go with. She was a year older than me. I never
had any sexual relations with her. She was a plumpish, dark girl.
Dark hair. I don't remember what color her eyes were. She weighed
about one hundred and ten pounds. She was the oldest child in her
family. I don't remember much about it now. She was a funny sort
of girl, a sort of mongrel I guess. There wasn't a Sunday she wouldn't
attend the church activities in Mount Abel. She had a brother almost
as old as I am now. He and I were always good friends. He was
not muscularly built; a thin sort of lad. He was the pet of their
father. He used to have more privileges than the other children.
He would never speak to girls. This girl's name was Amy. My
sister was a good friend of her sister.

Amy was the mother-type. She used to feel sorry for me. I was
a wild kid, fast-driving and all that. She used to tell me not to go
with guys who drive fast. She used to pity me. There really was
no reason for it. I don't know whether she is married now or not.
My sister corresponds with her sister but she never mentions Amy in
her letters. I hardly ever think of her now.

I feel as if I am in a daze or up against a big cliff. It seems somehow
as if my path is blocked.

> *In some patients, as in Harold, resistance is 'felt:' it is reported as a diffuse
> kinesthetic perception. In others it is more distinctly somatized and
> localized.*

I don't think of this girl anymore. O, once in a while I wonder
what's become of her. She used to mother me.

Before my uncle bought the farm he used to live across the road from their home. The first couple summers I never even noticed Amy. She came to visit my aunt once in a while but I was never in a position to talk with her. The third year I was there my sister introduced her. I used to get a lot of fun out of seeing how many girls I could speak to and what their actions would be if I spoke to them.

My aunt always tried to impress me with what a fine church-going girl Amy was . . . a typical saint. She probably married some farmer and then did what other farm girls do.

The last year I had no desire to go to my aunt's place but I wanted to get away from the city where I lived and spend a few months away from everything.

I used to go with a girl in the city. She was a small, thin girl, with kind of strawy hair. I don't think she weighed a hundred pounds. She was a year or two younger than I. She lived with her sister and brother-in-law and their four or five children and another sister. They all lived together. I knew this girl about one or two months. Her name was Lila, I believe. She was oversexed, very much over-sexed. I had intercourse with her several times. I don't know how I didn't contract some venereal disease from her. She was loose, I guess: she would play around with anyone who would say hello to her. She had very, very, very soft breasts. She became so—I don't know—very nervous and excited; her fingers and arms would twitch when someone would touch her breasts. She used to cry a lot. I don't know why. I used to spend a lot of time with her; had nothing else to do: didn't have a job. She always used to tell me that she was in love with me. She used to cry because she couldn't resist anyone who wanted her. She was the real reason I went up to Mount Abel that summer. I wanted to get away from her. When I came back I found she was going around with some Italian fellows who had gonorrhea. I never even spoke to her again. I just hung around and did nothing but think how I could get some money, maybe stealing here and there from cars and pawning what I stole. I don't know what gave me the idea for the crime I am in here for. I knew there wouldn't be much chance.

Just about two weeks after this fellow and I had been sitting around conspiring the best way to pull off this job he went to the probation officer. I was then on probation for a holdup. So there were some men from the FBI at the probation office when I came in. . . .

I never had anything outside; never cared if I had anything to eat or any clothes.

At first I didn't say anything but after several hours of questioning I decided. I knew they didn't have much proof, but I identified some of the things. Three months later I was tried.

But I really don't care about this. I am getting more benefit out of this institution than from 10 or even 20 years outside. If I were still outside I would probably have taken a gun and held up somebody. If they resisted I probably would have shot them. . . .

I used to go to High School outside. I went about two years to High. I was getting along alright. There was a teacher there who used to help me because of my eyes. She was the mathematics and science teacher. She was a thin, cold woman almost five feet ten, grey hair. A very fine woman.

In High I studied German; one and one-half years of German, a year or so of math, algebra, geometry and English. I always liked science. There is one thing I always tried to understand; one experiment about why water always reaches its own level. I am still trying to understand. O, I know now, but at that time I was always trying to understand. The experiment went like this: we had three glass tubes with a hose attached to the bottom of each tube. If you raised one of the tubes the water would sink in the others. Of course, now I know that it is due to the air pressure and the pressure of the water.

Our High was not very big, just about one city block. They taught everything there; mechanical drawing, engineering. I was never interested in anything very much, but math came easily. English seems to have been pretty hard.

I took German instead of Latin because of a girl. Ella. She sat across the aisle from me. I don't think I ever learned anything there. And I very seldom bothered Ella. I just fooled around the classroom and made a lot of useless noise. I guess our classroom was the noisiest in the whole school. They all had me marked down buggy. The German teacher was an old man. I can't recall his name; this was when I was about fifteen. He used to get terribly mad when we put a swastika on the blackboard. He used to get so mad he pulled his hair—what he had left of it. The class I was in was the most unruly class they ever had.

I didn't like English very much but I don't know why. I used to cut a lot of periods. I used to cut the first period in the morning and then not go back sometimes all day. My cousin was the same way. That's the one who is getting married. John. He's getting married soon. I never liked him very much. If he hadn't been my cousin I wouldn't have bothered with him.

I didn't associate with many people outside.

I used to go down to the river bank a lot. There was a highway along the shore of the river. About two hundred feet away from the Boulevard there was a steep grade, sort of a decline down to the river. There was a fence on the edge of the highway to warn the drivers about this grade. Often times I would sit on that fence and watch the boats go by. The river is not very big. We used to spend a lot of time on the water, swimming or boating. Often we would get a hitch back down the river again. Many times I used to just sit and watch the water, greasy and dirty. There was a big steel company on the other side of the river, and big swamps between the factories. We used to get boards and wood there and make a raft and take it out in the middle; and when a boat came along we'd pull up the anchor and put the boat on one side. The middle of the river always seemed to be the nicest. It was the coolest part.

Lots of boys from this neighborhood used to take girls over to the other side. Sometimes there was one girl to ten or fifteen or twenty men. I never did a line like that. I hate a lot of fellows for things like that and I hated my cousin. He baited this girl Lila to go over the other side. He and about twelve other fellows told her I was there. It doesn't mean anything to me now. But I thought then it was a rotten dirty trick for anyone to do. I used to get a lot of fun with girls, talk with them and watch their reactions and try my best to be a gentleman. There aren't more than one or two girls I ever hit. Lila; I hit her because she went over to the other side with my cousin. The other girl called me a filthy name. I hit her. I was drunk that night. O, I have had a lot of arguments with my sister, but I never hit her real hard. She would throw everything she could lay her hands on at me. But the next day everything would be alright. She could really curse but now she's changed. She's quite a lady now.

My little sister is twelve this month. I didn't even write to congratulate her. I wrote a poem for my older sister's birthday. It wasn't very good: it was pretty lousy. I used to write poetry when lying in bed at night. I should have written to my younger sister. I haven't seen her for three years now. She'll be a big girl when I leave here. All my older sister thinks of now is going places and getting all dolled up. I used to think the same way. She works now; gets about thirty dollars a week.

My mother was always very strict with us. Sometimes I used to stay out until eleven or twelve or one and when I came home I found mother waiting for me. She would be mad at me and sometimes hit me, and I would argue and explain to her. She wanted me to be home at nine. She thought when I didn't come home I would be out and be around and steal things from people. Maybe I would be doing that once in a while; the other times I would be playing pool in a poolroom, or getting drunk somewhere, or with a girl. She didn't like that because she couldn't sleep until everybody was home. She always held my sisters up to me as examples of good children. They were home at a certain time; why couldn't I?

My sister was working before I came here and she never went any place. The money I needed I'd borrow from her. I'd have to give her a long story and explanation. I don't owe her such a lot, about twenty dollars now besides what she's sent me here.

Prison doesn't destroy desire. I still have a desire for a nice little boat. I didn't ever like automobiles so well. I always liked a boat.

When I was getting finished with grade school I used to hang around with a bunch of ten or twelve kids. We were always hanging around together. I remember we used to break into lunch wagons and into a paint shop and a butcher store. I got two years probation, an extra year more than the other fellows. My father didn't say anything. I went back to school and three months later we were hanging around together again.

There was a railroad running about a block from our house. We used to throw stones at the engines and cars and at the signal lights and break open tool cases and locks. So we went back before the same Judge who sentenced us before. He just hollered at us. My probation officer got me out of it with one year probation. The other fellows got nothing. They just went home.

At that time they tried to do something for my eyes, so they trans-

fered me to a public school where they had a class for eye conserva-
tion or something like that.   But it was just a class where they sent
some of the kids who had some trouble with their eyes.   They had a
teacher assigned to help them with their studies, but we attended all
classes with the others too.   They gave us a typewriter so we could
type all our work and taught us how far to hold a book from our eyes.
We did very little writing and we wouldn't read small print.   We
attended class with children who had normal eyesight.   The other
fellow who got a year probation too was in my class.   We kept to
ourselves.   He went his way and I went my way.   In about a year
I graduated and went to High.   The reason I quit after two years of
High was that my uncle wanted me to come up to his place.   My
mother wanted me to keep on studying.   I didn't know what to do.
So I went up there only for a few months.   Then I went back to the
city. . . .

THE THIRD HOUR

Yesterday I felt as if I was lying on a cloud somewhere with my
head wrapped in cotton.   I couldn't move it.   It was as if I were up
against a big stone cliff or something.
Why I said that I don't know. . . .
Yesterday I couldn't move my head.   I don't know what it was.
I still remember lying on this bed, or on a cloud.   I felt as if my head
was wrapped in cotton, so soft and yet so hard I couldn't move it.
Sometimes it seemed as if my mind left my body and just went off
by itself. . . .

> *Where the association is unimpeded by resistances, this is a common
> experience among patients.*

I never had many friends on the outside.   Usually I'd hang out by
myself, go and sit on the guard-rail near the river and watch the river,
the dark, dirty river go by.   It rolls and rolls by.   Then the river
turns, it turns and you see it against the sky.   The sky so clean and
the water so dirty, just like someone took a paint brush and painted
grease in a straight line.
I used to spend a lot of time on the river near my home where I
had some small boats, just row boats.   I never had no motor boat.
And I used to play in the swamp, swampy, muddy grounds with

bushes and weeds and some sandy spots. There were old logs and pipes laying around. I used to go there with a .22 and shoot bull frogs. One time I put a match on a tank and I tried to hit this match but the bullets always went over the tank or to the side. I always had a liking for guns. I don't know why....

I used to get hitches on tug boats and barges and go up the river and back. I would just do nothing and waste a lot of time. Sometimes I would look for work but I would never find any. I never had a job, so I would just ignore it; wouldn't look for work at all; maybe spend a half day in a show and sleep a lot. It would get monotonous, and then I would read books. I used to read the wrong kind of books, I guess; detective magazines and crime stories just to pass the time. I used to listen to the radio a lot too. Most of the time to crime serials but once in a while to music. Not jazz music. Music. Music. Now I know it was classical music. I liked it. I don't know anything about it. I guess it is soothing to the emotions, makes a person free of everything.

I spent most of my nights on the outside with fellows. That was on account of my eyes. They don't blink at night.

When I was about twelve I used to hang around with fellows from my neighborhood and we used to shoot out street lights and lights on billboards with staples. There was a lunch wagon and we shot out its windows.

There was a fellow had a motor boat and we shot out all its windows and drilled two holes in the bottom of it. He used to go out fishing in it. One time he threw all the clothes of the fellows when they were swimming into the water, so that's why we got even with him. Me and another fellow one time stole a row boat, one that belonged to this fellow, and he threw a hammer and a saw at us but he didn't hit either one of us. We just ran.

There was a dock nearby where we went swimming and diving off poles. They were real high, forty feet or so. The water was deep there too. Maybe fifty feet. A lot of people used to go swimming there. There was a Park on the other side of the Boulevard from the river. I'd spend a lot of time there too. They had concerts in the summer on the baseball diamond and you would see the grandstand and the baseball diamond filled with people. Up across the street from the Park there was a stand where we used to get ice cream.

We'd steal from two to five gallons every week, sometimes two or three big cans a week.

After I got a little older, all the older fellows used to come around to the gang. I must have been about sixteen then. There was a young kid that got his leg cut off, the right leg at the ankle. That stopped most of the fellows from going to the railroad yard. Right along side of the railroad was a coal company that had a big trestle where the freight cars full of coal used to be pushed. That trestle was on a grade, and they would tie the freight cars so they wouldn't roll down. One time we unhooked them. They started down the grade and rolled and rolled and rolled.

There was a church school I used to go to, and an order of sisters that ran it. It was an Irish Catholic school. I couldn't see the blackboard and I was sitting in the back of the classroom. So I kept the other children from doing their work and used to get beatings for not having my lessons prepared. I think that me and another fellow—he had a paralyzed arm—were the worst two fellows in the class. I used to pal around with the best student in the class too. He used to live about a block away from me. I remember one time we were coming home from school about 4 o'clock and I got hold of a newspaper and was reading it. He made a kind of sarcastic remark to me: "Don't take the print off." I never forgot that and we were not such good friends again. I recall how he used to tell me that I might get in trouble, that if I did anything they would give me time. I didn't pay any attention to him and one time told him to mind his own goddam business. This boy used to have a blackjack that he carried around with him and one time he hit me on the toe. It hurt bad. When we were about twelve his brother showed me the gun he carried. This brother was nineteen or twenty then. He was like a gorilla, hair all over and big muscles.

It seemed then that I had to have a gun too.

We had a clubhouse in an old barn near the railroad station. There was a big sword in the clubhouse, about three feet long, and a big shotgun, a muzzle-loader with a double barrel. We also had some fur skins that we stole from a nearby leather factory.

To me a lot of these fellows in the gang seemed awfully stupid and dumb. For instance, one time we had a checkbook and none of them knew how to fill out a check. I told them how to fill one out and they all wanted to have a check.

When I belonged to this gang, me and another fellow found two cans of paint in the cellar of an old house. We threw a match into one of the cans and when it blazed we turned the can upside down. It started smoking and black smoke came. The floor was just dirt and pebbles and stone, and the black smoke was all around, and we were gasping for air. Finally we found the stairs and ran. We heard the firemen coming and they rushed into the house. After a while they came out and said there was nothing there.

When I was still about twelve we used to build big fires on the river bank. Sometimes we'd catch crabs in the river, over on the other side, and cook them. One time at Christmas we got hold of a lot of trees, about fifty or more Christmas trees, and we piled them on the river bank and lighted them. It made a big fire, a great big flame, maybe a hundred feet high. The fire engines came down and even the fire boat and they put it out.

We used to steal keys every place we could get them, automobile keys, garage keys, all kinds of keys. We got them and tried to open a lot of locks. I never went inside a garage we opened. We used to steal a lot of batteries right off cars and trucks and sell them for one dollar apiece. That's how we got some money.

One time we broke into a paint shop. We pulled two or three boards out at the back of the building. Two of the fellows went inside. There was a police station right across the street from this place. A policeman came from the railroad station and went through the parking lot behind the paint shop. He had a flashlight and we knew it. So I told them to put the boards back in place and we lay down flat so when he would flash the light he wouldn't see us. He went by and didn't even flash his light. He went right through to the police station. We got nothing but paint, some ink, some pens, some old junk.

I remember one time we broke into a butcher stop.

Shop. A slip of the tongue. Orthodox analysts would regard this as a potent manifestation of resistance.

There were a lot of cigarettes. One of the fellows took about twenty packs. I told him to take them all; there were about three hundred. When the police found the place where we hid them in the barn the cigarettes were missing. Somebody must have stolen them from us.

Before I came here we had an apartment over a tavern. There

was always a lot of noise and racket going on, but it was quiet when I came home at night. I would sleep, but the next day my mother would tell me about the noise and the racket. My mother now lives at grandmother's.

Directly across the street from my grandmother's house there is a lot. There are two garages on it. My father rents one of the garages and keeps one of his cars in the other. The other car he keeps out in the open. He said he bought this other car for my sister; my sister said to give it to me but he wouldn't do that, so my sister said she didn't want it.

My sister is about twenty now. She has a job: she likes to work and dress up and go out. She didn't go to High with me: she quit when she graduated from grammar school.

Me and Arty, the fellow who was on parole with me, used to hang out at a blacksmith's shop. We used to watch the blacksmith work and talk with him. About nothing, I guess. Then I stopped hanging around there. There was a trucking company right down the street from the smith's shop; they used to have crap games there. I never shot craps there: I couldn't see the dice.

I used to play pinochle with my cousin. He used to cheat me. My cousin John.

I'd stay out late a lot, go to a poolroom and play pool, listen to the radio, get drunk, do nothing at all. I'd stay out late and my mother would holler at me and hit me.

I got up early in the morning to get something to eat for my father before he went to work. I hardly ever spoke to my father. I don't know why. We never got along. He always jumped on me: he used to tell me how hard he had been working. Many times him and my mother would be arguing about me. I heard them but I made believe I never heard anything about it. When I write a letter home I hardly think of him and never even mention him. Sometimes my mother tells me how he feels: my sister does too. I never ask.

One time while he was busy fixing his car my mother told me to call him for supper. When I went to call him he didn't hear me, so I went nearer to call him again. He picked up a hammer and wanted to hit me with it. He said I had been cursing him. I guess I was about thirteen then.

I used to spend a lot of time at the park. There was a big bunch of fellows there on Saturday or Sunday night, all gambling and drinking, singing and making a lot of noise. Everybody would run in different directions when the radio car came around. I would go to the concerts there. All the girls from that neighborhood would go too. I tried to see how they would act when I talked to them. Most of them I discovered were just bums. I found that the girls who talked like ladies were the worst bums of all.

On Saturday and Sunday nights we had nothing to do and so three or four fellows would go to the show. We'd make a lot of noise and many times they threw us out. Whenever we would see several girls sitting together we'd sit near them and talk to them and make remarks until they got up and walked away.

Sometimes I used to just like to go and go and walk to the outskirts of the city. I liked to go away somewhere by myself. When I was at my aunt's home on the farm I'd go out in the woods sometimes and spend the whole day by myself. My uncle was the same way. He used to go and get away from everybody, way up in the mountains. It's cool up there, brooks run down the side of the mountain. In the winter I would go up into the mountains and chop wood. My aunt always liked to burn wood in her stove.

My uncle would eat a lot of meat. They always had chicken on the table and my aunt would find time to fry pancakes for him at every meal.

Sometimes I would go to my uncle's father's house. He had a big cherry orchard and on rainy or cloudy days when you couldn't do any work I would pick cherries. I'd eat more than I picked. I'd stay there all day long, just with my raincoat on. Lots of cherries in the trees. My uncle's father made cider and he'd get me drunk with it. My aunt didn't like it, didn't like it at all. There were a lot of arguments. He was an old man with grey hair and a grey mustache, an old thin man. He just said, "Well, it's nothing." My aunt used to yell and yell.

My uncle had a sister about two years and a half older than I was: I was sixteen and she was eighteen. She and some other girls would go out a lot. The fellows used to come around and take them out and lay them. One time, I remember, when she was in the kitchen, she called me in and she says she wants some love. I just turned around and I said, "No love today." And she said, "O yes, I forgot, you can't make love, you're blind." And I was so mad I held my penis and said, "This is blind too: it only has one eye." And my aunt heard it and came in and hit me. So when I came to go home from my aunt's house she came over to me and apologized. My uncle didn't say anything. That week I went home. I didn't want to be there anymore.

The last year I was there my father found some rubbers in my overalls pants. They were left from when I went around with Lila. He showed them to my uncle who burned them. My aunt told my mother and my mother hollered at me.

I can still hear my uncle's sister telling me that. I'll never forget it. She was not very fat: she had kind of brown hair with streaks of grey in it, or blond or something. She wasn't pretty: she was ugly. She had a friend who was big and fat. One time several fellows came to my uncle's house and brought a lot of whiskey with them. Everybody was drinking. Two of the fellows got drunk and they took the two girls outside but they came back very quickly. I don't think anything. . . .

The Fourth Hour

My mind is centered in this room. I can't seem to get out.

I am working with a fellow I don't like. He's a big, blond fellow, a Swede. He reminds me of a big ox. He hangs around with a friend of mine, Dobriski. They are pretty chummy. This Swede hasn't what's known as a gentleman's reputation. He's distrusted by many. He's taking the place of a fellow by the name of Mac. Mac is a young fellow about twenty: a quiet southern boy who doesn't say much. He didn't like the job; he sweated so.

Mac came here from G———. He tried to escape from there and got five years on top of his three; so he is doing eight now. He lost all his good time on the three years, but he turns up at the Parole Board every three months under some new juvenile law. He plays a lot of ball and sweats a lot.

The noise of that fan reminds me a little bit of a wind blowing in the trees and rustling the leaves. I am thinking of the wind blowing, the leaves rustling, on the side of a hill. I am thinking of the place where my uncle owns some land, about twelve acres on an island. A small river circles around and forms the island. One time I drove over a bridge to the island with my father and my sister. A little before that the bridge was washed away in a flood. The people had it fixed up again so that they could go over it with their trucks and cars. It was wet and slippery and the road was muddy. Our car jumped off on one side and my uncle's tractor had to pull it out.

I used to go fishing in that river with my uncle. He never said much: he was a quiet man who would kid you occasionally. He didn't do much hollering at anybody or anything.

A cousin of my grandmother's sister has a family in L———— and I have some cousins there. I don't even know their names. They have a little country place and six or seven children. Most of them are big now: two girls are married already. One of the boys I liked a lot. His name was Jerry. I had a lot of fun with Jerry. He had a little car and we would go skidding over the sandy places together. I would visit there a day or two. We'd go down and swim and row around on the water.

They live near a small town that has a nice beach. One of the girls who is married now was Sarah. She was not too thin and not too thick. She used to like to spend a few hours each night watching the stars when nobody was around. She would like to sit in a corner and pet with me too.

My uncle in L———— used to make a lot of wine and me and Jerry would go down in the cellar and steal maybe a gallon of it and take it to the woods and drink it.

I remember one time my cousin Riggs and I hung around for a while and then we started hitch-hiking. We got a hitch all the way out to L———— and we decided that we were going out to see how Jerry was doing. We stayed around for a few hours and then started back. While we were on our way to L———— a policeman saw us standing and waiting for a hitch. He wanted to know where we were going and told us to watch ourselves and be careful.

When I went around with that gang of fellows in our neighborhood we all had bicycles we stole. I stole about six of them I guess in my life. Several were stolen from me. I sold one or two. One I stole I scratched off the paint and I repainted it a maroon color. My father came down to the cellar where I was painting it. There was a fellow with me; his name was Jimmy and his uncle was a policeman; so this boy spoke up and told my father he gave it to me. He said his uncle was a policeman; that they didn't know the owner of it and his uncle paid for it at the cop's auction. He said he had no use for it because he had one already so he gave it to me. The only way I ever had a bicycle for myself was when I stole it and somebody lied for me to my father so I could keep it. I liked to take it apart, especially where the gear was. When it was greasy and muddy and dirty I liked to clean it and take care of it. I had it about a year and then I stole, I mean sold, it.

After I quit school I hung around with a fellow named Amos for a while. He used to work at a steel company across the river from where we lived. We used to hang out there, me and him. We'd get rocks and throw them in the windows and we'd wreck the joint. We'd steal all the copper wire, tear it out and break all the windows. One time I wouldn't go to school. Played hookey. I didn't go home for three nights. I stayed in there until my uncle found me and took me home. He was dead. I mean, he is dead now: got killed about three years ago. He was the best uncle I ever had. He used to tell me that whenever he got his bonus me and him would go together to South America. He died in February and they got the bonus in June. He was the best uncle I ever had.

Had the patient wished this death and is his praise an atonement for the wish?

He was always drunk but he was always good to me. My other two uncles, they were drunk too, always drunk. All the uncles on my mother's side of the family were always drunk. One of them is married and has a big family now, so I guess he stopped drinking. My other uncle, his name is Sam, he drinks now. He only works a couple of days a week as a plumber's helper. What money he gets he spends for drink. He isn't married: the reason is that he promised my grandfather that he'd live with my grandmother all the time and not leave her. He is about fifty-five now.

My aunt Louise, my mother's youngest sister, she is about twenty-seven, I guess. She's married and has three children. She always told me I shouldn't steal things from people: if I needed money to come to her and she would give it to me. But I never went to her and got anything from her. Riggs, my cousin, tried to get me to go to her so we could get money to go to the show; but I wouldn't.

He used to get mad because she wouldn't give him any money because she despised him. One time there were two cousins of her's from Buffalo visiting her. My aunt saw Riggs and me in the park one night and she called us over. I never saw them again afterwards. My aunt always told me how to act in front of people; to be quiet, not to act like a baby, never crack jokes. For about a month after that she always kept telling me that she was wondering what these girls thought of me. I don't know what I said, something kidding or some joke, but there was nothing dirty, no dirty intention. I remember one of the girls had a dress that looked like a parachute.

I remember once I got into a fight with a fellow they called Skinny. I was about seventeen then. Most of us when we grew up broke out of the gang into smaller gangs, five or six fellows in each. Well, we got into this fight one time. He was smaller than I, but heavier. He couldn't lick me and when he saw he couldn't lick me he tried to cut me with his belt buckle. He held his belt buckle in his hand and tried to cut my face with it. We were pretty good friends afterwards, got along pretty well. He and I were going to steal a canoe once from somebody's yard but one of us got afraid so we didn't take it.

Me and another fellow had a rowboat on the river. One time we went all the way down the river, about eighty miles. We took a .22 rifle with us. After a while we came to a real small motor boat with an outboard motor. We shot that boat full of holes. I wanted to take that motor but instead we shot it full of small holes, like pencil holes. Somebody stole the gun off us later. We had about ten or fifteen dollars between us when we went on that trip. After we got to the beach we couldn't find a good place to get off. The mud came up to our heads. We were out there altogether about a week, then we got sick of it and went home.

Sometimes I used to stay away three, four, five days at a time. Sometimes my father would hit me when I came home, sometimes he wouldn't; sometimes my mother would hit me.

When I was about fifteen, my father and mother had an argument and I think he hit her. I was so mad I couldn't see him. I picked up a poker about three feet long. My sister pulled it out of my hands.

My sister always was good to me. O, we had little arguments but after a day or so we started speaking again. I used to borrow money from her, but first I'd have to do a little talking and say, "Just

because we had a little argument you don't have to act that way."
She would always give it to me. I never could get a job anywhere
so I'd do a lot of reading and sleeping during the day and go out at
night.

Once in a while we would steal cakes from a bread company down
the street. On Saturday nights a lot of the fellows that worked in the
bread company used to have a crap game, so me and another fellow
were going to hold them up. We were going to take a shot gun or a
revolver. We never did. I don't know why.

When you look at a shot gun it looks like two big cannons looking
right at you. I mean a double-barrelled shot gun.

My uncle used to go hunting up in the woods. He used to take a
great big Saint Bernard dog with him. He never shot anything; just
go up into the woods all day long. He kept the dog to keep other
dogs away from his chickens. This was a great big dog, a monster.
Once I saw him shake a little pup and almost chew his head off. But
he was a good dog; he wouldn't bite ånybody, just bark.

My uncle had one of these farm battery radios. I would get to
hear it once in a while. Crime stories: Gang-Busters. I would hear
how the big gangsters got shot and I would laugh.

I smoked a pipe when I was on the outside and I'd throw the ashes
on the floor and get hell for it. I'd put the ashes in an ash-tray but
there was such a lot of them that my mother hollered at me because
she said I was smoking too much, so I started to throw them on the
floor again. Then she hollered at me for that.

There were big apartment houses near the Catholic school I went
to and on one of the streets there that bordered them there was a
very dark place. One night I held up a man and a girl in a car in
that place. I got caught. The man grabbed me and hit me in the
jaw. I got probation for that, five years probation. I must have
been about seventeen then. When I was asked why I wanted to
steal the car I told them I wanted it to go to Canada. That was a
lie. What I really wanted was the man's money.

I went to H——— Street School before going to the Catholic
school. I started at the Catholic school in fourth grade. The public
school on H——— Street was from kindergarten to the fourth
grade.

In the winter, on B——— Street, about two blocks from the

public school, a lot of big fellows from C——— and W———
Streets used to come around and throw snowballs at people. I got
one in the eye and had a black eye. I remember going to school with
my hat pulled over my face and telling them that I wouldn't come to
school for about a week.

I can remember that my eyes were blinking even before I had that
black eye.

When I was about six or seven I remember crossing a street when
the hot sun was shining. I ran into a street sign. I think, I'm not
sure, I got a black eye again then. The sun was shining so bright.
I don't know if I saw anything or not. . . .

THE FIFTH HOUR

It's hard. It's hard to get my mind way back in there. Hard to
remember. It's hard to put your mind on them and remember all
the incidents.

I was about six or seven. It was before I even started school, I
think. I used to run around on B——— Street, and I remember
we had a big yard and my father had a garage there where he kept his
car. We had a club house there too. It was Saturday night and
there was a young fellow named Fred something who lived across the
street in a four-tenement house. I remember it was getting dark,
not very dark; it was in fall or spring when it starts getting dark
around six o'clock. There was a touring car parked in front of a
house down the street and Fred and I were sitting on the running
board. I was talking to him. I don't remember what we were
talking about.

Some guy came along; he was about thirty I guess. He was drunk
and he started talking to Fred. I didn't say anything; I didn't
understand what they were talking about. They were talking like
that for about half an hour. Then Fred and the other guy got up
and we went to the club house. It was getting dark, about seven
o'clock, and we went in. We had made sort of beds from automobile
cushions and Fred and the other fellow laid down on them and they
started playing with each other. Fred was about seventeen; he had
dark hair, black hair. The three of us were in the club house. Then
they came around and started going down on each other. Then they
wanted me to go down on them. But I wouldn't do it.

We were in there about an hour, maybe an hour and a half. I remember when the fellow that was drunk came out he wasn't drunk anymore and when he walked outside of the driveway of the yard and he said to Fred he'd see him again.

When I walked out on the street to go home it was eight-thirty. My mother and my aunt were looking for me. I had straw all over me from the club house. The reason they were looking for me was they wanted to give me a bath. It was Saturday night.

I never said anything to my mother about that. . . .

I can remember back to when I was about four. I remember we were driving on a truck, my older sister and me and my mother and father. We were moving from our old place and we stopped at a farmer's house and stayed all night. I was about four when we moved to P———— Street, somewhere near C———— Street, and I remember there was a candy store I used to go to sometimes. I called the man "uncle," uncle something or other. Then from there we moved to B———— Street, where we remained about five years. I started to go to school there, in kindergarten at the H———— Street school. I was about five and I remember playing with blocks. There was a big room, and when they wanted to make classrooms they would pull the big sliding doors together.

I don't remember the teachers very well, their names I mean. The first and second grades are very hazy in my memory. I recall going to the gym class for exercise when I was in the fourth grade. And I remember belonging to a health class or something to build me up with milk, rest and the proper food. I remember also that the gym master made us stand at attention on a white line for half an hour sometimes. If we would talk in class the teacher would send us to the coat-room where we'd hang our coats and make us stand in that room all morning. I must have gone to this school until the fourth or fifth grade. Then I went to St. A———— School because my parents wanted me to be a Catholic. When I signed up for this school I think I had the classroom on the second floor, the first one to the left. I was about eight then and I used to wear knickers.

The sisters used to assign lessons and if you didn't have them done in the morning you would get whipped in the hand, and they forced you to kneel before a statue, the statue of the Virgin, in the dirt. I remember the priest used to have a crooked cane. One time he got a fellow with the cane around the neck and drew him close and then beat him up bad. Sometimes they made us all stay in. One time a fellow tried to get out through the window. I got whipped a lot.

We used to have a gang then. We'd pay our school dues, forty or fifty cents on Tuesdays. It was forty or fifty cents depending if you were Irish or not. I had to pay fifty cents, but the Irish kids paid forty. Many times we'd keep the money and go to shows.

One time my mother's godfather came to our house. He used to board there. It was in the summer time. I know because we used to have watermelon every week. This godfather always had whiskey. Once my mother broke some of his whiskey bottles on the step, the stone step of the porch.

I remember when my sister Anna, the youngest one, was born. I was in the next room to where my mother was. I could hear my mother crying and hollering. I was sleeping on a small bed. I don't know where my other sister was. It was when I was seven years old. Before the young one was born I remember my mother used to keep me on her lap and never let me go out. I used to sit and watch the other fellows outside. When it was six or seven o'clock she'd say it was too late to go out.

We had a victrola, about four or five feet high.

I remember one time I was sleeping in the front room, the parlor. Somebody was grabbing at the window shade. There was a man with a hat on out there: I know he was a burglar or somebody. Then I fell asleep. Next morning I told my mother about it but there was nothing missing from the house.

Down the block there was a small house. Nothing in front, just a few windows, no porch, nothing. I remember one time somebody's furniture was thrown out on the street from it. And there was another house on that block, a big red house, three or four stories high. We used to call it the red house. Everybody said not to go there because it was haunted. Next to that house was one with a big veranda going around one side and the front. I think a policeman or fireman lived there. We used to spin tops on the sidewalk in front of this house.

There was a Mr. Vanderbilt used to live in the big house next to us on the other side. I don't remember Mr. Vanderbilt very well. I used to see him when I was around twelve. The fellows used to find money around his house in the garbage cans, fifty and one hundred dollar bills.

A very common fantasy of infancy and childhood. Sums of money are to be found in garbage, waste, feces. This accounts for the orthodox analyst's view of money-feces.

They would find this money and then take it back. Three years ago, by accident, I found out from a fellow who should know that this Mr. Vanderbilt was connected with a big bootleg ring. I met this fellow who used to drive one of his trucks and haul whiskey for him. They used to smuggle it into the eastern part of the country from boats anchored off Atlantic Highlands in Jersey.

I don't remember Mr. Vanderbilt. Wait! Davis was his name. Davis. Davis.

The connection with large sums obviously caused this confusion.

He had a small wife who I remember better than I remember him. Yet I think he lived there alone and they had another house too. After he moved out there was a big fire in that house.

There were three or four houses that had a big yard together with no fences between. They had no inside toilets. We used to sit on top of the outhouses and sometimes shoot staples at cats. They had a lot of cats there, hanging around the outhouses.

Downstairs from us lived this lady who used to shave. She used to get dark in the face, like a beard. She had a son, the kid that got his leg cut off on the railroad. She also had two daughters. One time me and my cousin Riggs got one of the daughters in back of the garage. She was only a baby, about seven. I guess we just tried to do it to her. She didn't want to. She cried. Then Riggs hit her. So she ran away and told her mother, and her mother told my mother. I remember Riggs' father and my mother and his, I mean, her mother all sitting in the kitchen; and Riggs, he pointed at me and tried to tell them I was the one who hit her. I hated him then.

I don't remember my cousin Tony very well. He used to hang out with the older fellows, the big clique. He was about eighteen then. He used to steal everything he could get his hands on. He'd hitch on the back of one of the big pie trucks and steal pies and we would have a real feast. He went to live with my grandmother one time for about a week because his father was going to give him a beating.

There was a gang of kids in the next street who came over and had a fight with the fellows from B———— Street and I got in between. I got the worst of it. One of the fellows hit me with a piece of rope in the eye. He hit me in the eye. And Gimpy hit me one day with a snowball. Afterwards he swore to God he didn't do it. It was in the inside of a big house. I was just coming in and he was throwing a snowball out at somebody and he hit me in the eye. I remember Gimpy well. One day he got the loan of a bicycle and he took me out to a dump on the handlebars. We went looking for copper. That day I didn't go to school. When I got home I got a beating for not going to school.

Right at the corner of our block there was a fire-station, a hook-and-ladder company. Next door was a Presbyterian church and a big house, the preacher's house, and then another big house. On the bottom floor there were two stores, one a candy store and one a butcher store. One fourth of July a man came around and parked his car right across the street. He had a lot of cap pistols in the car and some of the fellows saw that and stole some. I stole one too. Afterwards my mother made me bring it back.

I remember the fire-engine parked on the street in front of the firehouse. The fellows used to blow the siren. We would press the button and blow the siren. We would press the button and blow the siren and pull the cord and ring the bell.

We lived a block from the river. I don't think the river is as dirty now as it was then. Once some of the fellows found a credit book from the store in the center of the block where we lived on B———— Street. They erased all the numbers and give it to me and told me to go in and buy some things. The man didn't give me anything because he saw that the whole book got written in before.

When I was four we lived on M———— Street near C————. My grandmother lived on C————. We lived on the second floor, and I remember I used to climb the stairs on my hands and feet: I used to help myself up with my hands. There was a store on the bottom. I think it used to sell fruits, vegetables and fruits.

I don't remember much. I don't remember much about liv-

ing in P————, but I remember coming on a truck, moving from
P———— . . .

THE SIXTH HOUR

A lot that I am telling you about comes back to my mind. Shall
I repeat things again?

I remember when I was eight or maybe nine years old. We were
still living on B———— Street. One time I went out toward the
river and I saw my cousin Riggs and another fellow come out of the
brewery warehouse. They broke some boards out of the side. I
was sitting there with a group of other fellows at the dock and a
policeman came over. He was there to see that nobody went in
swimming naked: and he asked the bunch of fellows if they had seen
anyone enter the warehouse. He asked me too and I said that I
didn't see anybody.

I used to spend a lot of time across the river in the swampland, a
big area of thirty acres. It was marshy and swampy and in some
spots it was sandy with brush growing all over it. We used to go over
and catch and shoot bullfrogs there, and sometimes we would swim
over with a hammer and some nails and get some logs and boards and
make a raft and come back with it. On the shore I remember it was
all muddy except some spots. When you stepped in the mud you
got in it up to your knees. Once a fellow stepped in the mud and
cut his foot on something.

We used to take a rowboat down the river about four miles or so
where there was a landing near a railroad track and big cars of watermelons used to come in. We always stole watermelons there.

I only saw one man drown in the river. I must have been fourteen
then. I remember the police pulled him out of the water. There
was a big crowd of people around watching. They put a respirator
on him to pump the water out but he was dead. So they put him
in a basket and put it in the ambulance and drove away.

The fellows from M———— Street had a clubhouse that was out
in the water. They put poles into the ground and on these poles
they built the house. You only could get there on a cat-walk and
sometimes they took the cat-walk down and you would have to go by
boat or swim. One time the police raided it, knocked the house
down, tipped it right over into the water. They used to have big

crap games in there and guns on the wall. Most of the fellows owned rowboats and some even had sailboats.

Right across the river there was E———— Hall which was owned by a politician named F———— where they had meetings once a month or more. Me and two of my cousins used to watch their cars so nobody would bother them till the meeting was over. We used to make a little bit of money that way, not much. Sometimes we would let the air out of the tires when we knew a fellow wouldn't pay us. This politician used to own a saloon of F———— Avenue. When I still lived on B———— Street I used to go to see a fellow once in a while who lived next door to this saloon. We would get in through the back of an apartment that nobody lived in. It was full of empty whiskey and beer bottles and on a bureau there was a cardboard box full of papers, just filled with papers. I remember digging in it and finding something hard way down in the papers. I pulled it out. It was wrapped around with paper and tied with a string. I broke the string and took off the papers and I found a sawed-off double-barrelled shotgun. Three or four years later, when I lived on M———— Street, I told another fellow about it and we went back there to look. We found everything still there, the bottles and all the papers, but the shotgun wasn't there anymore.

There was a fellow in that water gang who used to carry a blackjack. Several times he would get a dog or a cat and hit them with it. One time he threw a lighted cigarette into a parked automobile and the cushions got on fire.

There was a gas station near home and I hung around there a lot. One time I left my coat there and I had a pack of cigarettes in my pocket. When I came back and looked most of the cigarettes were gone, so I don't think I hung out there much more. There was a lunch wagon near that station and when I was about fourteen I used to break into a little storing shed in the back. They kept bottles of soda there and I would steal bottles and bottles of it. When I was about twelve I would steal milk from the milkman that came around at nights and used to put milk in the boxes that belonged to the stores. One time I walked down the Boulevard with two empty pint bottles and I passed the house of a fellow named Leeter who used to own a motor boat and chased us away so we couldn't swim around it. I threw the milk bottles right at the door and broke a window.

I sold my bicycle for four dollars because we wanted to buy an automatic and a .22 target pistol from a fellow. When we came to buy them his father had the guns and he couldn't get them, so me and my cousin Riggs spent the money. Another time when I was living on S——— Street I stole six dollars from a woman upstairs. Me and my cousin Riggs had a fine time for about two weeks on the money and they never found out whether or not I was the one who stole it.

There was a kid lived next door and when I was around twelve I got into a fight with him. He snuck up around me and hit me with a stick in the head and I hit him in the eye. Afterwards I took my knife and stuck it into his father's automobile tires and slit them.

Characteristically, retribution is directed against the father.

I used to hide my knives, a checkbook and things like that underneath our porch, and one time a fellow came and asked me for something. He couldn't find what he wanted so I went out to give it to him. My mother came out to see what it was all about and when I gave it to him she told him not to come back any more, and then she hit me in the head with her hand.

I remember long before my aunt married my uncle a friend of his used to come in with a truck load of onions and potatoes to sell them at the public market near our home. Sometimes he wouldn't sell all his stuff and he would come to our house and put it in the cellar. I thought I was pretty strong when I could pick up a fifty pound bag of potatoes.

One time my cousin Riggs and I went off on a hitchhike to near where my aunt lives and we got a hitch almost all the way to there. Then we waited a long time for another hitch and finally we started walking and eating apples that some farmer gave us. I have a dislike for that cousin. For some reason I never did like him but I used to hang around with him a lot. Anyway, I was real hungry and when we came to my aunt's house my grandmother who was staying there gave us something to eat. We were on the way home again when we met my uncle. My uncle Sam was coming up to see my grandmother and he told us to wait a while and he would take us home. So we waited and waited. I had about half a dollar in my pocket and we were waiting at the edge of town, so I told Riggs I would go to town and get something to eat again. When I came back I couldn't find Riggs. I waited for about an hour and he didn't come back and I couldn't find my uncle Sam either. So I went back to my grandmother's house because I thought that maybe he went back there for some reason. I found out he had left and I figured my uncle left too, so I stayed there that night, and in the morning my uncle spoke to me. He wanted me to go to work for him and he would pay me fifteen dollars a month. I had a big argument with my aunt. She was always quick-tempered; when she was mad she didn't care about anybody or anything. I always felt as if I was in the way there. She always fought or argued with my uncle. He just looked at her. Many a time she picked on me but I never said anything to her. I stayed there about three months that time and all the time my aunt was picking on me. She had one big argument with me. She wanted me to go to work on my uncle's father's place and I didn't want to. We had a terrific argument and I didn't wait for anybody: I just started to hit the road. That was alright too because two or three weeks before this my father wanted me to come home. He was figuring on getting a farm for himself. First he was going to get a farm on Long Island, a big farm: he was going to raise cauliflower or something; then he wanted to buy a chicken farm; then some other kind of farm.

The instability of the father is evident here.

I came home hungry and started eating all the cakes they had. My aunt Louise, she always made cakes for me; she sure used to fix up a cake! She is the one that always told me not to steal or take anything when I needed money, just to come to her and she'd give it to me; not even go to my mother for it. She was just a quiet, motherly type. My other aunt, Vanya, was just the opposite of that. She would always have arguments with everybody and she had a kind of wild look. She always combed her hair straight back: but my aunt Louise had nice hair, and she wore it nice and curly over the sides. She had curly hair like mine. My aunt Vanya has real black hair. She used to live with my grandmother before she was married. Once she and grandma had an argument and she came to our house to live for about two months. She bought our first radio, the first one we ever had, and she used to holler when anybody but her touched it.

She was very good to my sisters and used to bring them things.   Both my sisters had diphtheria about that time.   I never had it.

I don't remember much about when we lived on S———— Street. I guess it was four rooms and a bathroom.   I used to sleep in the front room, the parlor, and I would close all the doors and windows and listen to the radio until late at night; listening to crime stories and all the comedians I could get to hear.   If my mother heard it she would chase me to bed, but as soon as she went out I was at the radio again. I don't remember the kind of radio it was, but I know it was a cabinet set, a big one.   When my aunt went back to my grandmother's she took it with her, and about a week later we were so used to having one that we bought our own.

My grandmother's radio is a real old set; must be about twenty years old.   My uncle Sam always has a baseball game or something on.   He would rather listen to a baseball game or see one than any- thing else.   He used to drink a lot of coffee; he and my aunt Vanya would maybe drink a couple gallons a day.   I guess that's why she's so sensitive about everything.

Before my aunt moved she was living in my grandmother's house and my grandmother gave her the money to buy the farm.   My grandmother used to say she wanted her children to have places of their own and that's why she bought this farm for my aunt Vanya.

There was a small cemetery about a mile from the farm.   I was always afraid I would run in to it.   One day when I was walking in the mountains I ran in to it.   I didn't know what it was at first. Then I saw the stones and crosses.   It was in the afternoon but even then I didn't want to go all the way in, so I circled around it and kept on going.

In front of my aunt's property there used to be a big tree.   I spent a lot of time in that tree just reading.   My uncle used to say I must be in love with that tree to sit so often up there and read.

There was this girl Amy who lived right across the road that I told you about.   She used to look at me just like I was a younger brother to her.   She had a brother, a tough kid who got into a lot of fights. Once his friend made a crack about my eyes winking so I hit him twice, twice in the head, once with my left hand and once with my right.   He cried hard.   After that we were good friends.   I never had any of those fellows bother me or say anything about my eyes after that.

Me and Amy's brother Toby used to go out a lot together. We went to the town nearby where there was a roadhouse we'd get drunk in.

There was a farmer out there who seemed to like me a lot, Toby's uncle. He had a son about my age with a brand-new Terraplane coupe and me and Toby and him used to go tearing around in it. We rode fast. I drove it several times. It was light and easy to turn. Toby's father didn't like this kid. I guess he was afraid he'd get killed driving too fast, but I always got along with him. My mother didn't like me to go out with him either because she was listening to Toby's father. I remember once me and Toby and this fellow—I forget his name—started out to get a driver's license for me. Toby's hair was like mine and he and me had about the same build, so he was going to town and register in my name and they were going to take the Terraplane and make the test in it and get the driver's license for me. Somehow we didn't get around to doing it.

Me and this other fellow was also going to start in business. There was some money owing to me, about forty dollars from Toby's father for some work I did for him and about forty-five from my aunt. We were going to rent a blacksmith's shop and build platforms for truck bodies. They sell for about a hundred and a quarter. This fellow was very good at building them. We also had several ideas for making small plows and discs for cultivating. We thought we'd rent this shop and hire a blacksmith. Around this time my father wanted me to come back to the city. Later on I got into trouble time after time and so we never got around to it . . .

The Seventh Hour

There was an old brewery with a big chimney and we used to go inside this chimney and climb up the iron ladders way up to the top and look down. You could see the river from up there. From that height it looked like a creek, so small; and the railroad, right at the foot of the chimney; the tracks looked smaller than match sticks; and the train, the train looked like a toy train; and you could see the mountains far away, hazy and misty; and you could see all over our town and the town next to ours.

We used to go to C———— on our bicycles. There's a big park there with roads through it and bridges and a small pond for sailing with seaweed growing in it. The kids used to sail small boats. It wasn't deep enough to go swimming. In the evening it looked all nice and soft.

I get several thoughts in my head all at once. . . .

I remember back to a place where the B——— Company now stands. There used to be a small farm there next to the railroad yards. One time we hid a whole carton of playing cards there. There was a tin roof on the barn and we would run up and down, up and down.

When we still lived on B——— Street I once went with a fellow to take the lunch to his father where his father worked. We had to walk maybe a mile, and on the way we found some things, some metal things. I don't know what they were. We hid them in a sandbank and came back about three or four times looking for them, and we'd dig and dig and dig for them but we couldn't find them. They were long metal things with something like a pulley in the middle. They reminded me of a rounded sword. The other fellows used to have them and throw them. With practice it was easy to control them and you could make them stick in a tree.

One of the fellows had a car that somehow was charged with electricity. We used to play around with it and try to shock each other. When it rained we would connect it with a wet fence and when someone came along and leaned on the fence they would jump.

There was an Italian fellow who lived on this street too and one time I remember he had an argument with my friend. It wasn't a fight, just an argument. I wanted to get even with him and so I stole a pair of dumbells and a small sailboat from that fellow and hid them behind a pile of wood.

I used to play a lot with a gang that hung out around the Community House near the Catholic School I attended. There was a brewery across the street where we used to steal dry oats and put them down fellow's necks when we were in school. The sisters would make us stay in and clean the floors because the oats got all over them.

I used to hang around with a fellow by the name of Jimmy. He spent the summer at the shore with his grandmother. He was a blond-haired kid about my height and build, only he used to walk funny with his feet. One time I got sore at the girl I went with because she said something about his feet. He was in German class with me and we'd cut class lots. I didn't like to go to school very much and neither did he. We only went because we had to.

I'm hanging around with Perry occasionally here. The other guys kid me about him. I hate a lot of them. There's a fellow named Billings. I hate him. We were walking in the line the other day and he gave us a dirty look. I hate the ground he walks on. About a year ago I almost got into a fight with him. I never did like this guy Billings. He has a dirty, filthy mind.

I was sore at everybody today. I wouldn't even speak to my best friend. They think that because you talk to someone there is something under-cover going on.

Dobriski is the name of my friend. He plays ball with the institution. One time we were playing ball down at the other end of the yard when some fellow called Shanty said something about my eyes. I quit and walked away.

Dobriski is a stupid sort of fellow but he is kind and considerate to people. He reminded me of an old fellow I used to like to talk to who worked on the same job with me. This old fellow made parole about a year ago, and when he got out he went to see my people and told them how I was getting along. He was just like a prince, always so cheerful. He loved flowers. He is the first one besides you who ever took any interest and tried to make me understand that there is something else in this world than prison and crime.

The initial verbalization of positive transference. A triumphant moment!

I worked with another fellow who took the *Reader's Digest*. Once in a while he'd start an argument and after the argument had gone on for some time he'd bring out his book and prove his point. He would never start with the subject he was going to argue about; he'd start with something else, something entirely different; and then he would gradually bring it around to the point little by little. It would take him about an hour to reach his point.

I also worked in here with another fellow, Johnson. This Johnson, he was funny alright. He didn't like for anyone to criticize Sears-Roebuck where he once worked. He would get raving mad when anyone said Sears-Roebuck was a gyp-joint. He would work late at night and he used to come to my cell window when he was through with his work and look at my books. Every once in a while he would bring me flowers for my cell.

I don't read many newspapers, although some fellow sends me the *New York Times* every day. I just read its headlines.

Sometimes there is too much noise in the cell-block to do anything so I just stand by the window and smoke and look outside. The trees and the lawns look nice. Over the wall I can see the mountains. They look rolling, misty: in the evening it looks like a painted picture. Upstairs, from the auditorium, you can look outside and you see the whole countryside. It looks so nice and green: in the wintertime it looks white and snowy.

I remember when we were kids we used to have snowball fights and we'd snow-up the middle of the road to try and stop the cars from going through. And we'd build snow-forts. I recall we used to make big piles of snow and then dig little caves out of them and then we'd make a fire in them and they would melt down. One time we made a fire right in one of the caves: there was a lot of smoke in there. And sometimes the river would freeze and we would slide on our shoes right on the frozen river.

Several times I went down to the Bay for swimming when I played hookey. At the Bay we would have to walk through big fields of mud and we'd get mud all over our shoes and clothes.

Me and Jimmy used to go to baseball games at night. His uncle was a policeman and he used to talk to a fellow at the gate and he'd let us in and give us good seats, grandstand seats, right behind the batter. They would have all the lights on, just like daylight. And you could see the white ball and all the action, just where the ball is and how it goes. Sometimes when they would hit the ball it would go beyond the rays of light so you wouldn't see it and you wouldn't know where it was coming down. There was a score-board way out in the field, and above the score-board there was a clock. I couldn't see the clock; it was too far away I guess, but it was real big. I went a lot of times to these night games. I never ordinarily went to see games in the daytime, only at night. I used to like to see the white ball. I could see it anywhere. There was a net before the grand-stand to protect the people from the balls. Many times the ball would come over and hit the net and then roll down again.

Dobriski pitches sometimes; he also plays at first base. He's a pretty good ball player too. It is hard to play ball in a place like this because all they have to play for is an extra steak dinner once in a while and that's all. In a place like this there is always a lack of cooperation. Some of the fellows don't like this and some don't like that. One fellow is praying that the manager will make parole so he can get back on the team. He can't play ball very well but he tells everybody it's because he has bad eyes.

I've got another good friend, Carlson. He marks the score behind the batter; last year he wanted me to take that job over. He asked me if I wanted it, so I didn't tell him I couldn't see, only that I didn't want it. I didn't tell him why. Once he said something to me about my eyes and I didn't talk to him for about a month. Every time somebody says something about my eyes I always remember it later. I always remember. I use it as a basis for hating them.

I don't remember much about a dream I had the other night.

This dream was unsolicited.

All I remember is I was talking to some young fellow and he wanted to run away from the draft; so I told him it was better to go in the army for one year than in a place like this for five. I also remember that there was a war going on or something, and that there was also some fellow who wanted me to write a letter home to his mother. He was dying.

The writer holds to the general thesis that the first few dreams brought by the patient should remain undiscussed. Too often the patient is alienated by early probing.

This one that was dying was an older man: the other was a young fellow. I don't think I looked very carefully at them. The younger fellow reminded me of Perry, except that he had hair like Dobriski, kind of a dirty blond. I don't recall what the older fellow looked like at all. I was telling the younger one that it was better to be in the army for one year: that it was bad but not as bad as five years in here. The one that was dying was in one piece; I mean that he didn't have his legs or his arms cut off or anything like that; but there was a hole in his side, a pretty big hole. He wanted me to write a letter to his mother. He wanted to let his mother know but he didn't want anybody else to know. I can't even place the fellow. He wore a tin hat like they have in the American Army. I don't know how I was there or what place I was holding or what job I was doing. I don't even know if a war was going on. Things changed from one moment to the next. He kept hollering to write somebody a letter: he was hurt or something. While I was talking to the young fellow there was a freight train going by and he was going to jump on that freight train to avoid the draft. The train was going and going and going, and it looked to me as if there was no end to it. I don't remember seeing the engine passing, all I remember is that the freight cars were going.

These first dreams will provide an index to performance and will enable the examiner to estimate the sufficiency of the patient's grasp of the technique of reporting.

Sometimes I lie in bed and I can't fall asleep until about eleven. I get up several times to get a drink of water or to take a smoke and look outside. Sometimes I'm up till five-thirty in the morning. When I lie in bed like that and can't sleep often I write poetry. The words just keep going through my mind like waves, fine and smoothly. I can't remember a thing going through my head and so I write everything down in the night. In the morning I try to decipher what I wrote.

I remember in the dream the freight cars were all going, moving, moving. They made a rattling noise. I could hear it plain as day as I was watching the cars.

When I lived in T cell-block they had sliding doors made of bars. I was up on the third floor. Up there I would sleep until count-time: many times the officer would holler at me for sleeping late. I didn't like the place, someone would walk by and your mind would lose interest in what you were doing and turn to the person going by. Somebody was always playing some music, the same song all the time. I didn't like it so after about three weeks I moved out. I couldn't get any of my work done.

The only reason I moved up to that cell-block was that Dobriski was up there. We are always having a lot of arguments. He is a very fine fellow only he would burn me up a lot by talking to this fellow Billings or the one they call Shanty. If a person says anything or makes any remark about my eyes I always remember it. He purposely and deliberately agitated me by doing that. We had a lot of arguments about it . . .

The Eighth Hour

I had three dreams.

In the first one I dreamed I was on the road above the greenhouse here. I dreamed that I and a girl were going in there. We went in on one side and at the other end I saw my sister, so we ran out of one door and my sister came out the other end. She started rushing toward the girl with a whip in her hand. The girl didn't know what to do. My sister had a whip and I tried to stop her.

In the other dream there were some men with big hats. I can't place any other people or any of the characters. I don't remember much about this dream. There was a room with a big bathtub in it and somebody turned on a tap and hot steaming water came down on all the people. I don't remember getting any of the hot water on me.

In the next dream I remember helping a fellow provision a boat with food. I was going to buy a boat for myself, a motor boat, and I was going to cruise to Atlantic City.

I remember sitting in the show last night and it was real hard for me to see the picture. I was straining my eyes so much. The pictures were too bright, I guess.

The reader will note the cautious but active introduction of the writer into his role in the entire procedure.

L: *'Harold, suppose you start with one dream and tell everything that occurs to you in relation to it.'*

Well, I don't know who this other girl was. I think it was Lila. I remember my sister saw her one time with me and she didn't like her.

It was at the greenhouse in here. The greenhouse is about eighty feet long. We went in at one side and she was at the other, the other end. We came out on the road and my sister had a whip or something like a whip and she came running at the girl and it seemed she was going to hit her. I started holding my sister back. I wouldn't let her whip her. I remember distinctly the girl with the whip was my sister Marie, the older one. They were the only two persons in this dream. I remember they were in the greenhouse inside the walls and I remember the greenhouse, the road, the buildings and everything. My sister had a dark dress on. I think we walked in one end and saw my sister come out the other with a whip in her hands. She was holding it in two hands, the thick end was in her left hand.

L: *'Why would your sister want to whip you?'*

She wouldn't whip me, she was going after the other girl. She saw the girl with me one time and didn't like her. She always used to kid me about what ugly girls I picked up. I held her back. The other girl didn't know what to do, to stay or run away. My sister's got a bad temper, a really bad temper but I always can cool her down. I just talk to her and just cool her down a little bit. But she had the thick end of the whip in her left hand and the thin end in her right hand. She was holding it with her two hands. The whip was about four feet long. I held her by the shoulders. I held her back but I didn't take the whip from her.

I remember that time my sister saw me with Lila. My sister had a red dress on and the girl was wearing a pink dress and I had a white shirt and blue trousers. I don't know why my sister didn't like her. I guess she was ugly in a fashion: she had straight hair and my sister has nice curly hair, shiny. I remember all the kids I hung around with would kid me about her. They used to say that she was taking good care of me.

I think it was very funny. I remember very distinctly the greenhouse and the wall and everything about it; the greenhouse in this place and the wall in this place, everything in this place except the girl and my sister.

Most of the other girls I ever went with my sister liked but she disliked this one. I didn't go with this one very long, about two months or so. My sister really hated even her name.

All I remember is that it was daylight and it was in the summer, and the grass was so green.

They were the only two persons in my dream.

My sister is right-handed so I don't see why she would hold the whip in her left hand. I don't remember whether the girl was running away from me or where she went. I was holding my sister by the shoulders, holding her back. She was saying to me that I should get out of her way. After that I remember nothing about it. I think I woke up then.

L: 'Can you remember anything more about the second dream?'

The second one I don't remember much about. There were a lot of men, men with big hats, big hats like Stetson hats, and cowboy shoes. It was in a room or something. They had a lot of things like sprinklers near the ceiling set in different angles. It was a kind of bathroom with a sink and a wash basin and everybody was there. Somebody turned a knob and the hot steaming water came down on everybody. I don't know who anyone of them were.

In the last dream I had I can remember the place. It was at a dock where all the boats were tied up near C————. There is a bridge there over the river and before you cross that bridge you come to the place where all the boats are kept in storage. There were several people, a man and his wife and a small child, a girl. They owned the boat and were fixing it up to take a cruise. I was telling some girl in the party that I was going to buy a boat some day and I kept pointing out to her several different ones. I would like that one and that one and that one; and I would take a short cruise to Atlantic City for about two weeks or so.

I was in Atlantic City once or twice. I remember seeing the big pier standing way out into the ocean. I didn't like to go swimming in the ocean. I'd rather go to a pool. It's not so dirty and there is no sand.

I remember about ten years ago we went off on a trip up a river on an excursion boat. I think it was my aunt Louise, my mother, my sister and myself. We got on the boat somewhere and went straight up the river. It seemed like a river so maybe it was. With a river you can see both sides unless it is very wide. Maybe it was the Bay. The boat went out and then it turned around and came back. I don't think it was a river; if it was it was certainly very wide. There were big mountains where the boat docked. I saw people swimming and rowboats and sailboats. There were a lot of people on it but not many people swimming. It was a long time ago. I remember when we started from home. We were living on B———— Street then. There were only myself, my other sister, my aunt Louise and my mother. We lived near the railroad station and I remember we took a train there for where the boat was. When we got off the train we took a bus and went to the dock where the boat was and we went on the boat and then the boat started. I can't remember whether we went up the river or down or up the coast. I don't even remember why we went. I was very young then. When we came back it was dark. I recall the people dancing and looking down the boat through a small iron door into the engine room where I saw the wheels and the motors talking, I mean turning, and making a lot of noise.

A slip reflecting his awareness that he has been evading dealing with the dreams.

I can't remember the name of the boat but it had three decks. When we got there we walked up the mountains. There was a road, a dirt road.

This all probably happened when I was around eight years old. When we came back I was telling everybody about it. I remember one fellow saying he was going on a trip too. We were talking under a street light on the corner. There was a fire hydrant on that corner.

One of the fellows lived near that corner. He used to take barrel-staves and cut guns out of the wood. I remember some men once drained the sewer on the corner and found a cannon-shell, about a foot long and eight inches in diameter. I tried to pick it up; it weighed about forty pounds. The fellows used to lose balls in that sewer, baseballs and handballs. They got them out by chinning themselves in the manhole and picking the balls up with their feet. In the summer time the firemen would turn on the fire hydrant on that corner. One time I had a fight with a fellow who hit me in the eye and I was lying on that corner crying, right underneath the street light, the street light. It was shining bright in my eyes and everybody was looking at me. After that my mother didn't let me go out and I used to sit in the window and watch all the fellows out there playing.

One of the fellows and I used to have whistles. When we wanted to warn each other we would blow them. He was about three years older than I and I remember how he used to read books and I used to think how much smarter than I he was. I remember he used to diagram sentences and play a harmonica. He had an older sister who always used to sit and sew. I didn't see him for a long time and then when I was twelve I joined the Boy Scouts and found him in the same troop. . .

The Ninth Hour

I was just reading about a fellow who has been waiting to be hanged for thirty-two years. The judge died before his sentence was to be carried out so now he is still waiting to be hanged. I know about this fellow from another fellow I used to know; this fellow did about five years in the State Penitentiary and he told me about him. The one that is waiting to be hanged, he doesn't know what an automobile looks like, or a truck, or an airplane. He gets exercise about two hours a day and most of the day he is locked in. He smokes real strong tobacco, so strong it would even kill a horse to smell the smoke. The fellow that told me about him drove a truck for a bootlegger named Davis. I knew this Davis from seeing him in a brokerage

office in B——— Street. That's the main thoroughfare of our
town. He used to be at this office a lot. Up the hill a way on
R——— Street is the Court House, across the street is the House
of Records where I had to report for probation. My probation officer
drove an old Model A Ford; he had a son about two years older than
I and he lived near the High School where I went.

There was a candy store near the High where I hung out. I ate
my lunch there, not much, a bottle of coke and a piece of pie and that
was enough. I played the pinball machine a lot. One time I had a
fight with my cousin Riggs in the back room there.

Right on the corner across the street from the park there was a
little triangular lot. We had a clubhouse there, right up against a
billboard. There was an empty house nearby where we used to play
around. We took all of the fixtures out of it, the copper wires, the
iron, all the junk and sold it for the money we could get. Sometimes
we'd put dirt and rocks inside the pipes when we took them to the
junk man so that they'd weigh more.

> *Much inconsequential and repetitious material is omitted from this
> session.*

I don't know why we stole so many watermelons. We'd get whole
boatloads of them from the railroad cars down the river. I don't
know what we wanted with all of them. We couldn't eat them all.
I suppose we stole them just because we wanted to have something
to show.

One time I stayed out from nine in the morning until around eight
at night. When I came home my father spoke to me harshly. I
was never on good terms with my father. Maybe it was because he
was a little deaf and he couldn't speak English well and I couldn't
speak Polish.

> *The confusion and conflict as between immigrants and their children are
> well illustrated here.*

He never had much to say to me. Sometimes he would treat
me alright and sometimes he would holler and say something.
Sometimes I would hear him and my mother argue about me:
my mother always held up for my end. My sisters always held up
for my end. My sisters always got along with him. The oldest one

would sometimes tell him to go to Hell or something like that and he would just laugh. I would only speak to him when it was necessary, other times he just didn't say anything to me. When I was about twelve we broke into a butcher shop and stole a lot of things, so I went away for about three weeks to the juvenile home and when I came back my father didn't say anything.

I never liked to go to church. When I was at St. A———— School they made us go to church in the mornings and in the afternoons. Many times I said I was going to church but didn't go. One time my father saw me out in the street when I was supposed to be in church and when I got home he gave me a beating.

I don't know why but I didn't like a lot of the kids that went to school there. They were wise and I guess most of them were smarter than me. Anyway, I know I was the one that got most of the lickings and got punished for not having my lessons done or for doing something wrong or for doing something I shouldn't have been doing. I couldn't read very well and got several lickings for that. I wouldn't do any work at the board and got hit for that too. They sat me in a back seat where I couldn't see the board so I never did any work. I never told them I couldn't see the board. I never told anyone, not even my mother.

My mother and grandmother and sister used to make me go to church even though I hated it. Once I told my mother that it was all a bunch of lies, so when she was visiting me here she made me promise her I'd go to church once. I went once. It doesn't grasp my emotions, I guess. I always find some excuse for not going.

My cousin Emma and I were alone in the house together once. I was supposed to go to church and I went down there but couldn't tell whether it was over or not. So I went home and we were alone together. I played with her and was kissing her and I played with her breasts. That's as far as I got. I was about twelve then. She was reading some book, something about where babies come from, and playing the radio. I was sitting on the arm of the chair. She's about twenty-five now, married about three or four years. I never met her husband. She was always dull and uninteresting.

I know my cousin Joe's wife. She's a fairly beautiful girl. They have one child. She always seemed nice to talk to. She's short and has black hair. When Joe went to prison the time he got eighteen months she told me that next time it happened she would divorce him, but when the next time came around she just let things go. Once in a while my cousin Riggs would mind her kid for her when she wanted to go out and one time he was doing that he asked me to bring Lila up there. I didn't.

I always told Riggs that when I had girls I saw no reason why I should share them with him: he never did with me. He used to tell me about this girl and that girl and the other girl he was taking out, but when he saw me with a girl he would come over and try to get her on the side.

There was that cousin of mine from L——— that I told you about. She would like to sit in the car and pet or sit out on the porch when everyone was asleep, and sit and kiss. I used to tell myself that the next time I would go further and further. I still haven't reached the point yet. I guess it would be a simple matter for me to go as far as I want with her, but now I think she'll be too old when I get out, probably she'll be married.

There was another girl on S——— Street, Carol I think her name was. I used to have her every once in a while for about two years. She was always afraid she'd have a baby. My friend Willy always told me how he had her once up against a tree. I don't think I ever told him once when I had her.

Willy's sister was a little too fat for me. She would only let you put your arm around her neck and kiss her; that was the only thing she would allow.

Willy and I used to go swimming in the park and we used to pick up different girls, I guess mostly for the fun of it. We'd always go to shows together when he wasn't working. He worked at night, I think. We spent a lot of time in the early afternoon and evening walking up and down the main street.

I always dressed as neat as I could, especially in the evening when the streets were getting dark. I'd hang around the corner next to the school and would get drunk a lot. One evening—I guess it was the only time I ever got so drunk—I started drinking at about four o'clock, and it was about nine when I got down to a bench near the river front. I fell asleep and it was raining on me, so I swore I'd never get so drunk as that again.

My uncle liked to get me drunk, the one on the farm. I used to go down his cellar where he kept his wine and cider, and sometimes I'd siphon out the barrel he kept it in. He used to wonder what became of his wine and cider it went so fast. His father used to get me drunk too. I liked to go to his father's house. He had a lot of wine too.

My uncle Albert used to eat a lot of meat, all he ate was meat. He worked very hard. I want to be anything but a farmer and work as hard as he did. He worked hard all his life and he'd drink and spend his money only when he was a kid. His father worked hard too and he never had much of anything, just a home. Sometimes when my uncle worked plowing up the ground I used to think I like the country. But I don't like hard work of that kind. I guess he was born into it and he figures on staying in it.

I'm not interested in making a lot of money. The only thing is, I'm going to write a couple of books on economics. I'm going to change the *Communist Manifesto*. Of course I don't know much about it but what little I do know about it I know it's wrong. There are some things I know are wrong. For instance, I know Marx's theory on population to be wrong. Some people know a little something about economics and they always talk about this and that, but I know that when you take everything away from everybody that can't be economically sound.

Adam Smith's *Wealth of Nations*, of course that's a little too old. Sometime I'm going to rewrite that book and I'm going to change the *Manifesto* too.

This grandiosity is a typical psychopathic manifestation.

Marx criticizes religion but most of his preachings he took from Jesus Christ.

In a couple weeks I am going to send for both books, *Das Kapital* and *Wealth of Nations*. I don't know much about economics but in a couple of years I'll know enough about it and then I'll start working on them. Now I'm interested in this stimulation of industry, I mean the re-armament program, the stimulation of iron and steel and oils and many other manufacturing industries, airplane manufacturing for instance. I want to see what the reaction is going to be in a couple of years. There's going to be a real downfall. According to the inevitable law of change there's going to be a revolution or a reaction. There have been two industrial revolutions, one in England and one in America, and they have been helped along by two great wars, the Napoleonic wars and the World War. They speeded up production and as soon as the wars ended everything dropped. That's what's going to happen in this case, maybe not so hard. And I think many airplane companies are going to go bankrupt, and some of the companies making automobiles and trucks for the army. I don't think a big company like General Motors will lose anything. They have distributing companies over the whole world.

I try to talk to some fellows here who know something about economics, but I don't want to get like they are. Perry, for instance, always impresses on my mind the economic side of everything but it doesn't necessarily have to be the most important one.

Perry and I hang out together occasionally, once or twice a week. The rest of the time I stay in my cell and study. I don't think he goes out much. He tells me that he is bi-sexual and from some of his actions it would certainly seem that he is. I hope I never have anything to do with him sexually. I wouldn't like to do anything like that. A lot of my friends are asking me; they don't seem to be my friends now.

I don't talk to very many people: they irritate me. I like to go off myself and just think about nothing and talk to myself. Dobriski is a swell fellow but he is really too dumb for me to talk to about economics and that's the thing most on my mind. He doesn't care what I talk about.

Perry is willing to argue about anything with anybody. We eat together at the same table. I don't like the way he puts his foot under him on the bench. I don't like it. He sits on one foot. He always tries to get some argument stimulated. He gets a lot of fun out of trying to convert people to the 'only faith,' as he calls anything he says. There was a fellow yesterday, an ex-Communist from Boston. Perry tried to convert him. It was funny: his face got all red. . .

THE TENTH HOUR

This morning I was talking to a fellow outside my cell window who gave me some flowers and I put them in my locker. I didn't like flowers very much on the outside but in here I like them a lot. This old man Thomas also liked them a lot: he used to write poetry about flowers and tell me about his garden at home. He had a small estate and he would tell me about all his flowers, how they were growing and how they were arranged. He loved to sit and tell me about his experiences when he was a kid. He was quite a sportsman, it seems, participating in all sports, probably to make a living. He was well built for an old man, his arms and muscles were all hard. He liked to putter around flowers and take care of them; to see how they grow and grow different kinds, big flowers and small flowers.

When he left here he went to see my family. I don't know where my mother and father are living now. My sister was up to see me not very long ago but she wouldn't tell me where they live.

Everybody I talk to notices the improvement in my eyes since I am coming here to see you.

This was a gracious way of informing L of the transference. As a matter of fact, his eyes were unaffected at this time.

They are open a lot more than they used to be and they feel kind of hard in the roof when I spread them wide open. They don't blink much even in the sunlight now and I remember they used to blink a lot. Years ago I would have to hold my hands over my eyes to see but now I don't have to anymore. I wear glasses sometimes to keep people from asking so many questions. In my cell I have a very strong bulb so I wear glasses to stop most of the light. They're dark glasses, smoky. . . .

My aunt and uncle are the only two people that have so much land on that island. They work it themselves and if they don't make enough out of it this year they'll lose it all. My uncle is a kind of fellow who would rather fish than do anything else, but my aunt works very hard.

I remember once near their house when Amy's brother killed a snake. He was riding a bicycle and the snake was crossing the road and he ran right over it. We caught a lot of snakes around there.

There was a fellow named Mick who had an old Chevvy that we'd ride around in and go up and down the big hills fast. There used to be a lot of girls around there too and we had a lot of fun taking them for rides in the old Chevvy.

Toby's father liked hunting. He used to raise rabbits simply for the pleasure of letting them loose and then hunting them down. After he killed some we'd all have a big feast. One time we went to a carnival, me and my sister and this Toby's uncle. He took us into town and all he did was drink. I saved him from some of those sucker games. I told him how they work. It seems to me that anybody grabbing them is just a sucker. When I got home that night I remember I slept out in the grass.

I recall that me and Mick's brother went to see a fellow and we were in there talking about nothing at all. This fellow insulted Mick and I said something back to him and he got sore, so he started chasing us with a shotgun and we ran right through a big field of corn.

I like the country out there and I always thought I could maneuver around to fix myself with a small income, not very much, since I'd rather be up there than down in the city. There are too many people in the city, too crowded and too noisy; they run back and forth and you don't know your next door neighbors. Out there in the country you get acquainted easily, you know everyone and everyone knows you.

I only had a couple of fights up there. One was with a big fellow about my age who weighed more than I did. He came from the city to see someone for a week or so. He made a nasty crack about my sister and when I heard about it I started to pick an argument with him. I was afraid of him but I had to do something when I found out that he said something about my sister. So we started to argue back and forth and we started wrestling and I fell down and hit my head on a stone. Then we started arguing again and talking back and forth and he denied he said anything. Then another fellow verified it right in front of me. I stood on a step a few inches higher than him and I was scared and didn't know what do do. So I hit out and hit him right on the chin and he staggered back about ten feet and went down on one knee and I got more scared and I tried sic-ing the dog on him but the dog wouldn't do anything and I didn't know what else to do. So I knocked him down and I managed to get on top of him and I started beating him with my fists. I felt awful weak and tired but I kept hitting at him. I don't know what happened then. I think some other fellows came along and pulled me off him.

Another time I had a fight with Steve. He said something about my eyes and I hit him twice. He laid down and after that we were good friends.   We never said anything about it, never even mentioned it after that.

I got along with most of the fellows after that out there.   I remember I used to wear different kind of clothes than these fellows had. My clothes were clean after I finished working even.   I had a big wide belt with a lot of glass jewelry on it.   When I couldn't get out of going to church I dressed neatly to look my best and when I went there I would make eyes at the girls, looking at their hats or their hair. They'd feel self-conscious or something and I would laugh up my sleeve.   They'd look like they were trying to shrink away.

There was a fellow there who owned a garage.   He was making a racing car, a sporty racer with curves.   The wheels were small and it had mudguards and fenders and everything.   Every time I saw it I would want one like it.   There was a race-track nearby where they ran trotters and even cars and they would broadcast the races.   I used to listen to the broadcasts but when I was working my aunt wouldn't let me talk about it or even see it.

My aunt is a fine woman only she's quick-tempered and hard as steel.   I guess she works too much.   Most of those people there seem to me to be wasting their lives working, working, working all the time. It finally ends up where they haven't got anything.   That's why when the opportunity afforded for me to come to you and get straightened around and study and accomplish something I was willing to do it. I don't mind work, but when you waddle around in dirt all your life that's a different matter.   I've seen my uncle doing it year after year and he still hasn't got anything.   If he worked as hard with his mind he'd probably be a rich man.   Some people just go along and live their life, just following it, and they never try to get anything out of it.   One fellow was telling me that it was just a question of luck, that if my luck changes I'd be able to get out of here and steal money and get away with it, and if not I'd be just the kind to stay in jail the rest of my life.   He seems to think it all depends on the type of breaks you get: if the breaks are for you, alright; if they're against you it's just too bad.   But I know that it's possible to make the chance, to make it so, or any way you want to.   It don't come just in one day or one year; it may take five or ten or twenty years, and it sure is hard work building it they tell me.

There are some books in the library I would like to read but I haven't the time to read them. Time does seem so short. We spend a lot of time in bed, from 9:30 at night to six in the morning. Half of that would be enough for sleeping.

The grass outside my window is so nice and fresh when it rains. It smells so sweetly. The flowers bloom and everything is so cheerful. When it rains all the birds run along underneath the shower. I guess the birds just can't resist the water. . .

THE ELEVENTH HOUR

I want to tell you about a dream I had last night. I remember it yet: I forced myself to remember. I dreamed about this place. We were in the mess hall eating; I don't remember what we were eating; and I saw Lieutenant K——— standing at a post directly opposite from where I was sitting. The tables were not the way they are in the mess hall: they were lengthwise to the pillars, and my table was in between the pillars and the arch, and I was dreaming that I was directly in front of him and I was hollering for something to eat and he looked at me and smiled. Then I was dreaming that I went up and tried to get in school for the second period and I had to talk the officer into letting me go upstairs through the grille, and finally I went upstairs. It was only a few minutes to six and I looked into the typing room off the corridor and there was a friend of mine coming out of the class. There was a crowd of fellows and one of them was named Decker and there was another fellow (I can't place him) who was speaking Polish to me, and Dobriski. This fellow Decker used to be here about a year ago. And that's all I remember.

L: 'Can you report your associations to the first part of the dream, Harold?'

All I remember is that I was sitting at the table. It seemed that the table was in between the pillars, and directly in front of me there was Lt. K———. He had on a white shirt and a hat and he was standing at one of the pillars. It seemed funny because only plain officers stand at the pillars usually, and the lieutenants stand either at one end of the mess hall or the other. I don't know who was sitting next to me or who was sitting at the other tables. I think we were eating beans or something like that. I can't place it very well. I know it was Lt. K——— because when he smiles his face bulges out. There wasn't any noise or violence, just somebody hollering for something to eat.   I think it was supper time, and that was funny because Lt. K——— isn't usually there for supper time.

   L: 'Does this dream mean anything to you?'

   I'm not sure.   I see him in the mess hall occasionally but I see Lt. R——— more often.   I forget whether I have ever spoken to him but I have seen him without his coat; yet I've never seen him leaning against a pillar.   And the funny part about it was that the table was lengthwise, not the way the tables are arranged, but in between the pillars.   The table was right underneath the arch and he was standing directly in front of me, right against the pillar.   The tables aren't set that way.

   L: 'Now, Harold, you know that often the objects seen in a dream may symbolize something else, stand for something else.   We have got to try and discover what they symbolize.   One way to do this is to fix on one thing and speak of everything it brings to mind.   For instance, the table might suggest eating, eating might suggest a special type of food, and this might recall a pleasant experience you have had with someone while dining.   Now can you follow it through yourself?'

   Well, I worked for Lt. K——— for about two years and I have grown to like him a lot.   I don't remember hitting the table or anything, just hollering to him I wanted something to eat.

   L: 'Does it suggest that you were starved?'

   I don't know.   I don't eat very much.   O, I eat all of the pork chops and steaks I can get hold of.

   L: 'Was there any reason for you to be so hungry?'

   I haven't had a . . . I have been in this place for about two years now and I sort of forget everything on the outside.   I don't know. I can't place anything, can't see any meaning in it.   I think that's why the table was between the pillars underneath the arch.   That might suggest intercourse with a woman.   The table may be the penis and the two pillars and the arch a uterus or something.   This is the first time I thought about it.   I don't know what made me think of it.   If I was dreaming that, why would it be Lt. K——— who was in it?

   L: 'Are you implying that the business of eating was disguising a sexual significance?'

   I guess that's what I mean.   The sexual act resembles eating a lot. It's the satisfaction of a certain desire.   It's perfectly possible that in my dream this desire was disguised.

L: 'Well, let's start from the fact that this dream may have a sexual significance, the two pillars representing what you called the uterus, and the table the penis.'

Well, I know that there are different symbols representing different sexual organs. I read a book that said something like that. *The Outline of Mentality.* It deals with history, religion, sex, geography, everything. I remember it stated some of the sexual symbols like the number three, or a cave, or a window. I never realized that a dream would have a bearing on some thought like that. I never thought about it very much. I just tried to remember what I dreamed. It never occurred to me that. . .

I haven't had any sexual affairs with anybody in this institution. I don't think it's right for two men to do things like that.

Wait! Maybe that's why the Lieutenant was there. To stop me from. . .

About the other part of my dream, about going up to the classroom through the grille. I had to talk the officer into letting me go up; I had to show him passes and papers. I looked into the typing class and they were getting through with their class. My best friend attends that class. There also was one fellow I used to associate with, a fellow named Decker and there was another fellow who talked Polish to me. This other fellow started talking to me about my trial, about too much time I got, and about a fellow named Felix. I don't remember the last name of the person. He said, "Why don't you see Felix?" I can't place it anywhere. I don't remember if I ever knew anyone named Felix. It couldn't be Felix the Cat but that's one of the things I always read in the newspaper in the comic sheet. I'm not much interested in the news. I look at the headlines and once in a while glance at the editorials. If they are interesting I read them, but they usually seem one-sided to me. I look at the pictures and the maps and the funny sheets and the financial sheet. There is a column every day on finances by a fellow called B. C. that I read. I look at it and the business graphs. Pictures are alright. I like to look at them but I don't like strung-out articles. They can be condensed down to a few short lines if you ask me. *Life* magazine condenses everything down to just a few pictures and a little bit of understanding explanation. I like to read a little bit and have a clear understanding. I don't read everything in *Life*. Some people tell me it's the best magazine in the market. Maybe. I like to read

Fortune and the *Reader's Digest*.   I don't read everything in these magazines, just the things that interest me.   I don't read the *Saturday Evening Post* or other magazines like that.   I have a magazine now where they analyze the industries in Mexico.   I like to read something like that because I learn something.   *Fortune* carries a lot of advertisements.   You can learn a lot from advertisements too.   I remember one.   On a white sheet of paper they had a black spot in the middle, a black spot to attract one's attention, like making a black dot in the center of a circle. . .

L: *'Let's get back to the matter of your first dream, Harold.'*

> *If he had been allowed, he would have wasted the hour in just such evasive chatter as he was recalled from at this point.*

What I think about mostly in this institution is eating and studying. I don't think very much about sexual relations with anybody or with any woman.   I like to get my hands on a good meal once or twice a week.   I buy some pork chops and steaks from a fellow once in a while.   It doesn't seem enough to me.   I can't even steal anything, not that I look for anything to steal, I just do my work and leave. That's why I tried to get into the officers' mess a month or so ago, because there you'd get a decent meal, decently cooked food once in a while, fried or something, not always steamed like they do on the main line.

When my sexual desires get bad I satisfy them by masturbation. I don't get very many urges.   I guess you might call me a habitual masturbator for the past few years.   When I go to bed at night and my eyes are hurting from reading too much and I can't sleep, I get up and go to the window and look outside and smoke a few cigarettes. Then when I'm tired I lay down again and sleep and in the morning when I wake up I find my penis hard and, well, occasionally I get up early in the morning and try to hold myself back.   But when I feel the urge I don't care what's what, and I release the excess.

I've had a lot of wet dreams.   I remember one like that.   I was dressed up like a Marine, with a white hat and a white belt—one time I tried to enlist in the Marines—and I was in bed with four girls at the same time.   I don't remember much about this dream but it stood out in my memory because I was dressed like a Marine.

> *The orthodox analyst will recognize in this series many symbols of Don Juanism, anal-erotism, and wishful thinking.*

I find that when I wear shorts in bed I dream more often of women. When I don't wear any it's hard to have a discharge; the reason is that there is no irritation.

I can't understand how it was that I thought of the symbols, the two pillars and the arch and the table directly underneath the arch.

I can remember that the plate was dirty, but I don't remember if there were any knives or forks or spoons or cups, the people at the table, who they were. There were a lot of other tables around and every one seemed to be filled. I remember we had beans; I don't know what kind. The plate was dirty, sauce all over it.

I'll take steak anytime rather than beans. Can't see any connection there. I remember hollering at Lt. K———— that I wanted something to eat and he looked at me out of the corner of his eye and smiled.

I don't even remember if the tables were in line or how many people were sitting at each table. Lt. K———— was standing directly across the table from me, right under the arch. It seemed to me I was sitting at the second table from the end, at the center of the table. I wonder if that could have any bearing on the sex act? I remember the scar on the lieutenant's face distinctly. It seems to me that there were nine or ten other fellows at the table with me, and I remember there were fellows across the table from me. I don't know who they were and I can't place them. It struck me funny at the time because I knew that the tables didn't face that way, they face toward the arches, lengthwise, and no officer stands that way, leaning against a pillar. Why, any of the arches, the pillars and the arches in the entire institution, anywhere, might resemble a vagina. I don't know what made me think about that. Perhaps my going through the door, the grille, walking up to the education section might mean the same thing!

> The reader will note that the patient himself arrived at all interpretations of symbolic material naturally and spontaneously. The correctness of the interpretations from any point of view does not matter. What does matter here is the ease and facility with which these interpretations are made and accepted.

I don't remember who was sitting at the table with me. If I could only think! But all the fellows looked the same to me, their clothes were the same, their faces the same; the only thing about them was their hair. Their hair was either black or white. Perry's is black;

Yuggie's is white; Mike's is white, Don's is white.   Perry is the only one who has brown, black hair; the others are all white or blond or grey.

Dobriski is the best friend I have here, but there is nothing between us.   The most is that sometimes he puts his arm around my shoulder or I put my arm around him.   He is really a fine fellow, only kind of dumb.   He's just like a brother to me.   I used to argue with him but even though I felt like hitting him a couple of times we never had a fight.   Sometimes we'll get mad at each other and won't speak for weeks, maybe a month.   We've been good friends for about three years and I think we will be good friends for ten or fifteen years to come.   We don't argue like we used to; I guess we are getting older. He's about two or three years older than I am and he looks out for me. I don't like some of the fellows he fools around with, and I tell him I don't like them and to keep them away from me.   He does.   Now I see him occasionally in the mess hall and I wave to him.   One time he was sitting at the moving pictures with some Swedish kid and they were holding hands.   It made me so mad I didn't speak to him for two weeks.   I hated to see him get mixed up with anybody like that, but I guess he can take care of himself.   He's interested in putting up money and getting out a 'lovelorn' magazine when he gets out, so I gave him a few ideas how to get people to subscribe to his magazine, how to get a big list of names.   He seems positive about going straight when he gets out.   He has been in the reformatory for about two years but he's a quiet kind of a kid, doesn't holler or shout when he talks, but he always spreads his hands all over the table.

Perry is a fine fellow.   He's a little crazy of course.   He lives in my cell block and he doesn't go out very much, stays in a lot.   I seldom see him outside because he would rather stay in with his work and you can't even drag him out with a team of horses.   We have lots of fun converting a lot of fellows to any faith we want to, changing their minds to capitalism or socialism, lots of other things, just for fun, just to pass the meal away.

I have another friend, Carlson, and I sometimes see him on Sunday mornings.   He is about thirty and his mother has been to see my mother a lot since I am here.   I was around the ball-players a lot and I used to see him and Dobriski eating on Sunday evenings.   Carlson always asks me if I want a steak or something.   He's a very radical fellow, a real radical, radical as hell.   He's against everything, the

New Deal, the country, the place, everything. He's always got a joke up his sleeve he wants to tell. Sometimes when you talk to him he pretends he's asleep. That way he lets you know he don't care to listen to you. He's a smart fellow, no getting around that, and he's a chemist by trade. He gambled a lot and made a lot of money gambling and conniving, talking people out of things.

Carlson doesn't like Perry. Dobriski is different: he seems to say, if he's your friend he's my friend too. I never heard him criticize Perry. If he ever wanted to criticize he'd keep it to himself. He's the one fellow in the world who can get along with everybody, no matter who. I couldn't listen to a lot of things people tell him, all of their troubles. He's very anxious to start some business when he gets out and he offered me a partnership. He likes me a lot and he shows it. He'd kid me by saying my head was filled up, that my capacity to learn was too small, that I would have to stop. When he said that I didn't like it and I got mad. I know he did it on purpose. I didn't talk to him for three weeks until one Sunday morning he came over and sat down right next to me and put his arm around me. Perry didn't like that. Something funny going on here, something wrong. I guess Perry is alright; he is what he is, but I don't want to have anything to do with him that way. It isn't right. I wouldn't feel right. I don't see why when the days are going by just fine, rolling along, why I should do anything like that to spoil it for myself. We've been friends for a year, more than that. Sometimes he gets those moods or spells. Most of the time he hasn't any relations with anybody and spends his time with his books. Sometimes he wants me to go and check this or that in the library for him. I enjoy his company: I like to be friends with him. We've been friends for a long time and I don't want to spoil it by doing something that isn't right. It wouldn't be right for me. A lot of people know that Perry is bi-sexual. I never did anything like that with him and I hope I never will. It doesn't matter what they think of me, or what I think of them. Only what I think of myself.

When I get out maybe I'll get married. Maybe and maybe not. I don't think so. If I spend all my time with my work like I am doing now I don't think I'll get married. . .

THE TWELFTH HOUR

Well, I had another dream last night. I dreamed that I was on my bed half-asleep, and somebody was pulling the covers over me, shaking me I guess. That person was my mother. I got up and it was the same cell, the same cell I have now, everything was the same, only the blankets were different than we have here. So I got up in my cell and I got over to the wash-bowl and started washing myself, and I looked through the window in my door and right across the hall was Perry's cell. His light was on and he was washing himself. That's all I remember.

L: 'Can you associate to any of the objects or people in your dream?'

I don't know. Everything seemed the same in my cell as when I get up in the morning. The only thing is that Perry don't live where I live and nobody wakes me up or shakes me like that. The only person that did that was my mother; many times my mother would wake me up like that in the morning at home. The blankets in the dream were like those at home, soft quilts. Everything was the same with the exception of the blankets and my mother shaking me. When I got up the cell was the same and through the window I saw the light in the cell right across from me and Perry was in that cell washing. I could see him combing his hair and wiping his face. I remember somebody waking me, nobody calling me but somebody shaking me. The person was my mother and then when I got up no one was there. There was nothing changed in the cell. I think I was sleeping in the same bed in my dream. The dream had only two persons. My mother and Perry.

My mother was always kind to me. O, she gave me a beating every once in a while, but that was alright. Sometimes when I asked her for money and she wouldn't give it to me I would try to get on her nerves by walking up and down. She was always kind to me and my sister, like any mother would be. She always held up for my side when my father said something to me or when he talked to her about me.

Perry is a friend of mine, an acquaintance, that's all. I probably will never see him again after I leave here. I know him for a long time but I never dreamed of him before. Our association has always been pleasant. O, he didn't talk to me for a while because he doesn't like some of the people I hang around with, but now I get along with him alright. I always used to get along with my mother too.

L: 'Can you think of any connection between Perry and your mother?'

No, I can't, but I don't know. I like this fellow Dobriski very much. He reminds me of my mother, the wrinkles around his eyes are just like my mother's. He's short but well-built, with broad shoulders. His hair isn't like my mother's but his eyes, the wrinkles around his eyes, remind me of my mother.

I don't know the color of Perry's eyes, but Perry's hair is dark and the muscles on his arms are soft like my mothers'. Once in a while I have seen my mother look so downhearted and blue and sorrowful that I was sorry for her. When she looks at me that way it makes me want to cry. Perry is the same way; he looks so pitiful and helpless. My mother would tell me not to hang out with kids who got in trouble a lot. She wanted me to keep away from them. Perry is the same way; he always tells me to keep away from certain people, that I might get in trouble hanging around with them.

Many times I put my arms around my mother, always when I wanted to get some money out of her. I used to tell her how beautiful and young she looked. Finally she got wise to me and right away when I started doing that she knew I wanted something from her. But I never put my arms around Perry, not that I know of. Perry wants me to study harder and so does my mother. My mother is very religious and Perry isn't. I don't know what they like that would be in common. Perry hates coffee and my mother drinks a lot of it. My mother is mostly quiet but when my father argues with her sometimes she answers back, but not often. Mostly she's quiet, what you would call the timid type. Perry doesn't speak to anyone; he holds his head down most of the time. My mother reads a lot of books, mostly love stories. Perry reads books too but no love stories.

A lot of times I am half asleep when eating breakfast and Perry hits me in the ribs or punches me in the arm to wake me up. When he eats he holds his hands up by his face and mother does that occasionally too. She talked to me about biting my fingernails and Perry does the same thing.

My sister Marie doesn't look like mother at all. She has brown hair, is quick-tempered and ready to get in a fight or argue all the time. My other sister has blond hair. My father has black hair; but he's bald mostly.

Perry's nose is almost the same as my mother's, except my mother's is broader I guess, and she is shorter and stouter. I used to see my mother look so pitiful and occasionally Perry looks the same way; he looks down to the ground, his face so long, looking so blue.

I guess Dobriski reminds me more of my mother than Perry. He's about the best friend I have in the world. We have been friends for three years now. He pulled me out of a lot of arguments. He's never underhanded; never made any underhanded advances. The other day he motioned to me in the mess hall to come out and see him. He wanted to see me for something so I hurried up and went out. He told me he quit school because he had an argument with a teacher, and the only reason he wanted me to come out was that he wanted to look at me. We talked for about an hour.

I used to call him Gooch. Once I saw that name in a funny sheet so I put the name to him and he calls me the same thing. That's kind of childish.

My mother used to like that Amy I went with in the country. She had black hair and eyes like Perry. They were very beautiful. My mother liked her very much, she wanted the affair to go further, I guess. This girl was religious and went to all the church activities. I guess that was one reason my mother liked her so much. I put my arm around her once but I never kissed or touched her. . .

The Thirteenth Hour

During the last few days I have been having some trouble. Some of the fellows are talking. For instance, yesterday we were in the mess hall eating and a baseball player, a fellow by the name of O'Grady, he tells me I am losing weight. He insinuates by that kind of talk that between me and Perry there is something up, and all the people like that seem to believe like he does. My friends won't believe it. So I had some arguments and finally when I cursed them out a bit they came around and saw my point.

Perry was in one of his moods today. When he is in one of those moods he doesn't speak very much: when he is in those thoughts he is moody, downhearted, kind of pitiable. He don't pay attention to anybody, like as if he was in a daze. Yesterday morning he didn't seem very cheerful, in the evening he laughed and smiled a little, today he was very bad.

Every time O'Grady sees me he makes some nasty remark, the kind of remark I don't think he should make. My friend Dobriski gets in a lot of arguments like that too. When he did and I was around I'd talk to him and calm him down, kind of twist it around and get him out of it. He likes to talk about baseball. I keep quiet because I don't like this talk about baseball all the time: it gets monotonous. They talk and they talk and every second word is some cuss word to describe themselves or some other fellow. . . .

'All of the flowers are now coming up into bloom. They look so nice and pretty, and all of the birds and pigeons are all around the lawns in the morning. I get up as early as five, it's real nice and cool then, and I look out of the window. There's a bunch of birds around all the time and with them something is always going on, they're fighting or making a racket, especially the pigeons. Everything is so nice and fresh. I can hear the bugle blowing when they bring up the flag; it sounds nice and far away.

The calendar tells me that this is the middle of August. The months go by fast and there are only twelve of them in a year so the years go by.

Sometimes I look out of the windows at night and see the moon shining and the clouds around it. It's pretty hard to believe that the moonlight is nothing but reflected sunlight. The universe must be so vast: man's mind cannot penetrate it; millions and millions of miles. It shows that man is still very small. And the earth just keeps on turning; and the stars. It's very hard for some people to understand that the earth and the apple that falls out of the tree have the same amount of gravity on each other. They just see the apple fall out of the tree and they argue with you and think you are crazy. I used to argue a lot with fellows about how the universe is and things like that. Now I just back out of such arguments.

I like to read *Boat Magazine*. I just read it and look at the different boats. I like to go sailing. I'd hate to settle down in one place and just stay there all my life. I'd like to do this: buy a boat about sixty feet long, live on it somewhere along the water, somewhere in the north in the summer and the south in the winter, and have the work I want to do, all my books, my own library, and one other fellow on the boat with me to help take care of it. A boat doesn't cost much. I'd like to have one when I wanted to go somewhere. If I wanted to go to New York I'd go to New York: if I wanted to go to Florida I'd go to Florida. I'm not interested in making money, big cars and all that. I guess what most of the time I'm doing is dreaming, that's about all. I'd like to have a life of leisure. Of course I'd have to work, but I also want to do some of the things I like to do.

I don't want to tie myself down to one place and know that I have to stay there the rest of my life. That's one thing I dislike about this place. You have to do certain things at certain times. If you have stockade you have to stay out there, and you have to stay there in spite of the hot sun. Still I'm glad I'm here or I wouldn't be learning as I am. Of course, I haven't got very far, haven't even taken the first step on the ladder. But I'm going up. It looks so high up, so very far.

Dobriski kids me a lot; calls me dumb and stupid, and I make believe I'm sore at him and he laughs. The other day he motioned me outside. "I don't want to see you for nothing important," he said. "I just want to look at you. I haven't seen you for about a month." Then he told me how thin I am. Everybody loses weight in the summer, I guess.

Sometimes I get angry with him when he comes around with another fellow that lives in his cell-block. I chase them away. I want to have nothing to do with this fellow, I don't like him; I don't even want to talk to him. He irritates me. Yesterday Dobriski was playing ball and he came over to get a drink of water when I was going in. He said I was acting kind of funny. He said, "You don't want to talk to anybody; you walk around with a long face; you don't notice if anybody walks past you. I haven't seen you smile or have a good laugh in a long time." I think he just imagines it.

One time we were sitting in the dugout, me and Perry and Dobriski, and another fellow came over. Dobriski sat down by me and put his arm around my neck. I was sore at this other fellow and I didn't even want to see him, so I chased them away. Perry got sore because Dobriski put his arm around me or something. He said he didn't like it.

I always like to go out Sunday mornings, though, because they have the radio playing music. Perry likes music a lot too, but he can recognize any song that's being played and I can't. He says music is like a hot poker that singes your heart and soul.

I hate a lot of the fellows in here. I like to be by myself. O, I know them. I'm getting so that I don't want to speak to any of them and I don't want them to speak to me. I'd rather be alone somewhere, all by myself for a few hours. Yesterday afternoon I was alone for about an hour. I started thinking about some philoso-

pher who wrote that a lot of people have a liking or dislike for some
other people because, well, they say, "We would go and pay them a
visit if they didn't have that vicious dog in their yard." Most fellows
I guess are like that in here. One fellow says he's a friend of mine but
he told a couple other fellows what a fool I was. I told him I knew
what I was doing, so he started cursing me and called me all kinds of
names; so I started wondering how true this philosopher's idea really
is; certain people are just like a little vicious dog in the yard that
bites you.

Yesterday Perry was telling me about genius. I don't remember
anything he tells me different times. Thoughts go through my head
and I don't pay any attention to what he says. When he got through
I didn't know what he said and I told him so. He said he knew it but
kept on anyway.

There are so many different people in here. You can almost tell
the states they come from by the different customs and habits they
have . . .

THE FOURTEENTH HOUR

Sometimes I talk and talk and talk and don't realize what I am
saying. It reminds me of the times when I am alone with somebody
and I say something and they don't know what I am talking about.
I talk to myself a lot and I switch around to different subjects and think
about them but when I try to remember the first subject I can't.

I talk about different things with people, mostly trying to repeat
things I study. When I study and find something interesting and
then go on studying, I can't remember what I studied five or ten
minutes before. I'm getting some information about Mexico now,
something about their political and economic and social conditions
before and after the revolution.

I moved to another cell last night. There was an old fellow in
there before me who had crabs and all of the other guys were kidding
me about it today. I suppose it was just my imagination but last
night I felt all the time something crawling over me. I didn't sleep
very much. All the fellows were kidding me and laughed: they saw
that I hadn't slept much and they said I'd been chasing crabs all
night. I did sleep for a little while, though, and I woke at about four.
I heard people talking outside my cell window.

Thinking about a boat now reminds me of a submarine, how it goes down in the water and comes up. It is made for only one thing; to destroy. It produces nothing. These boats cost millions of dollars. War is bad. These sea battles, the boats run right through the water, through everything and over everything. They're the things man made to destroy himself. It usually ends up not by the man being destroyed, the man who made and built these objects. They're used to destroy other men, not himself. I can see the picture. A lot of these men swimming in the ocean, their heads bobbing up and down, and the boats going over them and past them. I don't think there will ever be any stop to it. They'll always keep on like that; but nature is a funny thing. When a pack of animals is together and one violates the code it is killed or ostracized, but man kills regardless. So does the rat. I always think that man and the rat are the two worst animals in the world. I think even a snake is better than either one. A snake goes on across the path and gets into the bushes and keeps going. One big country starts a war with another country, over a river or a mountain or a canal, and they fight over it, and they keep on fighting for thousands of years to come, over a piece of ground and some water. They shoot hell out of each other and the best one is the one who wins. All the way back in history there have always been wars over something, more territory, more land, markets, or something. These countries always are in trouble, always have something going on. The people of Mexico are always in the middle of a revolution, fighting, fighting, for nothing. A couple of men come into power; they take the money that they want; then they leave. It'll be like that through the ages. There's nothing new about it; it'll never grow old. As long as people are like puppets it will be that way.

I remember when I was in grammar school I had some puppets. I know how they work. You pull a string; they dance; they do anything. The only difference with people is that the strings are not visible; it's hard to know where it comes from, what makes them act that way.

I like to be alone, by myself. I find that although I don't know anything, I'm my own best company. I'm happiest when I am alone. I talk to myself and discuss things and I always have the same idea, one opinion of everything, so I don't do much arguing with myself. When I am alone I just close my eyes and let things go by.

This fellow Gordon is a tough kid. He thinks he's a big man because he gets in the boxing ring with someone. I think it's alright; it's a good sport; it develops their bodies; it makes them quick on their feet and teaches them how to use their hands.

I don't like to pick fights. I'm going to have one I'm afraid, and if I do I'm going to hurt the other fellow pretty bad. I don't want to fight: I might hurt somebody and I don't want to hurt anybody. As far as I'm concerned nothing is important enough to fight about, either here or anywhere, unless it's for sport.

I don't know very much what I think about, but usually something I have read in the past will come to my mind and I think about it and turn it around and change it and twist it around to see if I can get something out of it. One time I was thinking about the iron ore that Germany is getting from Sweden, and I kept thinking how they can get the ore out if the railroad it is carried on is destroyed. I thought and thought and finally I decided that the only way they could get it out would be by airplane. I told another fellow about this and he said I was crazy, so now I don't tell people what I am thinking about. I just think and let it go at that. Most people I know wouldn't understand what thinking is anyway. I guess they haven't done any of it. Most of them talk about baseball and then some more baseball.

It was always fun watching the fireworks on the Fourth of July.

A noise in the corridor initiated this train.

Most of my fun was in bringing them into our town. I would go to another town near ours, buy them, and bring them back in a rowboat. I'd cross the river by boat because then I didn't have to go by the bridge. One time I got caught on the bridge with a couple dollars worth of fireworks and they were confiscated.

I'd sit on the bank of the river on the Fourth and look over into P—————— where they were shooting off rockets, and I'd see the rockets going up and looking like small meteors. I'd get a lot of pleasure out of lying on the lawn at night just looking at the sky, the stars, and the clouds moving past the moon. It would illustrate to me the good and the bad things, how they come and go, nothing permanent.

Sometimes they'd have concerts in the park near where I lived, and I'd go somewhere away from the music, all alone, not very far but distant enough to hear the music softly. Nearby it didn't sound very nice, but from where I was it sounded so soft and sweet.   When you were away from everybody it was like the music was floating on the air, so nice.   When I played the radio at home too I always kept it very soft.   My father, he is nearly deaf, so he always turned the radio up loud, real loud.   I didn't like that and my sister felt the same way, so we'd go somewhere else and read.

People as a whole don't bother me.   Sometimes I like to talk to some sensible person.   I go upstairs to type my lessons and if anybody is in the room I can't work.   Some of the fellows up there are alright and I like to talk to them, but I just can't work when someone is around.   It makes it hard for me to read my notes with people around looking at me.   I tried to work several times in company.   I don't know whether they look at me or not and I keep looking around to see if they are watching.

I feel kind of sleepy.   I didn't sleep much last night.   I guess they were kidding me so much it's preying on my mind.   I kept telling myself that it was just imagination but something in the back of my head kept saying it wasn't.   These fellows had me coming and going and I didn't know which way to turn.   There's always something up in a place like this.

I looked out of the window and it was raining and the pigeons all got together and cuddled up against the building.   They perched up there under the arches, snugly and warmly, letting it rain.   They just get out of it.   They know the rain will be over in a while.   Man should learn more from them, only it looks like man learns more from the buzzard and the hawk.

It reminds me of a story I read one time of a bird that was trying to swoop down on a fish.   It was swooping down and got hold of the fish and the fish was too heavy, so the fish pulled the bird down underneath the water, and the bird drowned.   I don't know the significance of that but I guess people could come to their own conclusion about it . . .

The analytic implication in terms of resistance is obvious throughout this hour and especially in the closing paragraph.

The Fifteenth Hour

Doctor, would you mind giving me a little advice?   You probably know this: Perry is in love with me.   You know it.

L: 'Now, Harold, instead of me offering advice to you, suppose you just continue as usual with whatever occurs to you.'

Well, it's rather a funny and new experience, some fellow saying something like that to you.

Well, about a year ago Perry lived in my cell-block and ate at the same table with me in the mess hall. He always so arranged it that he was sitting across the table from me, so we had several conversations, and in the beginning I liked the fellow. He didn't seem to be like the other fellows; he was different or something: he would usually just sit at the table and not say anything at all during the whole meal; and then sometimes he talked about many things. I never paid very much attention to him. He always seemed a swell kind of fellow, not the sort who would get himself into trouble. I liked him from the beginning and we'd talk occasionally.

Then, about eight months ago, we were both waiting on an interview, sitting in the hall. We had to wait all afternoon and so we talked. He said something to me then. He didn't know me very well, yet he made a reference to something or other to bring out his point clearly, something like, "It takes more than a million pricks to satisfy me." These were his exact words, and it gave me a different slant on him. I never said anything to anyone about it, not even to Dobriski. I never even mentioned it to Perry afterwards either. You are the only one I've ever told it to.

We always got along after that. I never held it against him. I never tried to "make" him. I know a lot of people in here who are the same sort of fellows like Perry. I don't know: I can't bring myself to do nothing like that with another man.

And while we were waiting there for the interview he told me about all the troubles he'd got himself into: and then he got talking about different subjects, literature and art and things like that. He struck me as a fairly intelligent fellow, someone I would like to talk to. All I knew was that he wanted to go into the Industrial Shops, and there is a tough bunch of guys there. We were sitting there, waiting for the interview, and I was going to ask for an industrial assignment too, and I started to tell him not to ask for that kind of job. I had been refused sometime before on account of my eyes, so I told Perry not to go there. I didn't tell him why because I knew he wouldn't take my advice. So he got his assignment, and three weeks later he was out of there.

One of the fellows in the Industrial Shops who was the cause of Perry's leaving there made a bet with another guy that he couldn't make Perry before he went home.   Perry didn't like him so he couldn't have made him without a knife or a club, and I didn't want to see Perry hurt.   So I told him to watch himself and he told me he didn't like to have me tell him anything like that.   He got angry and didn't talk to me for about three months.   Maybe he wanted this guy to rape him.   Anyhow, while he was angry I began to hang around with my friend Dobriski again, and I didn't pay any attention to Perry.   O, we'd meet occasionally and say hello.   Then one time, about three months ago, I was sitting on a bench in stockade on a Sunday when Perry came up and started saying how sorry he was for not speaking to me for such a long time, and that he wished we could be friends in the future.   Then he told me he was in love with me.   I didn't know what to say.   It sounded sort of funny to me.   I didn't know whether to laugh or . . .

Sometimes I feel sorry for him.   He just doesn't seem to me like a girl.   One girl I went with always told me she was in love with me. I didn't think much of her, but I think a lot of Perry.   I don't think I'm in love with him.   He's a man like myself.   I like him a lot but there isn't any reason to be in love with a man.   I told him I didn't see how I could possibly be in love with another man.   Then he told me he was more feminine than masculine.

Perry doesn't talk to very many people.   If I got angry with him it would hurt me to hurt him.   He says a lot of things and I pass them over.   One time I took off my glasses just to rest my eyes for a while and he noticed my eyes fluttering and he told me to put on my glasses. I knew what he meant.   I knew just what he meant, and I was angry. I can't forget the way he said it.

I like him a lot but I don't want to do anything like he wants.   It's not what he thinks of me, it's what I think of myself.   I've never had an affair with a person like Perry in all my life.   It's not that I'm afraid, but I just can't bring myself to do it.   It's not because I don't like Perry: I like him very much; and I like a lot of other people in his condition; but I hate anything like that; I don't want to do anything like that with him.   ·He tells me never to say anything to you about his being in love with me.   Once in a while when we are walking along together he talks to me, and he says, whispering, "Darling," and things like that.   I just have to laugh sometimes; it's so funny.

I always liked Perry from the first time I saw him, but I confess that once in a while I get some flashes running through my mind, perhaps only for a half a second or so, little flashes of hate for him. I push them out of my mind. I just don't think about it any more. I don't believe I really hate him. I look at him sometimes and I just get these little flashes. I can't say when this happened the first time, maybe a year or so ago. We were sitting at the table and I looked up at him and I felt these little flashes of hate for him going through me, and I just shook myself and kept telling myself there was no reason to hate him.

He hasn't got a good reputation; in fact, he has a reputation for being a tale-bearer. Not only that; his reputation in here is that he is the sort of fellow that the other men are trying to play around with.

He's an altogether different person than Dobriski: he's quieter and smarter. Well, Dobriski is an older person, more considerate of other people's failings. Perry isn't. Dobriski talks with everyone. Perry won't: he despises most of the people around here.

One time he wrote me a note. It was funny. He called me, "My darling honeysuckle," and, "I love you with all my heart," and these names he called me were written over maybe twenty times, all over the paper. I didn't know what to say. Sometime I'm going to tell him this is just childish. He doesn't stimulate me like a woman would. But, I don't know; he says that when he looks at my eyes and sees me smile, fire runs through his blood.

He tells me he doesn't care who knows what he is and what he does. He just doesn't like people to talk to him. O, he's willing to have them say hello to him and say hello to them; and then he wants to walk by without pressing the matter further. I like to talk to him. He offers fine arguments.

When I moved back to T cell-block the fellows came up to me and they told me, "We don't mind you coming up there, but we don't like the idea of the Princess coming up." I told them that Perry was with me and if they didn't like it there was nothing they could do about it. I never told Perry about this. I never say anything to him that might hurt.

He eats like hell. He fills his tray way up at the steam table. I

Many clinicians have noted the voracious appetites and gross eating habits of sexual psychopaths.

kid him a lot about it. I don't eat much and he says that's because I sleep a lot and don't do any hard work.

I take a lot of kidding too. Some of the fellows around here have been calling me the Prince. It sort of quieted down the last few days. But everyone seems to think there is something up between Perry and myself. Everyone except Dobriski. He doesn't think so: he knows me and he knows that when I tell him something it's true. The reason I tell him the truth is that I don't care whether I hurt his feelings or not. Some of the fellows that talk to me emphasize the fact that I am ruining my reputation in here, but my reputation as a convict, as a prisoner, even as a right guy among the people in here is nothing to me. When I am outside I have a reputation, but in here I worry about my mind. Perry is helping me a lot. I'm learning a lot from him and I expect to learn more.

As long as I have known Perry he's kept only one friend of his that he had when he first came in. I was surprised when he came up and first began talking to me. He said hello and sat down by me and started talking. I would never be angry with him. I never really despised him. He's never touched me as long as we've been going around together. O, he's touched my hair occasionally and my arm, but it never went further than that. I touch his arm every now and then when we are getting in line. When we sit outside we sit some place where we are alone, where no one is around, and we talk together. Sometimes I listen while he reads, and usually a lot of fellows come around looking at us and they make remarks like, "The two lovers are outside," or something like that. Yesterday or the day before Carlson and some other friends of mine were telling me I shouldn't hang around with Perry, but I think I know what I am doing and what's the best thing for me. C———— is perfectly right in what he said about Perry today. I know he dislikes him and Perry dislikes C————. C———— says Perry likes to impress people that he has a little more intelligence than they have. One day he remarked to me that it was dangerous, that I might become like Perry, that I might try to impress people that I am smarter than they are. I know I'm smarter than a lot of them but I am dumber than most of them. One time Perry told me that C———— is too old, he can't think, his mind is all set. He knows Greek and Latin and when he gets into an argument he brings out his Greek and Latin and throws it at you and dazzles you; you don't understand what he said and it gives him time to think up a good answer for you.

I don't intend to stop associating with Perry. I think he's alright. He's different.

When I first came in here I didn't want to talk to anybody or bother with anyone. I just read a lot until Dobriski and I got acquainted. We went to school together and we lived in the same cell-block and because of this we became good friends. He doesn't like Perry very much but he tells me he does. What he means is that since I like him, he might as well like him too.

I'm having a lot of fun with this thing with Perry. He says he loves me and whenever he leaves me he calls me darling. He tells me that I am timid and shy, but I know I'm a lot cooler than what he thinks.

I hate people when they say something about my eyes. When I hear someone say anything about my eyes right away I guard myself against them. I don't care what they say, whether it's bad or good, it's always bad. That's why I like to keep by myself. I'm my own best company.

There is one other fellow I dislike very much because there was some trouble with him and some other fellows about a knife, and somebody did some talking, and then there was an incident about a crap game, and the officer in charge of the work detail where he worked accused everybody except this fellow. I hate this fellow very much. He reminds me of a cur or some other animal. The reason I let Perry say he is in love with me is to make him keep away from some of these other fellows like this one I'm speaking about. The one reason I listen to him and let him tell me those things is so he stays away from this other fellow. He's a young kid and he's doing a long time. He lost a year of his Good Time already and he's only been here a year. If Perry hangs around with him he'll get himself into trouble, so I let him tell me that he is in love with me as long as he listens to me. I told him I dislike this fellow and I told him why. I said I sure dislike anyone who takes advantage of other people when they are in a place where they can't help themselves. I said a man can't help himself in here. A fellow is just like a rat when he takes advantage. Perry knew what I meant. I was insinuating that he shouldn't say anything about anyone in here. He knew I meant that he shouldn't associate with this fellow.

Once in a while Dobriski used to talk about breaking out of jail and going to South America. So I would talk to him; first I would agree with him and after I had quieted him down some I'd switch back to magazines. He's a fine boy, big, blond, around twenty-five. When he had his birthday in November I got him ten cigars and wrapped them up and sent them to him with a note. He must have been happy to know that someone was thinking of his birthday. He's a very good friend and I don't see how I could have forgotten his birthday. Ten cigars mean nothing to me. I guess I could afford them but I couldn't put a price on all the friendship I have received from him. I like him but he takes advantage of me. When we get into an argument he is on my side and then switches over on me. One time I remember we were walking outside and he and another fellow wanted to play rolling balls down in the stockade. I didn't want to go and he coaxed me. Finally I decided to go. We were playing about an hour or so and got into an argument over some points. This other fellow said something about my eyes. I didn't like it and quit. That night I told Dobriski, "I don't have to tell you what you should do. You have to use your own judgment. If you want to hang around with this fellow, go away from me." So we didn't speak for a few months. I will never forget what this fellow said. It's easy for me to hate people if they mention something about my eyes. I agitate myself. I make it worse. I create a hate for them and I don't want to speak to them or even look at them.

If Dobriski does anything like that again I have to hate him. He's a fine fellow and all that so I don't think he'll let me hate him. We're friends, just like brothers. We've argued with each other, we've had some fights, but we never came to blows. He used to hang around with some people I despise. I despise their actions, their speech, their stupidity. Of course that's purely personal. They say something about my eyes that I dislike and I agitate myself and I hate them. Dobriski keeps associating with them and it hurts me more. About two weeks ago we were sitting outside, Perry and I, and Dobriski and another fellow came over. He knows I hate this guy: I told Dobriski to keep him away a long time ago. This Sunday he sat beside me I was sore and I got angry and told this fellow to go away. Dobriski put his arm around me and Perry got sore then. When they went away Perry said I should have more consideration for his feelings; not to make love when he is around.

That was funny. Perry imagines he is in love with me. He calls me a hypocrite, says I hurt his character. Some day, I guess, I'm going to take a swing at him, and I'm going to tell him he doesn't love me because he calls me a hypocrite. When Perry finds something wrong with me again I'll tell him that . . .

THE SIXTEENTH HOUR

I belonged to the Boy Scouts when I went to the Catholic school, and I used to pal around with a fellow by the name of Wally. He was a year older than I. We'd go swimming together and I remember one time we made a boat and his mother broke it up because she was afraid we'd take it out. My two cousins belonged to the same gang with us. Most of the fellows had air rifles and we'd shoot out billboard lights and street lights. When I hung around with these kids we played hookey a lot. I remember hiding my books in the barn, the club house, and then we'd go down to the river to swim and play around. We'd go into some old house and strip it of all metals and get some money that way.

I always had an idea that when I got older I would go to Annapolis. I was always trying to work that, but when I was hanging out with these kids I got into trouble, once and again and again, and everything started going wrong. This friend of mine, Wally, he kept out of trouble alright. When he and I were Boy Scouts he went to camp every summer for a month or two. Of course, I couldn't go: my father couldn't afford it. The years went by and I met him once in a while. He went his way and I went with the gang and here I am.

We had a fight once, me and Wally, and he picked up a milk bottle as if to throw it at me. I was cutting a piece of wood with my penknife, so I ran at him with the knife. I didn't cut him but he ran down to the police station and told some detective there about it. The detective knew who my mother was and he told her. Nothing happened from it though.

On S——— Street we lived in a two-family house and on the second floor lived a family with two girls who went to school while the man and woman worked. Several times I went up there and nobody knew that I was up there. I fixed the front door. There was only one way of getting upstairs and that was by way of the front porch and there was something wrong with the lock on the front door. It was very easy to open. I fixed it so I could get up there anytime. I remember one time I stole seven dollars. Me and my two cousins spent it all within a week. That was when I was around twelve. After this the family moved out and another one came in. They had two girls, about my age, and several boys. I used to play with one of the girls under the stoop underneath our porch, and when nobody was around I played with her further than most kids that age would.

She wasn't the first girl I had though. I don't remember who was the first one. It all goes back to when I was about seven or eight. Most of us young kids played together. There was a woman with one or two daughters and a son. The girls played with us and the son belonged to the big gang. One of those girls was the first one I had. Then I used to have Wally's sister, who was about as old as me. We would go to their house when nobody was around and undress and lay on the bed and roll around.

My cousin Riggs and I and another fellow got one of these girls around back of the garage and we were trying to lay her, and she hollered and screamed. My cousin Riggs wanted her to suck his peter. She was only seven and she wouldn't do it. When she got home she told her mother and I told you how Riggs said I was the one . . .

One time I took my father's straight razor—this was before my sister was born—and I started to cut wood off his bureau. When my father came home and started to shave he noticed it. I said I didn't know anything about it but my mother kept telling me to tell the truth. So I finally told the truth and got an awful beating.

Sometimes when I got a bad beating I used to cry and I felt as if somebody was singing in my ears songs I knew, and it used to make me feel worse.

I remember the first dog we ever had, a female called Nellie. We had her for about four years. One time she bit me when I ran past pushing somebody in a wagon. That's the only time she ever bit. I remember she used to run after cars and people. One time when she was having business with some male dog she got stuck and I remember my mother beating her. I don't know what happened to her pups. I think my father drowned them.

My father had a job driving a truck. It was a big dump truck.

My mother's godfather always got drunk. One time my mother

got sore because he got drunk too much, so she took all the whiskey bottles and broke them up. There was a store across the street where they sold bootleg whiskey and he'd go across every couple hours to buy a pint. It made my mother mad. I don't know why he left our house; there must have been an argument about drinking.

In B———— Street we had an old car in the lot. We'd blow the horn and raise hell with it, us kids. Once I was standing in the back of the car when I felt someone grab my ear. It was my mother; she was looking for me and she chased me away from the car.

In the big house where my cousin lived there is a big cellar, real dark, and a couple years ago somebody lost five or ten dollars in change and silver there. The kids spent a lot of time in that cellar trying to find that money, digging and digging, hours at a time. Most of it was never found. It's a very dark cellar. The big kids tried to get us little kids to play with their peters there. One fellow tried to get me to do it but I ran away. And we collected old bottles and put them up on a shelf in the corner. Then we'd take rubber bands and staples and break the bottles. We saved a big box of broken bottles to spread under cars.

There was an Italian kid that lived on the corner and we'd get in arguments with him so once we tried to get even and I stole a pair of dumbbells and a small sailboat from him.

I got a lot of beatings when I was young. The one about the razor was the worst, I guess. I remember I could hear somebody singing. It was going through my head. I didn't know what it was.

My oldest sister slept in a cradle in the same room with my mother and father. I slept in the other room with the boarder, whoever that would be. Most of the time it was my godfather, I mean, my mother's godfather. We had an old stove, a grey one with a black top and nickel-plated rims on the side, and the gas jet was right above the table. It was a big round table. By the house was the garage where my father kept his car. He built truck cabs and truck bodies and rebuilt sewing machines there. I was interested most in bicycles then. I used to steal the funny papers at home and bring them to a friend to let him see them just to ride on his bike.

We used to go to the movies every Friday night. The whole family would go. After father got paid he would come home to wash up, and then we would go to the show, every Friday.

When I was living on B———— Street I had a friend, Eddie, who was about five years older than I but always treated me like a brother. There was one person who really was a friend to me. His mother was taken away to an insane asylum. They said she had a fit and they got an ambulance and took her away. I remember that night they took her away. I knew his father too; he was a fine man.

When I got to be a little older, about nine or ten, I scrubbed floors for my mother. Before that I washed dishes. And I remember my aunt Louise used to get me to say my ABC's—I didn't know them very well—get me to say them while I was washing the dishes.

There was a family that lived in the big house. The man would get drunk and beat up his wife and his daughters. We'd listen how he cursed and beat up his wife. Then there was a fellow who lived directly across the hall from where Wally lived. He lived there with his real old mother. One time he came out in the street and he had a gun, and the people called the police station. The police came looking for him, and when they got there he was home on the third floor. They went up to get him and he jumped out of the window. You can still see his foot marks where he landed. There was also an old man in the neighborhood who rode a bike with hard tires. We'd kid his son because his father had to ride a bike while other men had cars. I don't think the kid liked that very much.

I never liked my cousin Riggs. I didn't like to have him around with me. We'd cut our classes and go to shows together; when I had money I'd take him and when he had it he'd take me. I didn't trust him though. I disliked him: I hated him for some reason or other.

Before I came in here I was going to buy a machine gun and another fellow and I had it all arranged. The only thing was that this gun had been stolen from a police car and didn't have a round cylinder. It was just before I came in here. I was going to get Riggs and several other fellows and we were going out and hold up a bank. If I had ever done anything like that with Riggs I would have killed him I guess. About a week or two after that I was picked up on this charge and that's how come it never came off. Now I hear he is married and settled down. Ha!

I never trusted him much. I never told him any of my business. I'd break into lunch wagons and steal soda and cake and pie and cigarettes. When I came home and the family smelled smoke from the tobacco on me I used to get beatings . . .

The Seventeenth Hour

I used to listen to the radio a lot when I was outside, mostly to crime stories and things like that, or comedians. When I'd come home I'd turn on the radio for an hour or two and listen to it. Many times my mother came in and hollered at me for playing the radio when I was supposed to go to sleep. I'd wait till she was gone and then turn it on again.

I never was what one would call a heavy eater. I like to eat a lot of potatoes, cakes, pancakes, my aunt's pancakes. She is really the only one that knows how to make them. They're delicious. I go for cake a lot. I like cake and good coffee. My aunt Louise always had some cake for me.

My aunt Vanya is entirely different from my aunt Louise. She's quick-tempered; we never got along well. Louise, she always reminded me of my mother; she likes to mother everybody even though she has three children of her own. Her husband tried to fix me up with a job at the A———— Co., where he is foreman or something. I went there but they gave me a medical test and I couldn't pass it. I tried to skim through it but they wouldn't let me.

I used to bite my fingernails. About four years ago, in the summer, I stopped for a while because I wanted to see if I could keep them. I did, and they grew so big they got in my way. So now I keep biting them again.

I don't like to season my food with pepper. I like to eat tomatoes with a lot of salt but no pepper. I don't like peaches, but I like oranges and grapefruit. I don't like greasy food, fats or things like that, and I don't like to eat more than is enough; I'm satisfied when I've had enough. Last winter I weighed about 155 lbs.; since then I've lost around six pounds. I know that eating doesn't make you gain weight; it's how much you eat and how you eat it. Now me, I drink about three pints of coffee a day. I don't eat much bread and don't drink much water.

I used to drink a lot of whiskey on the outside. When I was up on my aunt's place I drank a lot. Toby's uncle was a heavy drinking-man and he liked to go with me. He said that I was one fellow raised in the city who could drink more than most country fellows.

I don't like crowds. When I'm in a crowd it seems to me that everybody is looking at me. I used to go through crowds, especially on a sunny day, and figure to myself that they were all looking at me.

I used to be one of those wise-cracking kids. If anybody'd say anything to me I'd get sore and give them a sarcastic answer. I gave my mother, my sister, everybody, sarcastic answers.

If my mother really wasn't my mother I might dislike her. But of course she is my mother, and everyone likes his mother. A man

> *Here is a fine illustration of a commonplace of clinical practice. It gives expression to the importance of the superego (custom, tradition, etc.) in creating ambivalence. He wishes his mother were not his mother for reasons which we shall discover later. Cultural influence, however, enforces customary filial sentiment.*

only has one mother. Sometimes she would say things that would reflect on my eyes. I didn't like it, but we managed to get along alright. I talk to her: I like her. When I wanted to get some money out of her I'd throw my arms around her and kiss her and tell her how young and beautiful she looked. She always fell for it. But my sister is quick: she didn't fall so easy. O, she'd usually loan me the money, but sometimes it was a lot of trouble. Me and Marie got along pretty well. Once in a while we have an argument, then she throws everything she can get her hands on at me. One time when she saw me with Lila she started kidding me, kidding the life out of me; so finally I told her to shut up, and she got mad and started throwing her shoes and everything at me. My younger sister is about twelve now I guess. She's like any young kid, thinks she is tough, wants to fight with everybody. She's my father's pet. My mother always stuck up for me when my father said something to me. He blamed me for not getting a job. I'd look for work but I couldn't find any, so I got sick of it and didn't try any more. I didn't care much about anything. I didn't care.

I didn't have many clothes outside. I didn't want to ask my mother for any money to buy clothes with, or my father. The money I stole I used to buy things with for the fellows in the gang. I'd spend it mostly for whiskey.

My mother wanted to make me stay in. She didn't want me hanging around in the poolrooms and doing things like that. Sometimes my father would see me and then he'd say something. I never said anything; I never talked to him.

I'd stay up late and when it rained or something I would remain at home and read. Then my father would say something to me about a job; so I would go out into another room and get dressed and go out even if it rained. I'd sneak out a lot.

My older sister doesn't get along with my father either, only he doesn't say anything to her. She works. She makes about twenty-eight dollars a week and is only around twenty. I guess he won't say anything to her as long as she works, but as soon as she loses a job he starts talking. She was up here about two months ago and she has certainly changed a lot. When you say something to her she has a smart, quick answer, kind of sarcastic. I always figure that if I didn't know her and looked at a picture of her, she would appear to be a quiet girl. But she really talks and talks and talks.

I don't know what makes me think of Perry now. He's quiet; doesn't say much; doesn't talk to many people; doesn't get loud when we have an argument. We have some real good arguments, too. We argue back and forth and then he waits a few days and brings up the same argument again. He picks the place where I put my foot in it and ruined myself. He's funny some ways. I gave him a magazine to look at the other day and he took it to his cell and threw it down. He didn't even look at it and he started arguing with me: why was I always giving him such trash? So I took it back and I showed him what I wanted him to see. He started begging me for it after that. I didn't give it to him. When we talk, he does most of the talking. I'm learning a lot from him.

I kid him sometimes about my eyes. I tell him that deep down in his heart he doesn't like me because of my eyes. He almost cries. I am only kidding him but I think he believes what I say is true. A lot of times he asks me what I say to you and what you say to me. And I tell him a long made-up story, and then five minutes later I tell him a different story, and then I tell him a third story. He knows

The strength of the transference is well shown here.

I am lying to him. He doesn't ask me many things now. He knows we are talking about something, but he doesn't know what it is. He emphasizes that I should say nothing to you about him. I tell him I don't. He probably wouldn't say anything if he knew, but I wouldn't tell him. I find him a very fine fellow to associate with. He seems very willing to help other people in any way possible. We go out

together occasionally and he tells me not to listen to C————.
C———— has only one idea about everything and he wouldn't
change it.   He's afraid C————will take it upon himself to be my
guardian.

Most of the time when I was on the outside I'd hang around and do
nothing, practically waste away a lot of time.   I'd read junk, mostly
detective stories, mystery stories, just to while away the time.   And
in the evening I'd go out and get drunk a little bit when I was in the
mood.   I didn't care to talk to anyone: I didn t care what happened
to me or the world.   The world would go on regardless.

I never used narcotics.   I don't remember when I started smoking.
I remember I was smoking when I was about ten or so.   We'd cut
cat-tails and light them up and make out like they were cigarettes.
There used to be three of us who were pretty good friends, me and a
fellow and a girl.   She was big and fat, with dark hair, around eight
years old.   A nice kid.   Once when we were having some fun somebody asked her who she liked best, me or this other fellow, and she
picked this other fellow.   After that I didn't like her much, even
before she said that.   I guess it all goes back to my eyes like everything else.   You see, when I was about nine I started thinking that
people didn't like me because of my eyes.   I know now that many
people dislike others because of some physical defect, the way they
hold their head or keep their mouth open or something.

I didn't go out for any sport when I was in High.   I was mostly
interested in girls and cutting classes.   In the nights I played around
with the girls.   Never in the day because I didn't want them to see
my eyes.   When I went out in the daylight I always wore dark glasses
so they couldn't notice anything.   A lot of people have told me I'm
not a bad looking fellow and I know that girls would come up and
speak to me without my speaking to them first.

In the High School I attended I got along fairly well with my
studies.   I got left back in a grade in grammar school though.   But
when it came to passing a grade in High I passed it alright.   My
hardest subject was English.   I didn't like to read a lot of literature.
It seemed long and drawn-out and dry.   I'd read and read and finally
fall asleep with the book in my hands.   I don't know which was my
most favorite subject.   I guess science and biology and math.   They
were easy for me.   In the hallways we'd speak to the girls and say

their dresses were sticking out, but sometimes I'd be sorry and tell them they looked nice and then I guess they liked me a lot.

I didn't get into trouble from the time I was twelve or thirteen when I finished grammar school and went to High. I didn't finish High. I was about seventeen when I quit to stay on my aunt's place. When I came back I tried to find work. A few times I could have had a job but the eye tests always eliminated me. That's the way it went, so I got disgusted. I didn't want to go on, so I got in trouble again and again and then again and again.

I don't know what I'm going to do when I get out. I'll probably go to my aunt's place for a couple months. I know I've got a lot of work to do. I'm not worried about getting along outside, that's the furthest thought from my mind. I only know I'm going to do something. My aunt has a nice little place up in the mountains. The only trouble is that these people have a cemetery nearby.

Someday I'll just go back there and see how everything is. The world doesn't change much. The mountains don't change: the trees'll still be there . . .

The Eighteenth Hour

Well, Doctor, I am still biting my fingernails. I know I can stop it easy. I did once but every little while I do it again. I just keep chewing them.

I don't remember having any dreams. I slept good last night. It must have been the rain. When I got up this morning I felt kind of grouchy and I didn't talk to anyone until this afternoon. Last night I got into an argument with a friend of mine. He kept emphasizing something about my eyes. It irritated me and I got angry and couldn't control myself. Everytime he sees me he asks me not only once but five times the same question. When people say something to me about my eyes I get very angry inwardly. I used to tell them to mind their own business and control myself at least outwardly, but yesterday I didn't. I don't talk to a lot of people simply because they ask questions about my eyes. They probably mean well but it seems to me so many of them are asking the same thing. Every time they are asking the same thing. Every time they see me, even if they talk to me a hundred times a day, they ask me questions. I think men could learn more by observing than by asking. This fellow now, he means well. I haven't been in a mood like that for almost a year now. I've sort of got myself out of that habit. When I was on the outside I seldom talked to anyone in the morning. After lunch I'd say something but I'd seldom start a conversation before that. In here it seems just like one continuous day. Sometimes I feel just as well in the morning as at night. I felt entirely different yesterday and today. Perhaps I shouldn't feel that way but I guess occasionally it's alright for everybody. Not too often though.

There's some red dirt on the ground that reminds me of the kind of dirt at my aunt's place. I remember when I worked in the fields, haying or digging potatoes. It got so hot, like a hot stove. I didn't like it up there very much because I couldn't go swimming. The river was a little too swift, and sometimes it wasn't high enough. But I went swimming a lot at home. I spent a lot of time on the water, especially when I was about twelve. That's all I did most days when I didn't go to school, swimming in the summer and a lot of mischief in the winter. A lot of things we did I guess was just to show which was the bravest. A lot of the fellows ended up as I did; a lot of them have been arrested.

My cousin Joe did time, not as much as I am doing; and my uncle did time too. But they didn't do much. My uncle only did eighteen months because he took a gun from a friend of his who was drunk and the bartender saw it. Before he'd let the other fellow go to jail he went himself. But I guess my cousin Joe and me are the worst ones in the family. He was in reformatories a few times, mostly for burglary. One time Riggs and myself saw him somewhere near the railroad track behind a billboard jerking off. I remember I used to kid him a lot about it afterwards and he'd get so mad.

Here in this jail there's a fellow that was in prison with me before. I did six months for stealing some stuff when he was doing three months. He used to sleep with one of the colored boys there a lot. The other day I just hinted around about it to him: I didn't say any¬ thing much; and he got red in the face and mad as hell and he didn't know what to do. There used to be four of those fairies in there, four colored ones. A few weeks after I got there these four fairies came in. There were only about eight white fellows and fourteen or fifteen colored fellows in that jail, and the colored fellows slept on one side and the whites on the other. The white and the colored fellows had two dormitories apiece and they couldn't get at each other because at night there was a guard in the center between the doors in the hallway. He was supposed to sit there, and the dormitories were supposed to be locked up. This fellow would go and sleep with one of the colored fairies. He didn't get back until two or three in the morning. I just hinted around, more to kid him than anything else. He wanted to walk away but he couldn't go anywhere. Perry says I act like a hoodlum sometimes. He didn't know, but he saw the fellow get so red. Now he says he hates me because I'm acting like a hoodlum. He doesn't know that one reason I told this fellow that I still remember his experiences of about four years ago was that he goes with a lot of people like Perry. He knew what I meant though; that if he ever bothered Perry I'd tell a few people about his experiences. Now I don't think he'll ever bother Perry.

Dobriski says he dislikes my association with Perry. He says he knows there's nothing he can do about it but he dislikes it just the same. I like Perry because I am learning a lot from him. Why, I don't curse as much as I used to. I had a nasty habit of cursing with every second word. Now I'm breaking that habit. But come to think of it Dobriski doesn't curse either. Yet Dobriski hasn't got the vocabulary Perry has. Perhaps that's why my vocabulary is so small. I always said the same thing to people because they didn't interest me. You don't find many people in here who are interesting unless you look at them as cases like you do, Doc. To me, on the outside, people as a whole were just people. Sometimes I wouldn't speak to my mother or sister for three days at a time. I had nothing to say to them. I didn't speak to my father maybe for months. When it was absolutely necessary that would be the only time I ever would talk to anyone. O, I get along with my father and my mother and my sister now. I don't blame my father for being in here or anything like that. I don't say he's a bad father. I don't say my mother is bad either. The only reason I came here I guess was that I didn't care whether I was outside or in here. I did things that weren't right.

I used to think I was afraid of my cousin but I wasn't. I just disliked him very much. O, I palled around with him once in a while but I disliked him.

A lot of people used to see me and pass by and say, "Hello, Squint." I kept away from them.

Instead of interesting myself in something of value I went the wrong way. I took a great delight in having a gun, and when I had a gun on me and somebody called me Squint, I'd get so mad I'd feel like taking the gun out and shooting them. A lot of those fellows knew I had a gun on me too.

One reason I hated my cousin was that he called me that. When I leave here I guess I'll never see any of them again. Maybe my cousin once or twice, but after that I'm not going to see anyone again. I want to change the whole atmosphere of everything.

I never expect to get married. My cousins Riggs and Joe are married. I don't know why but I just don't like it. When I see all the trouble my mother had with my father and my father had with my mother over different petty things I feel that I don't want to get married and go through the same thing. I've heard a lot of fellows say that but after a couple months I hear they're getting married. Then they get in arguments and then they're sorry about getting married. I'm telling my sister not to get married to a fellow that hasn't got any money. She'd only get into arguments all her life when she wants something to eat and the children want something to eat. She doesn't want to marry out of her class. You can't take your class with you if you want to get anywhere. You've either got

The inability of the psychopath to cherish class loyalties, and his continual struggle to change his class is a generalized symptom. In this they differ from the conscientious social thinker who recognizes class distinctions and perhaps even lends his support in their eradication. The psychopath wants to change his class.

to get out of it for good or stay in it. I'm getting out. I feel sorry for those people but . . . I think they caused me a lot of irritation. I like them. I feel sorry for them. But I don't want to bother with them. I'll do all I can for them but other than that I'm through with them. When they came up here to visit me they seemed happy and contented; everything was going along fine; they were not worried about anything. I just feel sorry for them. If I had enough money I'd buy them things they need, but I have no money myself. I guess they are happy in these days in the state they are in. I won't try to make it worse for them: I'll try to make it as best as possible. My sister is working now, but I wonder what it would be like at home if she lost her job. I guess it would be the same as it was with me.

I used to worry a lot but now I look back and see how foolish it was. I guess if I had really wanted a job I could have got one. I didn't look very hard: I could have looked harder. I guess I just didn't care. I didn't care if I had a job or money or not. When I got any money I'd spend it right away. To me money always seemed a short-cut to get something you wanted. I guess money can't buy everything you want. I used to think of money as something to strive for: now I don't; it doesn't interest me that much anymore. I dislike it here. I dislike it because of the effect it has on my mother and my family, what they think and what people say and think of them. I'll never come to prison again. Never; not even one day. I didn't care whether I went to prison or whether I died. Now I want to live as long as possible, and I don't want to spend any part of the time in jail.

This institution that I spent six months in, there were four dormitories and there were stairs in the center between the four, and by the stairs there was a desk where an officer sat all the time. To the right of the stairs was the colored side and there was a wall between the stairs and the dormitories and a gate the officer would lock. Only about eight white fellows were there. These kids used to dance around at about three or four in the morning. It was disgusting to me. One time I remember there was a man who came in there dressed up as a woman, and the superintendent's wife cursed every time she thought of it.

I can't see it. I can't see people doing things like that. To me it's disgusting; that's why I'll never do things like that. These kids used to dance around. The fellow I am talking about who is here now got them to dance a lot: he was a regular wolf. They danced. They were just kids, about sixteen, all black. O Jesus! There was a light from the toilet on the white fellow's side. Yes; there were two dormitories for the colored fellows and two for the white and two sets of stairs, one leading up to the boy's place and the other to where the girls were. The light from the toilet came into the dormitory and there was enough of it to see everything. These kids used to dance around on the floor there. I got a kick out of it, the way one of them used to sing. I couldn't go for them; not only because they were black but because they were just like me. I'm not an angel or a minister or a reformer. I've never done that and I doubt if I'll never, I mean ever, do it in my life. I look at it in the broadest sense

The over-protesting and the slip of the tongue here of course betray the latent, repressed homosexual elements.

possible.   I just feel sorry for them.   They can do as they please.   I don't dislike them or hate them: I just can't bring myself to get mixed up in anything like that.   I guess I dislike wolves.   They don't seem like men to me, more like dogs, animals.   I guess I let my hate run away with me.   This fellow, I was just warning him that if he ever bothered Perry I would tell a few people what he did, about his relationship with the colored boys, and it would go very bad with him; he wouldn't like it a bit; everybody would laugh at him. . . .

We used to sit at mess, four at a table.   They only had a small dining room; there were about thirty tables in it.   They made the four fairies sit together.   They'd never let them sit with anybody else. The colored were on one side and the whites on another.

Three or four days before I left that place I got in a jam with an officer.   He was all alone at night.   There were about forty fellows he had to take care of and these dormitories were small; they would only sleep about sixteen.   We had small beds there, the same kind we have here; the kind you can pick up, throw the legs under and pile up.   They had been trying to separate these fairies and the officer wanted me to sleep by one of them.   I didn't like it.   They had a little cage there with an iron floor, and I told him right out that I didn't want to, that I'd rather sleep in the cage.   So he called me out and closed the doors and then he hit me and I fell down the stairs.   I don't remember falling but I remember waking up.   I slept by the fairy all right, at least I lay in bed but didn't sleep all night.   The next night the officer was all right.   He spoke to me and told me that he was sorry he had to hit me but he had to show the others that he meant business.   I didn't blame him.

A lot of these kids tickled me.   They'd walk up and down and sing and dance.   At night they'd dance naked.   During the day they danced with their clothes on but at night they danced naked; not in their dormitories where the officer would see them; they danced in the dormitories where the whites were.

One fellow slept with one of the niggers almost every night.   After the lights were put out at about ten o'clock he waited, and then that was his cue to go and sleep with one.   I could never bring myself to do anything like that.

When I was in here only a few months I told Dobriski that if I ever heard that he had been playing around with anybody I wouldn't speak to him anymore. Why, it's not manly. I don't do it. I dislike it. Ah, no, not me. I'm not an angel but I'm not that bad, maybe because I like myself, like myself too much. Maybe I like some of these kids here but I like myself more. I have nothing against these kids. Most of it is mental anyway. What they do is their own business. Whenever Perry says something like, "I love you, darling," or something like that, I tell him I hear an officer coming. He thinks my hearing is hypersensitive. I go one way and he goes the other. He really thinks an officer is coming. He notices I am running away from him. I really don't run away from him, though; I run away from myself. I'm not going to get myself stimulated too much to do something like that. I think too much of myself. After all, no one in the whole world likes me as much as I like myself. Why should I give myself reason to hate myself? One reason why I hate a lot of guys is because they believe I'd do something like that. When I first came here a lot of fellows came around and tried to start something with me. They got straightened out pretty quick. I haven't had any trouble with anybody since. Dobriski never as much as mentioned a thing like that to me. If he had we wouldn't be such good friends. One time he made a crack about me. I dislike to wear a top-shirt to my underwear and I was kidding him that he was an old lady about keeping warm. I asked him if he wanted some red flannel stuff to keep warm. My shirt was unbuttoned and he could see I wasn't wearing any underwear, so he said that I was going around just like a whore with no bloomers on, ready to drop my pants at a minute's notice. I was so sore I almost hit him a couple of times. I didn't speak to him for months. After that we cooled down and now we are friends again. He doesn't ever say anything to me about Perry. He knows I wouldn't do anything. I don't care what people think of me. I only care what my friend thinks of me and what I think of myself. He has proven himself the only friend I have in the world. When I was outside with him one day some fellow came up and asked me, "How's the Princess?" I knew what he was insinuating, Dobriski didn't. I don't know if he thinks anything about it; he doesn't say. He gives me no opening to say anything to him about it. He dislikes my association with Perry and he tells me that if there was something he could do about it he would do it. The other day I was just kidding him and I asked if he would like to trade places with me, if he would like to be as good friends with Perry as I am. He says he doesn't want to trust himself in that position. I guess that's one reason he doesn't play around with anybody, because if I ever found out he did it would be disgusting to me. I wouldn't talk to him anymore in my life. I don't see anything in it. You may think this is just to cover up but I don't care. It will be a long day before I do anything like that, with Perry or anyone else. O, I know a lot of people who are homosexuals, still that doesn't mean anything to me. Another reason why I wouldn't do anything like that is all the months of Good Time I'd risk to get something that you pay two dollars for in a whorehouse. . . .

THE NINETEENTH HOUR

I remember part of a dream I had last night. I was dreaming that I was moving downstairs to the first floor of T cell-block. That's funny because I used to be on that floor and didn't like it there so I moved upstairs. And I had something like a cello and I was bringing it into my cell and I was stripping the strings of the cello. I don't know how many strings; I guess there were three thick ones and three thin ones. I was taking them off and trying to put them on a real small guitar. I don't know how I was doing it. I remember there were three big thick ones, and they were separated by the thin ones, first a thick one then a thin one, and I was trying to put them on the guitar. I never had a cello in my hands and I don't know how I came to be carrying one. I remember I took the strings off the cello and put them on the guitar. I didn't touch the cello. It was standing against the wall.

L: 'Harold, you will remember what I told you about the technique of association. I want you to associate as well as you can to the items and events in that dream.'

Some time ago I started learning to play the guitar. There was a fellow, Al, who used to play it from five in the morning to five at night, all the time. I kidded him a lot about it. He'd come around and ask me if he could have the instrument and finally I gave it to him. All he would do was sing. I can see no connection there. My uncle Sam had a banjo in his home; I don't know whether he ever played it, At least I never heard him. I don't know why I dreamed about moving to the first floor again. I was awake at four-thirty and then fell

asleep about six. When I was awake I remember wishing that I
wasn't in this place because something very funny happened to me
yesterday. I was through working about six o'clock and Perry came
up and kept calling me down to his cell, and he argued with me and
pulled me. I argued with him for about fifteen minutes and finally
I gave in, and he got me in the cell for about two minutes. Then the
bugle for school blew for the second period, so I started thinking
quickly and told him I had to go outside to see somebody. So I
left him and ran out. Outside the fellow I was going to see was
playing ball. Dobriski. So I stayed out there waiting for everybody
to go in, and after about five minutes Perry came out. He was mad:
he looked as if he was going to kill somebody; and he came over and
told me I had two alternatives; to stay in the cell with him or stop
speaking to him. I don't know what will happen now. I figured
it would happen sooner or later but not so soon. I suppose it will
have to be the second alternative. He was so mad and so angry I
didn't know what to do or say. He kept repeating he was through
talking to me, and he was cursing me out. I felt embarrassed. I
went upstairs when it was time to go in and got into my own cell. I
was thinking about it all night. You told me not to make any crucial
decisions without talking to you first and I guess you meant about
him too. So I tried to forget about everything and just let things
go by. This morning I was cheerful and friendly and didn't mention
a thing about it. I don't know why I am telling you this but you
said you wanted to know everything.

He was so mad, so mad he was almost crying. Honestly, he was
almost crying, and trembling and nervous and irritated.

I usually stay in my cell after working and try to do some of my
own work. When he came upstairs last night I thought he wanted
me to go out, and then he started mentioning my name, calling me
down to his cell, and we started arguing. I told him the officer was
coming five or six times. It didn't do any good. He kept telling
me every time it was alright. Finally I did some quick thinking
and I said I had to see somebody. When he came out I knew he was
mad and he knew I was lying, that I got out of it by a lie, and I was
afraid. I must say I think I handled that situation pretty well.
I don't think he'll try that again for a little while. I think it's something different now. You see, I know Perry hates people and that

he doesn't talk to anyone. He thinks more of me than he does of anyone else: he really likes me: and I think he thinks more of me now than if I permitted him to do anything like that. I don't know what came over him. He grabbed my shirt and started mauling me and pulling me into his cell. I told him he was foolish, acting like a child, a baby. I told him to keep his feet on the ground. I like the fellow a lot but if he doesn't want to talk to me anymore I don't know what I can do. He's a fine fellow regardless of the way he's constructed and I don't hold it against him. I just don't want to do anything like that with him. This morning he was smiling and laughing and joking. I don't think I'll say anything to him about it. I'll just forget about it and let it go by. I don't want to do anything. I'm all mixed up; I don't know whether I'm coming or going. My eyes hurt and my head aches.

L: '*Let's get back to your dream, Harold.*'

Well, I was figuring on stringing the wires of the big cello on the little guitar. I was only dreaming about myself. I was moving all my things downstairs and I was carrying this big cello. It was really big. I had to tip it to one side to get it in my cell. I stood it up against the wall and started to strip the strings from it, winding the big strings, and trying to put them on the small guitar. I don't remember seeing anything else in my cell except the bed. I don't even remember seeing the locker; nothing but the bed and the big cello against the wall. The cello was a big thing. The big thick wires were almost like cables; the thin wires were like thread.

I was figuring that I'd hook the strings on the end and tie them around the little halters, but those strings were so big I knew it was wrong. They were about nine feet long and the thin ones only about three feet. I don't know why I thought I could get the big cables on the little guitar. I thought I'd tie them around the little pegs at the end.

That's all of the dream I remember. Maybe there was more but I don't recall.

L: '*Do you think the strings on the cello and the guitar stood for something, Harold?*'

They might have but I can't place it. I remember I stood the cello up against the wall and I was sitting on the bed, stripping off the strings. It was a big thing: the strings were as fat as a man's penis.

I used to know a fellow that played the cello. I never touched one
but you never can tell; I had one in my hands in that dream alright.
All I know is I was sitting on the bed and the cello was standing in
front of me, and I was pulling the wires out of it, the big thick wires.
I was figuring to turn the cello over. I didn't know how to get the
big cables on the guitar. There was something wrong there. The
wires on a guitar are not like they were on this cello. On a guitar
the thick wires come first, then the next thick and then a little thinner
and so on down to the last real thin one. On the cello there were
three real thick ones and three thin ones. The thin ones were in
between the thick ones. Maybe the cello had something to do with
me. It was husky and strong like a man, like me.

L: '*Now, Harold, suppose we start from the proposition that the cello
had something to do with you, was husky and strong, manly.*'

(Silence.)

L: '*Well. Where was the small guitar while you were stripping the
big cello of its strings?*'

I laid the small guitar on the bed.

L: '*If the big cello had something to do with you, what had the small
guitar to do with?*'

Maybe there's a female part of me. Yet I don't think there is
anything feminine about me.

L: '*What do you suppose the small guitar had to do with?*'

Maybe Perry. Christ! It sounds as if I'm getting in the middle
here.

Well, I was in Perry's cell only about a minute. He put his arms
around me, that's all. I said somebody was coming, and somebody
really came by. He wasn't on the bed. He was standing right there.

L: '*Tell me. What was the shape of the cello and the small guitar:
were they shaped differently?*'

The cello was like a big violin. The guitar was a little different
in shape, wider and thinner than the cello, more graceful, like a lady.

L: '*Well, try to continue the association. You had this object, a big
cello, a large object, with a deep tone, manly. Now you felt you had to
strip the big object and try to fit certain of its qualities to the smaller
obiect. This object was small, 'like a lady, graceful.' And you thought
there was something wrong about it.*'

I think I understand it now. I get the point of the dream.

L: 'Can you suggest anything else, Harold?'

Well, we might take it this way. There is a big, powerful man, a business man, with money and power, and there is a pauper that has nothing, no strings on the guitar. You strip the powerful man of his strings, his power, his money, and apply it to the small one. It would be a useless job though. But this man has nothing to do with me, my life. There might be other reasons but I don't know. The first interpretation sounds more logical. I like Perry a lot but I don't want to do anything like that with him. I want to help him all I possibly can but there's a limit to everything. I guess we're at the limit. I don't want to make any excuses. I knew what he was like and I even knew he couldn't control himself. I knew he hates people and likes me a lot. I guess he wants to do it because he likes me. I think he is himself stronger in some ways than I am, mentally at least.

L: 'What exactly do you think Perry wants to do with you?'

He wants to do it himself. Of course, I know about his bisexual condition. I had a feeling he wanted to, well, I—Well, I have a strong suspicion he wants to—to suck my peter. I don't want to . . . He is like that. One time we were talking outside about our relationship now. He said, "I'm in love with you. We're having a fine courtship," and that he is really a female. I guess that's what he wanted. I guess that's right about the dream. The cello is me and the guitar is Perry. I couldn't make my manliness fit his femaleness. It wouldn't go. The strings wouldn't fit. I couldn't do it. They're kind of alike the cello and the guitar, just like me and Perry are both men. The strings don't fit.

Jesus Christ! A fine courtship!

THE TWENTIETH HOUR

This 20th hour provides a neat firsthand account of the inner state of a psychopath during a period when he is tensionally supercharged and ready for an explosive episode.

Harold appeared to be very tense and upset at the beginning of this hour. He was slightly late for his appointment: his clothes were disheveled and his hair uncombed. For the first time since the initial session he had to be told to lie on the couch.

Things haven't gone so well with me the last few days. I am aggravated and irritated by people; my nerves are on edge. I am just

blowing off excess steam, I guess.   I feel like hitting some fellows.
Still I control myself as best I can.   I worry about a lot of things.   I
haven't felt like this for a long time.   When I first came here I was
like that: was in a nasty mood almost every day.   Then I taught
myself to put off these moods and not to stay in them.   O, I guess
they're alright once in a while, but when they come too often it's not
good for anyone.   I used to feel like that sometimes on the outside.
Sometimes I wouldn't speak to anyone in my family.   I'd get these
moods when I just wanted to be alone and not talk to or see anyone.
What made me feel like that I don't know.   I guess I felt tough, real
tough; at least I thought I was tough.   I'd wander around anywhere
and when I was asked something I wouldn't even answer.   This
wouldn't last long though, sometimes a day or two.   I'd want to do
nothing but sleep and get away from everything and everybody.
When I was up at my aunt's home I felt like that once in a while.
Why I don't know how to explain.   I just wanted to get away.   I'd
get into some argument with my aunt and I'd want to forget about it.
My aunt would want me to do something or go somewhere and I didn't
want to do it.   My aunt is alright, only when you see some person
for a long time, see the same person all the time, you somehow want
to get into an argument with them.   Not that I have anything against
my aunt and uncle out there.   They struggle hard for a living.   My
uncle sometimes gets in the same kind of moods that I do: he doesn't
want to speak to anyone; and when anyone talks to him he grunts.

I don't know when I first started to be that way.   I guess I must
have been about sixteen when I got into those moods.   When I was
in school before that I was cheerful and friendly except once in a while
when somebody said something about my eyes.   I used to hang
around with a fellow who was just like that.   He never said anything
to anybody.   If somebody said something to me about my eyes I
would probably leave but the next morning I was just as cheerful.
I don't know why I'd let it irritate me.   I guess I couldn't help it.   I'd
get nervous if somebody would talk to me because I thought they
might say something to me about my eyes.

Carlson said something to me about my eyes the other night so I
told him, "Why don't you shut up and mind your own business?"
I haven't spoken to him since.

I don't get that way very often.   I think that's the reason I dislike
my father.   I don't dislike him: I just don't want to speak to him.

Once in a while my mother would call me a blind bat or something like that in Polish, or my sister sometimes would say something.

I used to hang around with my cousin Riggs and he'd call me names like Squint.   I don't know why I hung around him, I disliked him so. I never committed any crimes with him because I hate him so much.

The obverse ('Only with those whom I love can I commit crimes') enhances the significance of this amazing statement. As we shall see, Riggs was a father-substitute and thus hated. What Harold means is that the forbidden (criminal) act is the forbidden (sexual) act and—for persons like himself—can only be performed with mother-surrogates as a substitutive means of gratifying the hidden wish.

One day I had an argument with him and I hit him.   Now I don't even remember what the argument was about.   O, yes; we were going to High School and there was a candy story where we hung out, and we were in the back room where they had some tables and chairs.   I swung on him and hit him and he staggered back; then he hit me; then we waited, and he swung no more and we cooled down.   One time, when I was still going with that girl Lila he tried to get me to bring her to his brother's house when there was nobody home.   He figured I would do it because there's no one there I guess, and because I am his cousin.   But I wouldn't do it: when I had a girl I didn't like to share her with someone else.   A lot of fellows when they got a girl would have a long line-up, sometimes as many as fifteen fellows. I never did that because I didn't like them.   They'd get a girl at night and one of the fellows would play the girl up, and then a whole line of fellows would follow him, maybe a block away two fellows and another block away two more, strung out way behind the first guy.

I didn't like to have my father and mother interfering with what I wanted to do.   When I was around seventeen I thought I could handle everything myself as well as anyone could.   I didn't think I was very smart but I thought I was smart enough.   This fellow that I told you I was going into business with knew another fellow who used to make different kinds of machines.   He made a machine to punch out nickels and he did time for it.   He knew how to make all kinds of machines.   My friend would go and start a conversation with this fellow so we could get some ideas out of him.   We would try to work it to get his ideas for ourselves.   That was one time in my life when I really wanted to do something.   After that I went back home and started to hang around with another bunch of fellows and it was the same thing. We used to steal cars and then we'd go out for a ride. I personally never stole a car myself, that is I never got in it and drove it away. I drove stolen cars plenty of times, and I held up people in them. One time Riggs and I were going to steal a car and we got in it and started it and it was in reverse so it backed up against a truck. We just went away and left it there.

Riggs and I used to gamble and when we won money we'd spend it going to the devil, buying whiskey, seeing shows. I don't know what's happened to him. I know he found a job as a bell-hop in a hotel and as far as I know he still has it. I guess he was afraid of me. I carried a gun. I didn't carry it all the time. Nobody ever knew when I was carrying it until, I guess, some of the fellows would see a bulge in my pocket and then they knew that I was carrying it. They thought I carried it all the time. I never got searched by any detective. I always felt I was safest in a big crowd with it. I guess I did it because I wanted something to keep the fellows away from me, and when somebody would say something about my eyes I would get so mad I didn't know what to do. I guess I've had about a hundred inclinations of shooting people. I had several fights about my eyes. When somebody would say something to me about them I would burn up and rush up to him. When I got in a fight I wouldn't wait for anybody to start at me; I'd grab him by the throat and hit his head against the street or the side of a building or anything. When I fight with somebody I don't see him. I just feel him, my hands around his head or his throat.

There was a fellow who stole a bicycle; he came to our house and let another fellow take my bicycle, the bicycle I stole. So I got sore and when this fellow came around I rushed at him and banged his head against a fire hydrant. I didn't hurt him very bad but he went home and told his mother, and his mother came to see my mother; and I couldn't say anything because I didn't want my mother to know that I stole the bicycle. I managed to get out of it somehow, I guess by a licking. I didn't get very many lickings. When my father gave me one I remember it was pretty bad, but when my mother licked me by hand it wouldn't hurt. Sometimes though she would throw something at me, just like my sister.

Once in a while I like talking to people. It depends on who I'm talking to. When you say something about my eyes, Doc, it means nothing.

Yesterday another good friend of mine was asking me about them. I told him to keep quiet. I don't think I'm very sensitive about my eyes; I just have different periods when I am more sensitive, that's all. Last night I was up in the library and I was looking at a book catalogue. It was in very small print and I held it close to my eyes and ran my finger up and down the page. Perry came over and said, "Tell me what you want to look at and I'll get it for you." The way he said it made me so mad I walked away, and this morning I wouldn't talk to him.

I agitate myself when I am asleep. I even dream about him. I had a dream last night that we moved from one cell block to another. He moved to the first floor and I moved to the third floor. I was so mad I was cursing everything and everybody. I am not sure it was Perry but it must have been some good friend of mine.

L: '*Tell me all you remember about your dream, Harold.*'

Well, I remember we were living right next to each other and one day he got notice to move and then I also got notice to move to the same cell-block. He was going on the first floor and I was going on the third because we were living next to each other and they wanted to break us up. I was sore and cursing everybody and telling everybody even the Associate Warden that I wouldn't go. I was cursing and so mad.

I consider him a good friend of mine. As for living next door to each other, that might mean close association. I guess I didn't like the idea of having us separated, him on the first floor and me on the third, keeping us away from each other. I didn't want anybody to interfere with our friendship.

L: '*Can you think of anything more?*'

I lived in T cell-block when I first knew him over a year ago. He was on the second and I was on the first floor. I don't remember anyone else being in the dream. I think it was him; whoever it was had hair like his.

L: '*Do you see any special significance in the fact that he lived on the first floor and you on the third?*'

Well, I live on the third floor now and Perry lives on the second. We didn't like the place we were living before because the kids were pretty wild and tough. In the dream I was running up and down cursing somebody, and I was yelling I didn't want to go. When I woke up I thought I was in T cell-block; that's how real it seemed to me.

I don't think Perry really dislikes me; I think he likes me a lot but being separated by a floor may have some significance.

We almost got into an argument. I was thinking over what he said about the book in the library and he said it in such a tone I felt like pushing him away and telling him to stay away from me. But I didn't say anything to him about it: I even acted sort of cheerful.

L: *'What were the exact words he said to you?'*

He said, "What are you doing? Let me look for whatever you want." I was looking at a book catalogue real close because it was in very fine print. When he said that, in my mind I knew what he really said was, "You can't see well enough so let me do it." Maybe that may have led up to the dream. This morning I was angry with him at the breakfast table but this afternoon we were both cheerful. We were kidding about eschatology or something like that and he was a lot of fun. Yet he must have noticed that I didn't feel so well.

I can't place anyone else, only Perry. We were living next to each other, our cells were next to each other, but he doesn't really live next to me. I was dreaming that we lived in P cell-block and were moved to T. He went to the first floor and I went to the third. I don't see how that could be.

I guess I could consider him my friend. I think that maybe something came between us and stopped our being close friends.

L: *'What do you suppose could come between you?'*

I don't know what could have. I like the fellow: I will, always. I don't want to do anything with him but I still like him. I don't know about the dream. Maybe it was because of the book in the library. Why should I dream I was angry?

L: *'You wanted to stay close to him?'*

Yes; he is my friend.

L: *'And you feel that something intervened between you?'*

That's it, but I still feel that I am his friend and he is mine. I know that when I was dreaming our cells were close together. Of course, there was a wall between us; still we were as close as possible. Maybe something widened it. What it could be I don't know. I don't feel in any way angry with him.

L: *'Perhaps you felt somewhat alienated by the actions you spoke about yesterday.'*

No; I don't think so. Some day I'll tell him that I won't go with him for that.

I don't feel that there is any meaning, any significance in the dream. As far as I am personally concerned there isn't any meaning.

L: 'You will recall, Harold, that he moved away first. Perhaps there is some significance in the fact that he moved first? That, in other words, the alienation begins with him; that he perhaps felt alienated, rebuffed, by your refusal to go into his cell with him?'

O, he was angry, very angry. I remember when he left his cell to come out to stockade about five minutes after I left him, how he looked as if he was ready to kill somebody: there were daggers in his eyes. He said I had two alternatives. He said, after all what am I going with him for if I can't do anything like that, if I don't want to; and if I don't, never to speak to him again. I said if he didn't want me to speak to him that was alright, but the next morning he was o.k. and I never mentioned it to him again.

I dreamed that our cells were next to each other, there was a wall between that might keep us from being too close; then we were separated by a floor. That's probably why I became very angry, because it separated us. He moved first, then I got notice to move. I didn't want to move out of my cell. We have been good friends for a year: he probably likes me more than he does anyone else; maybe he is in love with me. I kid him once in a while. I give him a look: I look at him and smile, and he walks up and down. When I smile at him he just can't sit still. As long as I can avoid those situations I get along with him. That was the first time he did anything like that. He hasn't said a word about it since. Usually I try to think about something to argue about with him so he doesn't say anything. For instance, this morning we were waiting for our turn to come to get in line and I thought of something a fellow once told me about eschatology. I figured he wouldn't know anything about it but he did. He always gets you somehow. He said I should do more of my own work before I talk about things like that. He says he knows something about everything. Sometimes I kid him. I tell him how smart he is and pat him on the back. He likes that.

As for the dream, I don't know. We don't live next to each other. I'll tell you how it is: he lives on the second floor and I live on the third. Our cells are not directly above one another; there's a cell between us. We talk to each other out of the windows once in a while.

I was really angry with him. He hasn't said anything since and

I'll probably never tell him; I'll probably just forget about it. When I start thinking about a person, the first thing I think about is what do they think about my eyes.

L: 'All along you've said you resent any reference to the condition of your eyes.'

Not always: not when *you* say something, for instance.

L: 'Well, most of the time. Doesn't that lead you to believe that you are anxious to hide, not only from other people, but also from yourself, the nature of the thing that lies behind the condition of your eyes?'

I see what you mean. Probably I can't think of what caused it. I see what you mean. You know I don't care what *you* say. To me you are the psychologist. I don't dislike you when you are talking like this afternoon. I look on you as someone different from other people. I'm willing to do my best for you.

L: 'Then you are willing to accept that statement?'

L: 'In other words, you hate to have anyone remind you of the thing that precipitated your condition.'

But . . . I don't know . . .

L: 'Either you don't know it or you don't want to know it. Which is it?'

I think the more precise definition would be the second one. Maybe I'm afraid of knowing it. That seems the best. I don't want to know it; yet I want to bring it out, bring it out if I can.

I don't know why some people tell me that they are coming along better. I don't want to listen to it.

Perry says he wishes you weren't working with me.

If I could only think of an answer. It's got to come out somehow.

I don't remember much about my younger days. O, some small memories, little bits of pictures, but there was so much.

I believe I told you as well as myself the reason I so much dislike homosexuals. I don't dislike Perry but I hate a lot of these people they call wolves. It all goes back to that incident in the clubhouse when I was about eight or nine. I think it all goes back there. I think it was an important part of my life. It caused me to feel about sexual acts the way I do, but it couldn't have been the cause of my eyes being like this, because I distinctly remember that my eyes were like this when I was that old.

I was always believing in my mind, ever since I was ten, that when I'd get to be twenty-one I'd either be dead or my eyes would be fixed.

This common belief of late childhood and early adolescence is designed to satisfy a basic need for expiation. It is an invariable component in the obsessive-compulsive adolescent personality structure. Underlying it is expectation of punishment for the phantasies preliminary to or accompanying masturbation.

Something always told me that. Now I'm past twenty-one and I'm not dead and my eyes are getting fixed.

I don't know whatever made me think of that. I used to go to see different doctors and they'd prescribe glasses for me and things like that. Once the Board of Health sent me to an eye specialist and he told me I would grow out of it before I was twenty-one. He said my eyes would be almost perfect and I believed it. Still I always had some doubts. I don't know how I figured I'd be dead or have my eyes fixed. I'm not dead, but I'm in prison.

I feel that I have told you almost everything in my life but there is something, there must be something missing. The things I mostly talked about were the things I did most. The things I did only once and the things I intended doing are unimportant. I forget about them. I can't remember them. The same things every day. When I go back further, to when I was ten or less, I have a picture in my mind of the class room . . . and the teachers, the pupils, how all the desks were lined up. I can see that . . .

The Twenty-first Hour

I had a lot of fun out at the shore with my cousin, a very nice kid. She liked to sit out on the lawn at night, looking at the stars, sometimes until two o'clock in the morning. I know she liked me a lot. I went pretty far with her. Not too far, though; just far enough that I know I won't have any trouble with her when I leave here if I ever see her again. If I ever see her again. I doubt if I ever will. . . .

I think I was about eight when I had a girl for the first time. I remember it was one of two sisters. I know it was when we lived on B——— Street. We lived there from the time I was about five, maybe younger than that. I remember we lived on F——— Street and moved from there to B——— Street and lived there for a few years. My father had a garage there and in his spare time he assembled cars, put them together and sold them. Well, back of the garage, between the fence and the garage, there was an old cab body that had a seat in it. I think it was on that seat that I had the girl. I don't remember how it was. Most of the kids used to play there. I remember it was late in the afternoon when I started playing around with her. She was about seven or eight. I don't know if she went over to the same school as I did. I think she went to St. A————— School when I went to H————— Street. I don't remember which girl it was, one of two sisters whose brother got his leg cut off on the railroad.

I recall several other young kids too. We were about seven or eight and we used to sneak out of class into the cloak room with cigarettes and smoke them. There was a kid everybody used to joke around: he was a barber's son and he always had hair tonic on his head. Everybody used to kid him about it.

One time I was going to the corner grocery store for my mother. I remember I went into the wrong store. It was a funeral director's place I went into instead of the grocery store. I don't know why I went in there. I knew just how many stores the grocery store was from the corner, and I knew where the funeral parlor was and still I went in there. The man didn't say anything to me. As soon as I went in I knew it was the wrong place.

We had a clubhouse behind the billboard, raised up against the billboard with the planks laid across the base and a hole in the side to get in. We had pictures of naked women all over the walls. I wasn't the oldest fellow that belonged to this gang, nearly the youngest. Most of the others were ten or twelve years old. They used to make little guns, I guess you call them catapults, to put snowballs in. They were made just like a shot gun, thick and round, and they used to put rubber bands inside for snowballs. You pull them with a cord from the rear and shoot them out. One time we were trying to dig a tunnel from the clubhouse to the yard. We dug a hole first and started to go in toward the lot, and then one day it rained and everything caved in and we had to fill it all in again.

I can remember when Wazeki's mother was taken away to the insane asylum. I looked out the window and saw the ambulance there. They put her in a straight jacket and put her on a stretcher and covered her with a sheet. That's what they said; my father and mother were talking; my mother was saying how sorry she was for the woman. I can remember her. She always was good to me. I only knew her a little while. She was raving and hollering and pulling her hair out, my mother was saying, and her husband was having her put away. Wazeki was about twelve then, I guess. He had a sister that I used to lay in bed with a lot when I got older. I'd go upstairs where they lived when nobody was home and start kissing her and putting my arms around her. I was about ten then. I don't remember much about her mother being taken away. I was sleeping then on the davenport in the parlor, and my father and mother were in the window looking out and talking. There was a victrola in that room. One time I got a licking from my father from cutting it. He had a straight razor and it was hid in a bureau, and I took it and chopped the bureau and got a licking. Everytime I remember that I can hear somebody singing and the victrola playing. I guess it only made me madder.

My youngest sister slept in the cradle in my mother's room and my mother's godfather and I used to sleep on the davenport. One time when I was sleeping I heard somebody at the window. I looked and I saw a strange man with his hat pulled over his head, and he tried to open the screen. I don't remember what happened then. I fell asleep: next morning I told my mother.

One time when I was about six I was sitting on our front porch and I remember I s——t all over the porch, right through my clothes and everything. . . .

There was a fellow by the name of Jimmy and he and my cousin Benny and myself hung around together. This Jimmy had a sister Lolly, a skinny freckled-faced kid, shy. One time we were at a dance hall and I was drunk and I saw her with Benny and I started kissing her on the floor; stood right in the middle of the floor and kissed her, and Benny got mad because they were engaged. I know she liked me. My cousin Riggs tried to make her but I don't know if he succeeded.

Benny and me used to go to the show together late at night. One time we went to a show and we came out pretty late in the evening, and when we came out Benny had a knife on him and he dropped it. He was about twelve then and I was ten. I hadn't spoken to Benny for a long time, eight years maybe, then one time I saw him in the

park near our house. Lolly was with him. She worked where my
sister and my cousin Riggs did and he'd tell me how he tried to make
her. I didn't like that; it didn't seem right to me when one cousin
was going to marry her that the other cousin should try something
like that.

I didn't like St. A————— School much. I was the worst kid in
the class and I always got punished for everything, because I didn't
have my lessons done, because I didn't learn my lessons, because I
wasn't doing this or that. I was a regular customer for getting
slapped with the ruler on my hand. I don't know why my mother
made me go to that school. They had a very fine pastor there in the
church and he was also in charge of the school and everyone had a
good thing to say about him. But when I got there they had a
mean priest. He hit the kids with his cane. Once I saw him give
such a beating to a fellow that the poor kid collapsed.

In H————— Street School in third grade there was a young
teacher who had a habit once in a while of putting one of the kids
under her desk. It was a big desk and a lot of the kids wanted to go
in there thinking that they could look up her dress; so they'd make
noise and the teacher would put them there. I was there once but I
couldn't see anything. This teacher also would send all the kids who
made noise into the cloak room, so sometimes even before we made a
noise we'd go in the cloak room and smoke a couple cigarettes. We'd
buy these cigarettes for a penny; not real cigarettes but cubebs.

When I was about thirteen in the seventh grade there was a girl
that lived on M————— Street who used to sit right behind me and
across the aisle. She used to spread her legs apart and pull her dress
over her knees. She was not very pretty in her face. There was
another one that sat across from me in the same row too who had
black hair. She was real pretty and once in a while she'd pick up her
dress too. The first one, the blond-haired one, lived on M—————
Street and she would ask me to come over to her house but I didn't go
because they had a pretty tough gang of kids there and I was scared
of them. When I got older these fellows disliked me: they hated me
because they were afraid of me. Once in a while I would hang out
with some of them. I committed crimes with some but they never
bothered me and I never bothered them . . .

The Twenty-second Hour

There was a small community house near the school where I went quite often when I was about seven. It had a room where all the kids played checkers and dominoes and things like that. They'd show movies in the summer once a week outside where there was a big yard. I don't know who sponsored it. All the kids from the neighborhood would be there. It was before they had talking pictures. They'd hang the screen on the side of the garage and they'd set the camera about a hundred feet back. I don't remember much about that. I don't remember much about any of my ambitions then. I know we played soldiers a lot. Putting tin hats and aluminum pots on our heads for helmets was a lot of fun, and we'd use wash boilers for shields and wooden swords.

One time I found two cocoons on a twig on the branch of a tree and I kept watching them for a week or two. Once when I came I found them open, but I looked and looked and didn't see any butterfly or anything. I was always wondering about that. When I took the empty cocoons off the twig they were sticky-like and silky.

Around this time my mother took me and my sister to a drug store on the corner of B———— and F————. We had little red sores all over our chests. I don't know what they were. The druggist gave us something and after a few days it went away. I guess I was never very sick. My sisters had diphtheria but I never had it. When my sisters had that the younger one slept in the baby carriage and the other one in the crib.

I don't remember if my little sister ever had measles. That's what my mother told me was the cause of the trouble with my eyes: that I had the measles and I went outside. I don't know where this happened, either in B———— or when we were living in P————.

When I was small I'd go with my mother when she went shopping, and sometimes I'd get lost. I'd walk off by myself. I used to think other women who were dressed like my mother and wore the same kind of coat she had were my mother. It made me feel embarrassed when I got lost like that. My mother would find me and then she'd say something about my eyes, why didn't I stay there, and she'd curse me in Polish.

I didn't like to go away with my father and mother anywhere. I would rather stay home. When I was about twelve we'd go down to the shore almost every Sunday. There wasn't much down there for me. I guess I'd get wet playing in the sand, that's all. I liked to go swimming but I didn't like to go with the whole family, just with one or two other fellows. My mother didn't like for me to go out; she just wanted me to stay home. Often when I was telling her that I was going out swimming with somebody she would holler and jump up and down. She was afraid I'd get into an accident or something. I guess she is a little different with my sister now. She lets her go wherever my sister wants to go. If I had no money my cousins Tony or Riggs would always let me have the money to go down to the shore for two days or so, but she never would let me go. It was not because of the money, I always managed to get a couple of dollars, but she always would say that my father would say this or that, that he wouldn't like it; so to avoid a lot of unpleasantness I wouldn't go. When we lived in B———— Street once in a while we went on these Polish picnics out in the country. I didn't like to go very much. There was only one place in particular I liked to go because I could sit by the lake and watch everybody in swimming. I was too young to go in swimming I guess.

It'll be good to get in the water again, to get in a lot of water, to get your feet way down on the bottom, way down. . . .

Sometimes another family would go with us in my father's car. They had a kid about eight with who I hung out when we went to picnics. They lived in another town and we used to pick them up on the way and take them with us. This kid and myself hung around together and watched the men have crap games. We used to spend a lot of time in the double toilets on these picnics. There was a partition between the men's and women's toilets and we'd go in there and spend hours looking through cracks in the wall. If we could make out somebody doing something we'd think it was great. I can't remember this fellow's name. When we got older, about twelve or thirteen, he gave me a watch. I lost it and my grandmother gave it to my cousin Joe when she found it. This fellow also won a shotgun in a raffle. I was going to buy it off him or steal it if I could.

The reason I like shotguns and things like that is that I like the noise. I feel it in my hand when it shoots, the vibrations. When I had a gun on me I thought I was better than other people. Girls didn't like guns, so in a conversation sometimes I would take it out and they would scream, they were so afraid of it.   I used to have a .32 short with six or eight shells in the cylinder, the break-open type. I paid eight dollars for it.   It was a small gun with a short barrel and a big handle.   I used to carry ten or twelve extra bullets in my vest pocket.   I'd keep it in my pocket and practice how quick I could draw it.   I'd look at myself in the mirror and point it at me and see how vicious I looked.   When I looked close at the barrel it looked like the mouth of a cannon.

My mother sometimes found things in my bureau drawer, black-jacks, brass knuckles, and the parts of a gun.   There was something wrong with the trigger of this gun.   She almost killed me with it. She wanted to break my head.   She hit me on the shoulder with it a few times and then threw it away.

When I was twelve I had a blank gun I bought for thirty cents from a fellow and I used to put .22 shells in it.   You could only put one shell in the barrel: when you shot it you had to take the empty one out and put the good ones in.   I'd always remember to put my coat in the closet when I had the gun in it.   One day I forgot and when I was sitting there reading or doing something I saw my mother going over to the coat.   She went through the hip pockets but didn't look in the breast pocket where it was.   I was really scared that time. Later on a fellow borrowed this gun and kept it.   No; I broke it.   I shot it a few times and the bullets were too strong for it.

I don't know when I first started to carry a gun.   I figured I just liked to carry it and as time went on I always wanted it with me, like a fellow would want to wear a tie or have his shirt sleeves buttoned. I don't remember the first time I liked to play with guns.   We were always playing cowboys or something like that.   It reminds me of a picture in the paper where kids are playing with toy pistols in London. We were just like that.   We'd make wooden guns with rubber bands and play with them.   We'd steal automobile tires and cut them up and make rubber bands out of them.   We had a lot of fights that way.

I like to throw knives too.   When I was older, about fifteen, I didn't think much about guns and knives but when I was thirteen I hung around with a bunch of kids and we'd find things, like knives, and play with them.   The other day I picked up a fork in the mess hall.   There was a cardboard box on the table about ten feet away. I threw it left handed and it sunk right into the box.   I guess it was luck.   I don't think I could ever do it again.

When I lived at my aunt's house there was a fellow who had one of those knives they put on the end of a gun. I can't think of the name. It was easy to throw and when you threw it, it would stick in. . .

The reason for this lapse of memory was analyzed. Unfortunately, it cannot be dealt with here.

THE TWENTY-THIRD HOUR

I am going to tell you good news today: we had steak for dinner; that was good.

Patients frequently 'telegraph' in this way their intention to reveal material of importance.

I just thought of this: you know, I don't ever remember seeing my mother undressed, but where we lived at B————— Street we didn't have a bathroom and we'd take baths in a tub in the middle of our kitchen; and when she took a bath I would see her back. I don't think I ever saw her fully naked. I used to sleep with my sister in the cradle. She was about seven or eight I guess. After that my mother always kept us separated. When we were young I—I used to do things that were not—not exactly right. This was long before my other sister was born. When she was born I was sleeping in the parlor. We had four rooms then: my mother's and father's bedroom, the kitchen, the dining room and a parlor. In the parlor there was a small day-bed and a davenport. When my mother's godfather boarded with us I slept with him on the davenport. When he wasn't, I slept on the small bed. In my mother's room there was a cradle. My sister used to sleep there. Sometimes both of us would play in there if we were in the cradle together and I don't know if my mother ever knew anything or not. But when we moved from B————— Street she kept us separated.

L: 'What do you mean by "whether she knew anything or not," Harold? What was it she would know?'

I don't know if my mother ever knew that I did anything like that to my sister. . . .

Well; I guess I was about ten and my sister about eight, or maybe even younger. We lived on B————— Street and sometimes we used to go to sleep in the cradle together. It wasn't exactly a cradle; more like a junior bed. It was big enough to hold both of us and sometimes my mother would make us take naps together, sometimes on her bed, sometimes on this cradle. When we slept together like that I used to get my hands all over her. I must have, well; I . . .

My mother and father slept in the big double bed. I think my father was working driving a truck and I don't know if we went to school then. I think I did. It was in the summer so we had to stay home and sleep in the afternoon, sometimes in the bed, sometimes in the cradle. Usually we would go to sleep together. I remember we had pillow fights and things like that. I know I . . . . , that is, I used to put my hands all over her and, well, I—I had intercourse with her several times. At least five or more times. We slept together a lot. I think my mother knew we were doing something like that. When we moved from B———— Street we never slept together again. I think it was when we went to sleep one time and my mother came in and my sister had her legs all over me. From then on mother must have known; she never said anything though.

I know there was some girls in the neighborhood I used to screw but I never did anything like that to my sister other than when we were sleeping together.

I remember when I was about eight or nine how my mother used to take baths in the kitchen in a tub. Sometimes she would call me in to wash her back. I didn't like to do it. I didn't see her completely, but most of her body. Sometimes I didn't want to wash her back so she'd swing around and hit me. I didn't like to do it, but when my sister took baths I'd see her completely naked. I don't think we ever took baths together. I know for certain of one time when we were sleeping in the cradle together that we had intercourse, and I remember dimly lots of other times.

Sometimes when the godfather was not with us there would be another fellow boarding there. He was a guy about thirty or so. I used to wear pajamas and when I woke up in the morning my peter would be sticking out and he would hold it. I remember he would hold my peter in his hand. I was a little kid then and I would try to duck away from him when I'd see him. He was living with us when the man tried to break into the house. I don't think he was asleep when I woke up and saw the man at the window. I guess I fell asleep again. I don't remember much about him. I just didn't like it when he would untie my pajamas and open them when I was asleep, holding my peter like that . . . I never told nobody before. I never liked to sleep with him but my mother made me.

I never saw my father naked. O, I saw him in his underwear a lot, but not completely naked. And I never remember seeing my aunts naked.

I do remember telling my mother, "Why don't you get Marie to wash your back?" but she'd swing around and hit me and yell, "You do what you're told!"

When I was younger many times I figured that I couldn't get along with my sister because of something I had seen or done. I knew a kid about sixteen who also laid his sister and he disliked her very much. I always thought maybe Marie dislikes me. Maybe she does. I don't know whether she can remember back that far. I don't think she hates me and I don't hate her though I think something like that could create hatred. . . .

When I was about ten I used to see girls partly naked, with nothing on under their dresses and sometimes they would pick them up and they were naked from the waist down. I saw lots of them, my sister too. She always hung around with some of these girls and she'd pull her dress up too. Wazeki's sister, I'd see her a lot. I used to lay her on the bed and take most of her clothes off.

When I was pretty small the kids in school used to talk about being under the teacher's desk. I was underneath there once but I never saw anything so I didn't want to be put there again. It didn't interest me any more. The way I got to be put underneath there was this: I ran out of the class room into the cloak room knowing that the teacher would put me underneath the desk. I just knew that most of the other kids were there so I guess I wanted to go too. I stayed there about ten minutes and when the teacher came after me I talked back to her in a nasty way, kind of sarcastic, and she said, "What do you want to do, stay here all day or go under the desk for ten minutes?" So I went under the desk. When I came out the kids were all snickering and motioning to me whether I'd seen anything, and at first I didn't say a word. I put my face in my hands and my elbows on the desk and didn't speak a word. When the kids motioned to me I just shook my head. This was in the morning and in the afternoon I told the fellows I didn't want to go again. I was sitting there all cramped and it hurt my neck and I didn't see anything. After that, some kid would go under the desk occasionally and then I'd get the feeling that I wanted to do it again, but I never got to do it any more. I remember I saw part of her knee and her leg, that's all. I don't know if I saw anything of the white-clothes she had on; her dress was blue, I think. She wasn't an old teacher: she was pretty young, about twenty-five or six, and she was fairly well built. I didn't know much about build then, though. I remember one time she came over to my desk to help me out with some work, and when she bent over I could see down her dress. Not very much, but my imagination saw more. I looked down her dress and when I looked up I saw that she was staring straight at me and I didn't know what to do. She must have figured that I was looking. She was pretty good to me, that teacher: she never hollered.

L: '*As a matter of fact, Harold, it is true, isn't it, that you don't like to look at the female genitals?*'

Yes; that's true.

L: '*Do you know why?*'

I guess so. I guess my sister and my mother . . .

I know why. When I went with that girl Lila on the outside, I used to play with her breasts but I would never reach under her dress and play with her genital organs. And when I laid her it was always at night, never in the day time. At night I didn't have to see them.

L: '*What do the female organs remind you of?*'

The first time I saw my sister naked it reminded me of a man without a penis. The first time I saw her naked she was getting out of a bath, if I remember right, and I knew she wasn't like myself. I didn't see a penis. It was something strange. I never asked about it. I always got in the habit of waiting and watching to see what would happen. When I went with Lila I liked to play with her breasts but she would get so hot she'd reach inside of my pants and play with my peter; so I'd lay her down and have intercourse with her. I used to dislike seeing her skinny legs. I probably thought that it looked like a man with his penis and testes cut off.

L: '*Who would be most likely to have cut them off?*'

Why, the father or the mother or the doctor, or whoever helped the mother to give birth to the child. I don't know; maybe I was scared

Note the order of primacy in which potential castrators are placed.

when I was young of something like that. I don't remember just now if anybody threatened me. I know there was a young kid who was ruptured, and once my father and mother were talking in Polish about him. He told her about the belt he wore and he motioned about his body to show her. I saw it, and when he told her I understood a few words, and he motioned to show her how the belt was going around him to hold his penis up.

I don't know but I think that's what most of the kids tried to see when we were in school in the class room where they were all trying to get under the teacher's desk. The older kids used to say that it was a fur cap or a teddy bear she was hiding there. Most of the kids tried to see it.

I don't think I ever saw my mother completely naked. I always tried to get out of washing her back. Sometimes when she swung at me I'd see her breasts. I only saw her genitals a couple of times.

I never saw my father completely naked.

When I got older I got some respect for my sisters. I never did anything like that to my younger sister. Even now I treat her as a baby. When she was a couple of months old I didn't like to look at her when she didn't have her diapers or panties on or something. When she was covered she was like any baby, cute and sweet.

I have a cousin named Rose who was about eight when I moved from B———— Street to S———— Street. She was living with my uncle on F———— Street and she used to come over and play with my sister. We had a back porch and between the back porch and the ground there was a foundation that held it up. It was blocked off and we had a clubhouse there, me and some of the fellows. We used to hide there and collect bottles and junk like that and we had a carpet in there. I took her in there and had intercourse with her once. That was the only time. She was a nice little girl but I never liked her after that. Then I played a lot with the girl that lived upstairs. Her name was Peg. She was about twelve, older than me at the time. I'd take her down the cellar and I liked her a lot. To me she always seemed a nice girl, pretty and everything like that. The cellar was dark and dreary and damp. I never played with her much outside, in the light. It's only in the dark when I touch women. I guess when I got to be a little older I knew what

women are for. I don't know how I learned. I guess I learned
from my cousins. I learned everything else from them.

L: 'Which cousins do you mean?'

I mean my two cousins Tony and Riggs. The oldest cousin was
doing time for highjacking a truck when I came in here. He's the
oldest and has a wife and child. Then there is Emma, she's married.
Tony got married before I came here and Riggs, he'll be married soon.
I dislike both of them.

L: 'Why do you think you dislike them?'

I'm not sure. I remember one day Riggs wanted some little girl
to suck his peter and when she hollered he told his mother I was the
one. I don't know how it worked out but I know I got a beating for
it.

L: 'But you disliked him before that?'

I might have. It's all jumbled up. He tried to catch up in school
with me: I was two grades ahead of him and he went to summer school
and things like that. He failed several times. I am only a year
older than him. Tony is a year and half older and he was only one
grade ahead of me. I don't know if that's the time I started hating
Riggs. I know I disliked him because he called me Squint. I only
went with him because I had no one else to go with. I remember we
used to steal things from a store across the street, apples, any kind
of food that was laying around. When I quit the Boy Scouts I
started hanging around the gang that he and Tony were in. I
played hookey a lot with Tony when I was at St. A——'s and
we'd hang around the railroad yards. Then I started with Riggs.
We played hookey in High. He used to gamble a lot and most
always win. I never caught him cheating but I knew he cheated.
I'd see him winning all the time, and I'd take my gun out and lay it
on the table next to me and he'd look at me and at the gun and a little
while later he'd start losing. Then when I got what I wanted I'd
quit. I didn't want him to cheat me. Some times when he wanted
a little money to get in a card game or crap game I gave it to him,
and when he'd win we'd buy cigarettes and spend the afternoon in a
show. That way I got along with him.

One time we were thinking of holding up a bank. He wanted some
money and I was out for the same thing. There were a lot of bank
hold-ups going on then around our town and we thought we'd plan

one too. I told him I could get an automatic rifle and we'd buy some shotguns and saw the barrels off. But I was always afraid that he'd squeal or something. I would never trust him even though I would go with him. I was always watching and waiting for something to happen. I came here before we could pull that job. We were figuring on a lot of things then. We were going to try and hold up some armored-car guards when they walked in places to collect money. We couldn't get the cars so we were going to get the guards. If we had a couple sawed-off shotguns we figured they'd be afraid. But I didn't trust Riggs very far. I knew he'd let me down: he's done it time and time again.

He's more the burglary type. . . .

THE TWENTY-FOURTH HOUR

As far back as I can remember I didn't like my father. I would never speak to him other than when it was necessary. For some reason I disliked him and I couldn't talk to him. I would tell my mother and sister to say things to him; I'd tell them and they'd tell him. My sister always got along with him. I got along best with my uncle. He and I were going to South America together when he received his bonus. He had a wife but he hadn't lived with her for eight years. He didn't get along very well with my father either. I guess it was because my father was quick-tempered and would argue with everybody. I know my father worked hard and didn't get much pay. He would always complain about something hurting him, his back or his head, and my mother babied him a lot.

When I was around twelve I got into trouble by breaking into a store with several other fellows and I went to the Juvenile Court and they sent me to the Home for three weeks. When I came back my father didn't say anything to me. He knew because my mother told him, and yet he didn't say anything about it. I figured he must be a pretty swell man if he didn't say anything to his son after he spent three weeks in a reform school. When I was older, around seventeen, he always wanted me to get a job. Whenever he'd see me he'd ask if I was looking for work. Usually I would lie to him and say yes, but he knew I was lying so he would turn around and call me a liar. That's why I would always try to be away from home when he came from work. I'd hear my father and mother arguing about me many times.   When I was around seventeen I didn't have any job, no money, fed up with everything, so I figured I'd get money as easy and as quick as possible.

L: 'You were saying that your mother babied your father.   Were you jealous of the attentions she showered on him?'

When he had a sore back or something I didn't like the way she was so sorry for him.

L: 'Did you resent your mother's attentions to your father?'

I always thought it was useless.

L: 'Did you ever have any distinct resentment against your father about that?'

I think the only reason she was attentive to him was so he shouldn't be angry and start arguing with her.   He always argued with her, that's the reason.

My father used to have two cars.   He used one to go to work with; what the other car was bought for was because he wanted to get my sister interested in learning to drive and taking out a license. So one day she said to him in front of me, "What's the matter with him?"   He said that he bought it for her, not for me.   I guess I disliked him more after that.   I guess he dislikes me too.

L: 'Why do you think he dislikes you?'

I guess he couldn't hear very well so when he said something to me and I would answer him so he couldn't hear it he would think I'd given him a sarcastic answer.

L: 'Have you always disliked him or was there a time when you felt differently towards him?'

I've always disliked him.   He would always argue with somebody about something: he'd pick on me and my sister or my mother.   Jesus! He'd even argue with my grandmother.   I disliked him even more for that.   Why should he argue with an old woman?   But maybe there was a time when I liked him.   I never talked to him because I felt he couldn't understand me.   There are loads of reasons.   One time I called him in to supper when he was fixing his car.   He had a hammer in his hand and he said he would hit me in the head with it. I was about thirteen then.   I didn't say anything, just let things go by.   He told my mother about it and she argued with him.   I could hear them.

When we lived on S———— Street we had four rooms; a kitchen,

two bedrooms and a parlor. There was a door from one of the bedrooms to the parlor. I slept in the parlor sometimes and they slept in the next bedroom. My sister slept in the other bedroom. I—I— Sometimes I used to. I was sleeping in the bedroom next to their bedroom and I used to hear them moving over and—preparing for intercourse. Sometimes I heard my father tell my mother to— move—over and—and put her—legs up and . . . I hated to hear it. I would put the cover over my head and try not to listen. An action like that, it isn't nice for a son to hear. Many times I heard my father say to my mother, "What the hell do you think I married you for?" I'm not sure if I actually saw them doing anything like that.

There was marked overt resistance while the patient was speaking of physical relations between his parents. He twisted and squirmed on the couch, bit his lips and grimaced frequently.

L: '*How do you suppose you would have felt if you had seen anything like that?*'

It's pretty hard to explain. I guess I hated to see him do anything like that in front of everybody. Sometimes when my sister used to get beatings from my father or mother—when she was younger she used to get hit sometimes for not listening to them—she would sit in the room crying, and I would go away by myself. I didn't like to see her get hit. My sister is a good girl. She works. She gives all her money to her mother. She doesn't play around with boys. My younger sister gets beaten a lot though. My mother beats her because she talks back. My mother is a timid woman; she cries right away. I guess I feel sorry for her, so I wanted to get away from everything and everybody and I'd leave home. I left home a lot of times; I can't remember how often but it was plenty.

L: '*If you had seen your parents during any intimacy, Harold, how do you suppose it would have appeared to you?*'

Well, it appeared that my father was hurting my mother. I guess it might have a lot of different meanings. Maybe I did see my father and mother do that. I can't recall. It must have been way back before I can remember. It might seem vulgar, brutal, filthy, dirty, or what not.

L: '*Is that the way a child would think?*'

Well, whenever we had to take a leak when we were little kids we would consider the penis dirty, nasty. My mother might have said that. She taught us that the genitals were dirty: she said that the penis was dirty.

I don't remember ever seeing my father naked. He strikes me as being the poor illiterate and ignorant European peasant type that come over to America to get something. They leave over there because there is nothing for them. He's a good mechanic but he doesn't know how to read or write. He has a big chest and a neck like a bull. He has a kind of pugilistic appearance. If I had ever seen anything like that it would make me feel as if he was hurting my mother, that he was choking her, killing her. But sometimes I know, when he was home and I was old enough to realize some things, I saw my father put his hands on my mother's buttocks. It didn't exactly appeal to me. I didn't think it was right. I guess I did feel a little resentment against my father for touching my mother.

L: 'You felt he shouldn't do it?'

I disliked it when he did it in front of everybody. My mother would always tell him to look out for the children but he didn't care.

L: 'And you resented the fact that he handled your mother that way?'

I certainly did.

L: 'You felt he had no right to?'

Yes. But when I got older I saw it in a different light. I guess I know right from wrong.

L: 'You were jealous of him?'

I must have thought that my father could at least be decent enough not to do anything like that in front of everybody.

L: 'You thought of your father's relationship with your mother as distasteful?'

When I'd hear them in bed, hear them talk and him coaxing my mother I hated to listen to it. I'd put the covers over my head and try to shut out everything: sometimes I'd recite nursery rhymes to myself, just to forget, just to forget. I still sleep with the covers over my head. I hated to listen to it. I didn't want to. I didn't want to be around. I wanted to be away from there. I'd pull the covers over my head.

I don't remember much about my father and mother before that time. I got one severe beating from him for ruining his razor. He really beat me up: he lifted me from the ground and let me drop on the floor.

My mother told me that when they were first married he'd hit her. I hated him for that. I guess my mother was married to him about a week when she says she left him. They were living in B—————— then and she came running back to my grandmother's; and my grandmother chased her back. My mother was about sixteen when they got married. Sometimes I wish my grandmother hadn't made her go back; she's had a very unhappy life with him.

Maybe he really is not as bad as I say he is. Maybe he treated my mother o.k. He always argued with my mother about me; why didn't I get a job, and this and that. When we lived on S—————— Street, when I was about eleven, my mother would close the door between the parlor and the bedroom where I slept. She'd come in the room and just sit, read a book or look out the window. I didn't hear anything when she closed the door, but sometimes when it was warm the door would be opened and I'd have to sleep underneath the covers. Sometimes when my father came home from driving a truck he would have some kind of joke he would be aching to tell my mother, and I knew it must be a dirty joke of some kind. He would tell my mother to remind him to tell her and my mother would say, "If that's the kind of a joke I think it is I don't want to hear it." I knew it was a dirty joke when he would say anything like that and I disliked it; he shouldn't say anything like that to her. I guess I hated him. I remember when I was about eight or nine I was learning to ride a bicycle and there was a fellow that wanted to sell his for three dollars, so I asked my mother to buy it for me and she told me to ask my father. I didn't have guts enough to ask him; so finally I mentioned it at the table and he said, "What do you want to do, get killed?" So I never asked him for anything again. I have often wondered why I didn't want to ask him for anything. Now I think that's the reason.

I know my father used to chase a lot of women. My mother told me. My mother was born in this country and she could read and write and speak English good. I got along alright with her. My mother, my oldest sister and myself were always more like companions. O, we had a few arguments, but they were nothing. Sometimes my mother told me about the things my father used to do: how he used to hit her when they were first married. I was old enough then to think about such things. I didn't form any hasty opinions.

I think the reason my mother's godfather left us is that he had an argument with my father.

My father doesn't drink or smoke but my mother told me that he used to go around in his car picking up women. I don't know if she ever said anything to him. She said she knew he was doing it.

I'd tell myself when I saw how my mother and father fought that I'd never get married.

I always used to dress neatly, clean clothes; my mother always saw to it that we were clean. She'd try to help me with my ABCs, teach me how to add. My father never did anything like that.

Often I'd go to sleep on the davenport and when I woke up my mother'd be there. I guess she came in during the middle of the night to see if I was comfortable. She'd cry a lot too. She'd argue with my father; he would holler at her so she'd go somewheres by herself and cry and pay no attention to anybody or anything; and she would take my sister or me on her lap and cry. She'd never tell us why she was crying.

He used to say things about my eyes and curse me out.

My sister was a tomboy and he would say things about cutting off my penis and giving it to her.

L: 'Do you remember him actually saying that?'

When I was around eight or under he would say things like that. He was always telling dirty jokes. I feel there is something there. He said something like that. He used to say those kind of things then, lots of things.

L: 'Such as . . . ?'

A lot of dirty jokes. He would hint around at the table. When he was telling dirty jokes I didn't like to hear him tell them in front of my sister and myself. I didn't like to be around. My mother would holler at him to be quiet. He said something about cutting off my penis and giving it to my sister. She was a tomboy when she was a kid and he'd tease her about it. She'd fight with all the kids. One time there was a kid about my age she had a fight with because he said something about my eyes. She would always hold up like that for me when I was young. I know my father used to fix cars and he made a car once out of an old taxi. He changed the body and painted it up and sold it. I was afraid he'd change my body too. He always said he wished I was the girl instead of my sister. He likes her best. I remember when I was eight he said he wished she was the boy: that she was the best one; she would fight anybody and was afraid of nobody. He always said I ran to my mother in case anything happened. He would say I was the girl and she was the boy. I remember one time we had a dog, a little dog named Nellie. He would tell me that he would sic the dog on me and the dog would bite off my penis. The dog was a wild dog: she'd bite anybody; and she used to listen to my father and do what he told her. I don't know whether he actually did sic the dog on me but he said that once or twice. We had the dog for about two or three years when we lived on B——— Street. She got killed by a car: she always chased cars. I guess I was under eight when he said that. He used to threaten me about this dog. The dog bit me one time when I was running past the alley. He said it once or twice in Polish, never in English. In Polish he said he'd sic the dog on me so she'd bite off my penis. I remember one time at the table he said that. My mother came to my rescue and scolded him for saying it. Then she started telling me that Nellie wouldn't bite me and she called her over and told me to pat her head to see she wouldn't bite me. It might have been when I was seven. I remember I got along with the dog better after that: she was always with me. I was very small then. I guess my sister wasn't more than four.

I can see it all; like a picture. My sister, real small. I can see my hands. My sister has dirty-blond hair, straight, cut in front. It seems so real to me. I can see the knicker pants I've got on and I feel so small in the chair. My father looks like he always looked to me. I have a distaste for his appearance; he always needs a shave.

L: 'When your father made that threat, do you remember how you felt? Were you afraid he'd carry it out?'

Yes; I was afraid he would. I didn't know what to do. When he said that my mother was sitting on the other side of me. She told my father, "What do you want to say things like that for?" She touched my knee, put her hand on my knee and touched it and said, "Don't worry; Nellie wouldn't bite you." Then she called the dog over. The dog was dark-colored and white underneath the chin and neck and throat, and the dog's tail was wagging as my mother was patting him. She told me, "Pat him on the head, Harold." I was afraid of dogs for a while after that. His tail was wagging and she kept patting him and saying to me, "He won't bite you." The dog looked at me with such pitiful eyes and he put his head under my leg when I kept on patting him.

L: 'Was Nellie a he or a she?'

She was a female dog . . .

THE TWENTY-FIFTH HOUR

When I was about eleven, maybe twelve, Riggs and myself were in the clubhouse together and we were masturbating ourselves, not each other. There wasn't any discharge. I don't know if this was the first time or not. I guess it was to find out who could discharge first. We were talking on the street about masturbating and we went into the clubhouse to do it. I don't think either one of us finished. I have a hard time thinking about how it was when I was younger. I can remember that though. Then we went down by the river that day after we left the clubhouse. It was in the afternoon and we swam until around five o'clock, then went home for supper.

I have another cousin, Benny, who just got married not so long ago. I remember he stole twelve dollars once off his brother. We went to the show together and I remember when we were coming out of the show he dropped a big knife he had; dropped it on the floor and the manager or someone took it away from him. That day before we went into the show we bought a big bag of cakes and cookies and we ate all through the show. I was about nine then.

I am trying to think back further than that. I think my cousin Benny and me laid the same girl once. I'm trying to go back a little further than that.

About my masturbating I don't remember much other than the incident in the clubhouse. Well, I left H———— Street School and went to St. A———— School. When I was in about seventh grade there was one girl used to sit in back of me who would always pull her dress way up over her knees. I was looking at her and all the fellows sitting around by me. We all had hand mirrors and held it in our palms so we could look back there. This girl knew it, and one time she gave me an emotion. She held her hand as if she was holding a penis and she was moving it back and forth about an inch or so. She asked me to come to her house on M———— Street to see her, but I was afraid to go. I was afraid of the gang on that street.

My favorite occupation was playing truant then. I'd go swimming or just lay around and do nothing. Sometimes I'd go to the show.

I was about nine or less and there was a young girl, one of two sisters. Back of my father's garage there was a cab body with a seat in it and we were sitting on it. I started playing with her knee and then putting my hand under her dress and playing with her genitals. She kept pushing my hand away and saying, "Stop it!" After about five or ten minutes I had intercourse with her. First she consented to play with my penis and, I don't know, it gave me such a tickling sensation. I saw her a lot. We'd go in the cab body and play on the seat. I remember she used to lay across the seat and I'd lay on top of her. Sometimes after I was through she'd feel my penis for a while; it was a funny, tickling sensation. I remember when I'd go to bed sometimes my penis would be hard and I'd imagine she was playing with it, so I'd play with it myself. I guess that was how I masturbated the first time. We used to be in the cab body a lot together. I was in the first section, the front of the cab body, myself, and I was imagining that I was driving the cab and I had my hands on the steering wheel. She came through the back of the garage and sat down on the seat beside me. She began pushing the shift on the car back and forth. Then I went to the back and I was jumping up and down on the seat. She came back and jumped up and down with me. She laid down first and I put my head on her chest and started playing with her. I guess that's how it happened the first time. I was real small then. When she moved away there were several girls there; O, a lot of them. My father's cousin had been in the World War and he had a part of a soldier's equipment, a gun and a gas mask and things like that in the cellar. I used to parade with those things down there. Sometimes I would get down there with some girls and maybe I'd wait until everybody would go away except one of the girls and me. Then I would start playing with her and then I would go in one of the corners and masturbate. It seems to me that I liked that tickling sensation. I remember I used to go around with a big hat on and the gas mask in a sack over my shoulder. I would try to make one of the girls and if she didn't want to I would go in the corner and masturbate. I used to wait until everybody was out of the way.

I also remember now one time we were in the clubhouse. I was about eleven and Riggs told Tony how we were masturbating on the second floor, and Tony looked at me and said, "That's what's wrong with your eyes. You jerk off too much!" So then after that I'd get the feeling that everybody looked at me and knew I masturbated. Another time I broke some lights and padlocks on the railroad with some other fellows and we had to go to court. One fellow in that gang said that the matter with my eyes was that I was masturbating too much. I didn't go with him after that.

L: *'Did you think there was any truth in what they said?'*

I guess there was.

L: *'And do you still think so?'*

I still do whenever somebody says something about that.

L: *'When somebody says something about your eyes?'*

That's right.

L: *'You feel that your masturbation is betrayed by your eyes?'*

That's right. When I was in County Jail that time waiting for my trial there was a doctor there who was taking morphine, and he said that if he saw me on the outside he would think I'd be taking morphine. There was another guy there, an Italian fellow, Beanie we'd call him; he hinted around, he didn't specify, he didn't say anything right out, he kind of squinted and said, "What kind of needle do you mean, Doc?" Another fellow made the same remark that time when I was in the County Jail. I used to have the feeling that people knew I was masturbating when they looked at my eyes; they would squint their eyes and it seemed to me they had a sneer on their faces. I despised and hated them. Maybe that was just natural but that they were making fun of me would be always in my mind.

Sometimes I used to masturbate more than necessary, but I don't know what's necessary. I figure I never cared whether I did it too much or not enough. When I got older, about sixteen, I didn't masturbate much, but after I got in trouble I masturbated a lot, and between the ages of sixteen and eighteen also a lot. Perhaps I still think that's the reason I committed all these crimes—sex, masturbation. I don't know. I didn't give a damn. I didn't care whether the world would stop or keep on going. I kept telling myself that I wasn't afraid to die. What did I have to lose if I died? One reason

Note the psychological proximity of masturbation and death; also of eye and penis.

I committed all these crimes was because I didn't care about anything. When I was going to High School I bummed around with a fellow named Jimmy and after I got in trouble he said that one reason I held people up and things like that was that I was masturbating too much. I didn't talk to him again after that either.

When I lived on S——— Street there used to be a girl, Carol, who hung around with my sister a lot. She was about thirteen and I was fifteen. Sometimes she'd come around to our house to see my sister and I'd wait on the front porch for her. I'd lay her right inside the house or on the porch when it was dark. I had her a lot. After I quit school I went up to stay at my uncle's place for about three months. I masturbated there a lot and when I came back I didn't see Carol. I didn't hang around with her anymore because I began going with some of the older guys, fellows that were in the gang with me when I was about twelve years old. That was a big gang. There were about thirty or forty of us. I hung around in poolrooms then and got in bad company. We'd go to the railroad yards and pitch horseshoes most of the day and play pinochle. Then I started drinking because there was a kid that used to belong to the same gang and his father drank a lot. He would be going up and down all the time getting beer. That's the way it went on. He'd always give me a couple of bottles and when we had a bit of money he'd buy wine and whiskey for us.

I didn't masturbate very much before I was sixteen, at least not as much as I did after sixteen. When I quit school I tried to get a job. After leaving my uncle's place I didn't know what to do. I started to read a lot of junk, *Spicy Detective Stories*, and soon, when I was stimulated by a word or two, I would go into the bathroom and masturbate. I'd read *True Detective Stories* and look at the pictures of nude women and masturbate. My cousin Riggs had some book— I don't know what it was, it said, "Printed in Habana"—about two French girls. It was really dirty. It was a kind of thin book, only about thirty pages, and it had a lot of dirty pictures in it. I remember I read it on the street near the railroad tracks. After about fifteen minutes I went home and I masturbated in the toilet. I couldn't get control of myself, couldn't hold myself back. It was a dirty book.

The real reason I would try to avoid talking to my father and mother is that I felt they knew I was masturbating. I'd make believe I was reading a newspaper when they wanted to talk. I guess I was ashamed of myself. Sometimes I wouldn't speak to them for a couple of days and my mother would ask me what was wrong. I'd say, "Nothing."

When I was about seventeen, one time we started up to see some-body in the country. They had a girl around fourteen. She was nice. I tried to make her but she ran away from me. So I went into the toilet and started masturbating. My father caught me. He didn't say anything.

One time my probation officer asked me how many times I mastur-bated. I told him, "O, once every three or four weeks." Later I managed to see a report he made out to that effect where it definitely said, 'habitual masturbator.' I guess he figured that my criminal career was due to that. I never did like that man: I guess I never will.

When I was small sometimes I would lay in bed and it used to give me a small tickling sensation. It's hard to explain it. I know the first time I had intercourse with a girl it gave me such a thrill, such a tickling sensation. I always wanted to do it then. I used to get Carol as much as possible. She was always afraid she'd have a baby though. She had a sister about four or five years older than I was and when I was seventeen I used to hang around with their brother once in a while. One time we went out to clean an old gun I had and this girl, Carol's sister, was sitting there wearing a thin dress with nothing on underneath. I could tell. Carol's brother went to the back of the car to look for some tools and I was talking in front with her. She pulled her legs apart so I could see the genitals. Why did she do that? I tried to make her but I couldn't. I always tried to get next to her but she was older than me and would only go out with older fellows. I used to think about her a lot when I was mastur-bating . . .

THE TWENTY-SIXTH HOUR

I can only think of one place and one time when there was mutual masturbation. It was between myself and my cousin Tony. I was about twelve then and it was in the park. The toilets were in dif-erent sections with doors that latched down. We got in one of the toilets and pulled the latch down. I don't know how it came about but that's the only time I can remember. When I was still living on B——— Street there were some fellows in the cellar one time

and we were all playing.   I ran in a part of the cellar and they called
me over.   They wanted me to play with their peters.   I ran away.
Riggs was with me and we both ran into a bin.   I don't know what
they were doing but when they asked me to turn around I ran out,
my cousin Riggs right after me.

Me and Jimmy had a girl together once.   I made her first and he
went after me.   That's the only time I ever shared a girl with anybody else.   I can't seem to remember if there was any more.   When
we had the clubhouse that was rigged up behind the billboard we had
a lot of pictures of naked women there.   Sometimes five or six of us
in the gang would masturbate there, but I don't think there was any
mutual masturbation.

L: 'Was there ever any mutual masturbation with a girl?

Only with Lila.   I guess I was around seventeen then.   She was
always hot.   I would touch her and right away she would jump
around and tremble.   Just touch her breasts and she would start
masturbating you right off.   She always wanted to do that.   I spent
a lot of time with her, most of the afternoons.   I'd get up and sit in
the park with her and start playing with her and she'd have her hands
inside my pants.   I remember stroking her genitals several times but
the odor of my hands was not very pleasant.   I dislike that odor.
Sometimes when I said goodnight to her, when I took her home, in
the alleyway, I would stand with my arms around her and rub her
genitals through her dress.   She had real soft breasts, not hard at all,
real soft, and whenever I'd touch her she'd tremble all over.   She
used to tell me she loved me and wanted to get married, but I didn't
like her very much.   Sometimes when I was broke she'd buy me
cigarettes and things I needed.   She wasn't very pretty but she was
passable.   I must have had dozens and dozens of intercourses with
her.   She just liked for me to touch her.   As soon as I touched her
she was all ready, ready to pick up her dress.   A lot of guys knew I
went with her.   They always thought I was getting my share and
they wanted part of her too.   I got in several fights over that.   Sometimes I would take her home and she'd cry when I'd leave her because
I'd see some fellows watching her and I'd be afraid to do anything to
her when all the other fellows were around.   She'd cry when I'd leave
her without having intercourse with her.   I'd stand up in the alley
way and I would stroke her stomach and her genitals, not for long,

just for three or four minutes. But I don't know; I didn't like very much to stroke her genitals. Once or twice was sufficient and she was ready for intercourse and I'd go ahead. Sometimes she'd try to hold me back for a while, but I just couldn't.

When I was about ten though I used to play a lot with Wazeki's sister. I don't know if there was any mutual masturbation there but sometimes when we used to play hide-and-go-seek I used to hide with her and I'd reach under her dress and play with her. I guess I did that to every girl I had intercourse with because that would come right before the intercourse. When I held Carol in my arms on the porch she'd take my hand and rub it against her genitals. There was no mutuality there.

I always liked to play with girls' breasts before anything else. I did that most with Lila. Sometimes I'd walk with her and put my arms around her and touch her in the breasts, and right away she'd start jumping. I never had intercourse with my cousin from L——— but I played with her breasts. I never stroked her genitals. I used to sit outside with her and just look at the stars and the sky.

L: 'Harold, do you recall any mutual masturbation with your sister?'

No; I don't think so. I don't think my sister ever touched me but I don't remember. I doubt if she ever did touch me on the penis, not even when we had intercourse.

When I did that six months in the County Jail there were four fairies in that place. There was one young kid who always used to come around. I didn't like him; he seemed displeasing to me and I didn't want him around. I never wondered about things I had done but about the things I was going to do, might do. Something like that wasn't in my plan for the future then. I never had affairs like that with anybody; that was the first time in my life I had come into contact with anyone who was bi-sexual. They were nice kids. I didn't hold it against them that they were constructed as they were but I just couldn't seem to go for it.

L: 'Can you think of any other sexual acts committed on you, or that you committed?"

You mean such as—sodomy?

L: 'Any acts, with women, with girls or boys.'

Never with anybody. It's distasteful to me. The only place I touch anybody is their arm or something like that, not their body. I don't like anyone to touch me. I dislike most of the fellows around here that call themselves wolves, because I think they are not men, they're animals. I don't think I ever had anybody do anything like that to me, and I never did anything to anybody else in all my life. When I was young I used to think that even intercourse with women or girls was something bad, something wrong. I never committed sodomy on women yet, nor on any man. I had opportunities alright. It seems to me just as bad or even worse than—having intercourse with colored women.

I don't like to get in positions where I might lose control of myself. I wouldn't like to have any affair with Perry. I don't like such positions, not because I dislike Perry but because I don't want to bring myself to do things like that. When I was doing time in the County Jail I used to see these fellows dancing around, singing something. I just can't see being different from myself.

L: 'Has fellatio ever been committed on you?'

Not by a woman, by a man, when I was about nine years old. That's the only time I can remember. It just doesn't seem right.

L: 'Harold; whom do you imagine you see, whom do you think of when you are masturbating?'

O, I don't know. Sometimes a blonde, sometimes a brunette, sometimes Lila, sometimes my cousin from L————. Usually it's some girl I know.

L: 'Ever anyone else but a girl?'

Some girl I imagine; a girl with real blond hair. I don't think I ever even knew a girl with really blond hair.

L: 'A girl like your sister, or one of your aunts?'

One resembles my aunt or my sister. Certainly I don't think about it when I am conscious like I am now. I have one aunt who is beautiful, but she's married and has three children. I respect my aunts and my sister of course. They all have brown hair, and Lila had brown hair too.

L: 'Well, let us take a slightly different line. When was the last time you masturbated?'

I—about two weeks ago.

L: 'Whom did you think of then?'

I don't know. Sometimes I sleep in my underwear and when I

am moving around it's like tight around me.   I blame the underwear; sometimes it irritates me and I have a lot of dreams about different women, and when I wake up the bed is all wet.   About two weeks ago when I masturbated it was a dark-haired girl, like Carol.   I think it's just a girl and I just want to get it over with because I think to myself that it's better to get it done with than to be irritated like that.   Other times I start thinking when I am lying in bed, thinking about some girl and some of my experiences come back to my memory and I—I just try to change it.   I don't remember who it was I was thinking of last time but she looked like Carol.   It's pretty hard to remember all of them.   Usually they have real light hair or real dark hair, but I can't tell the colors.

Sometimes I tell myself I shouldn't masturbate.   I masturbated a lot when I first came in here, now it has quieted down to about once every five weeks.   I tried to tell myself at first not to; to wait for about six weeks and then go to some person and have them— and—have them do it to me; but I didn't for about four weeks, but I never went to anyone to have it done.   I used to tell myself that if I see one of these people I won't have to worry about masturbation, but I don't see them.   I palled around with Dobriski; he is still my best friend.   He used to tell me that he had to control himself every time he saw me, but he never made any improper advances towards me because he knew I disliked that stuff.   I can't swear that Perry did anything like that with anyone.   That afternoon he called me in his cell and started coaxing me. . . .   He still tells me every once in a while that he loves me.   I don't know what he has in mind, whether he thinks I might loosen up, might weaken.   A lot of fellows are asking me how he is, how I like it.   I don't care if nobody knows the truth about me in here as long as I know it in my own mind.   I don't care what they think.   As far as he is concerned I know he is bisexual.   He is nicely built and good-looking, but I have no desires for him.   Anybody has a penis: if he had no penis it might be different; he wouldn't be in here if he didn't have it.   There are other people like that in this place, some of them are my good friends, fine fellows.   Not that I don't dislike it: I don't want to do it in the first place because I might like it.   You know, if I did anything like that I—I couldn't look at the person.   That's what I tell myself.   Maybe I might do it if I don't have to see the person.   I wouldn't ever do it so long as I would have to see the person.

I'm having a lot of fun with Perry. He's very fine company for me. He's starting to curse: I really kid him about picking that up from me. I guess a lot of fellows do think there is something between us but I know in my own mind that nothing has happened. Now there is no longer any opportunity for him to put me in the position he did that time, so I don't think he'll try it again. But he is not the only one like that here. I don't talk to a lot of them, not because I dislike them but I just can't see anybody hanging on to the end of my penis like that; even imagining it is distasteful to me. If I ever do it once I might do it again and keep doing it. That's why I can't even do it once to find out what it's like. . . .

When I was in the Catholic school in the seventh grade we'd hang our coats up in the hall and when school was up we'd walk around and get our things, and I remember the two lines, boys' line and girls', would mingle for a few moments, and most all the kids including myself would try to touch one of the girls. She was a nice girl, nicely put together, but very open with herself. She didn't care if some of the boys felt her up when she was walking in the hall. There was nothing to it for her. One time in the auditorium she was sitting a couple rows behind me and when I turned around for some reason or other I saw her with her legs wide apart and not a damned thing on. It was in the balcony and the seats are on a slope so I had a good view. I told all the other boys and they all wanted to change seats with me.

The church used to have little carnivals visiting them once a year so we'd hang around this carnival for about a week, going to find out what we could in different tents. There was one tent we peeked in one time where a girl was changing into a bathing suit, but she was always behind a screen and we only saw a shadow, just a shadow, that's all . . .

THE TWENTY-SEVENTH HOUR

Well, I don't know; I dislike coming into this room anymore. It's starting to wear on me I guess.

L: 'Harold, I want you to know this. Your dislike to come into this room and the fact that it is starting to wear on you have a sound reason behind them. And the reason is this; it is a sign of strong resistance. In other words, you are framing a line of resistance against disclosing certain things it is perhaps more comfortable and less embarrassing to repress, keep hidden, even from yourself. The only way you can conquer that

*is to do it anyhow.   The final benefits to you will be greater in proportion
to the amount of resistance you can overcome.   Do you understand?'*

Yes. I do. . . .

I had a dream a few days ago.   I was dreaming I had four or five
teeth in my mouth with large holes in them, so I wanted to go to a
dentist to have them fixed.   He wanted to pull them but I wanted
him to fill them.   I don't know whether he filled them or not.   I was
arguing with him: I didn't want him to pull them.   It was right here
in the hospital.   I dreamed it was this place and I came to this dentist.
I don't recall which of my teeth had holes in them, there were four or
five of them, and they were large holes.

L: 'Can you associate to any of the objects or events in the dream?'

On the outside I never had any teeth filled.   I would let them go
until they started bothering me or turned black.   Then I had them
pulled out.   I used to be afraid to go to the dentist, afraid to hear the
buzzing drill I guess.   It frightens me somehow.   When I do go
through with the ordeal I feel like a brave man, and kind of shaky.

*L: 'What possible interpretation can you give to the dream?   You
know by now that in a dream certain objects perhaps symbolize things or
people.   What significance does this dream hold for you, Harold?'*

I don't think that the teeth have anything to do with people, but
maybe they stand for people that were around me.   I didn't want
them around me; I wanted to clear the matter up.

L: 'Yet you went to the dentist?'

Yes; but he wanted to pull them; I wanted them fixed.

L: 'In other words, he wanted to use a more drastic method?'

Yes; drastic.   It might represent people.   I don't like people very
much.   They disturb me; they irritate me; I don't want anybody
around me.   When he wanted to pull the teeth I wanted them fixed.
It was different from my usual way.

*L: 'You wanted to preserve your teeth, allow them to remain in your
mouth?'*

I suppose you mean preserve things as they are.   I guess it's that
I want to keep my eyes in the same condition and not get myself fixed
up.

*L: 'Your teeth were in bad condition; they had holes in them, and you
. . .'*

That may represent certain things in my past history that I haven't
discussed completely or haven't told you about, I guess.

L: 'And the dentist?'

He wants to bring them out and not cover them up.

L: 'And whom do you think the dentist represented?'

The dentist represented—you, I suppose. It seems all jumbled up to me. I have an uncle outside who is a dentist: he fixed several of my teeth. I was always afraid of the dentist. I would rather have the teeth hurting me than have them taken out.

You probably figure that the reason I'm acting lost is that I indulged in some abnormal sexual activities. I don't know why I am lost; I don't know why you think I am lost. You didn't say so but I think you sometimes think that. I am trying to figure it out. I didn't

These words were uttered in a vindictive, almost baleful manner, reflecting the negative transference that had developed out of Harold's sincere attempts to overcome the resistance.

like to associate with people. I don't like them. I'd walk on the streets with my head down so I wouldn't have to look at them. They probably figured that I didn't want them to look at me, but I just didn't want to see them.

I don't like people with hair on their bodies, all over their chests and their arms. They seem to me like animals that didn't get all the hair off them, like fur. My father, he was big-chested and he looked like a gorilla. When he looked at me I would avoid his glances. I disliked him. Some people tell me I am shy and timid but I don't believe so. I guess my father always looked on me as his son. He must have given some thought to me. I disliked him, for what reason I don't know, even when I was older, old enough to realize what some of these things are about. I realize my father and mother are married and when I was old enough to understand what marriage is composed of I don't think I looked at things in such a sense. I can remember that even before I was ten my father always appeared the same to me as he does now. I dislike his physical appearance I guess, and perhaps because sometimes he would holler at my mother. I used to get angry about that. I don't know whether or not he ever beat my sister but I know he gave me more than one good licking. He works hard; he doesn't smoke or drink. He drove a truck for some company when I was around nine and one day he went to take a load of wood to somebody's house. I remember I got in the way and got hurt. He said something I didn't like to hear. He said, "Why don't you watch where the hell you're going, you blind one!" He said it in Polish. I don't think I ever went with him again. He begged me to go along with him when he got his new car to see how it rides but I didn't go.

I remember the first dog we ever had. Her name was Nellie. He brought her home one night and never said where he got her. She would follow him around every place he went.

Sometimes when I got in a fight with some kid, he would find out about it. He'd give me a beating for fighting, and then he would complain that I was like a girl and would never fight.

I just dimly recall how we moved from P———— on a truck my father owned. We drove for a couple of days and one night. The first night we stopped at a farmhouse. I remember stopping there in the dark and going away the next morning. My grandmother owned a house on C———— Street and we rented one nearby. I guess I was under five then. I remember I used to go upstairs by helping myself with my hands. The reason I walked that way was that I fell down those stairs once. I don't know whether it was because I couldn't see the steps or what, but I fell and was crying because I bumped my head and my mother picked me up and took me to a candy store and bought me ice cream. I guess it was like the time I was coming from the street where my grandmother lived and hurt myself. I was running across the street and the sun was shining, bright, real hot. I had sneakers on and the heat was burning the soles of my feet, and I ran right into a small iron post. It was about five inches in diameter, not a big one, just one of those cheap posts, and I hit myself in the forehead or the eye and it swelled all the way up.

My grandmother owned that house. I can see it. She lived on the third floor. I guess that's where my grandfather died, three years before when I fell. I don't remember ever seeing him. I—He was buried in his uniform. I can imagine I see him now. He's lying in the coffin with a big sword over his chest. He was an officer in the Russian or German army before he came to America. A big sword across his chest. My grandfather was German; my grandmother was Polish. He had one of those big pegs on the top of his uniform hat. Somebody is holding me in their arms to look at him. I think it is one of my aunts, Vanya or Louise. My father is there and my mother with my sister; my mother with a little bit of a baby in her arms. My father and my uncle is there. My grandmother is in the other room praying. I see my father there too. I might have been two or three then. My eyes are wide open. MY EYES ARE OPEN!

I didn't cry or anything. I was just looking at him and at everybody in the room. My mother is crying. She's much younger, no grey hair or anything. Her hair is brown. My father looks the same; he hasn't changed very much, only he's lost his hair.

My eyes were open then. My aunt was holding me. Whichever one it was, she was telling me to look at my grandfather, he was going away for a while. I know it happened in the room with the old-fashioned curtains on the wall and old-fashioned furniture, and there was a wedding picture of my grandmother and grandfather on the wall; and I know there were candles lit, they were shining bright, two big ones, one on each side. I must have been about two or a little more than that. My eyes were open and the room was kind of dark. Then somebody took me in their arms and into the other room. My grandmother was in there praying and crying. There was a lot of chairs around the table. I know I was old enough to walk because they put me down and I was walking. I wasn't crying but I know my mother was. I can still hear my grandmother sobbing. . . .

I saw my uncle in the coffin when he was dead but he looked different. He looked all white. My grandfather looked very much alive. He had that big sword, it was at least three feet long, right across his chest. My uncle didn't have anything but a plain ordinary suit on: he didn't look like my grandfather. My grandfather had his soldier's hat on. He was older than my uncle when he died. I was around eighteen when my uncle passed away.

You know, when I was about ten I didn't realize that my eyes were squinting and closed. I always thought that they were open just like anyone else's. I'd look in the mirror and I'd see them open, always open; and when somebody said something about them I never knew if they were lying or kidding me. I got into the habit of putting my hands over my eyes to shut the sun out. I don't know if I did my usual amount of winking then or not. When I had my hand on my eyes I would be able to keep them open. When I went down to the river I used to do that so I could see the boats way out in the middle, the steam boats and tugs. They were pretty small and far away but I could see them.

I remember we used to get fish, small fish: we had a lot of fun catching them.   One time I was giving some to a kid on his porch and his mother and father were talking about me, my eyes.   I was listening to them while I was talking to the kid.   One of them was saying, "What a shame!" I guess they didn't think I'd realize what they were talking about.   I didn't have much trouble about them when I was going to school.   I remember the kindergarten class in the gymnasium room; how I built houses out of blocks.   The sun would shine in through the kind of high windows and it would make me wink and blink.   One kid asked me, "Why are you winking so much?"

I started at W———— Avenue school when we lived at F———— Street.   My mother held me by the hand, and Tony's mother and Tony went along with us, the first day I went to school.   Then, after a couple months, we moved to B———— Street and I finished kindergarten there.   I only went in the afternoons.   I'd get up late, around eight, and after my mother cleaned the house I'd go off to school.   On B———— Street my eyes used to wink.   I can't remember if I squinted and blinked them before that.   And I can't remember anything about P————: all I can remember is coming from there. I was around two or three then.   We had everything we owned on a truck and we came to live near my grandmother.   There was a park near her house and my grandmother would take me and my sister for walks there.   My sister was in a baby carriage.   I just ran around but sometimes I'd take a nap in the carriage too.   Sometimes both of us would ride in the carriage, me and my sister.   This all happened when we lived on F———— Street because I remember going up and down that street.   I must have been two then.

L: 'Harold, when did your grandfather die?'

About twenty-one years ago.

L: 'Do you remember the year?'

In nineteen-nineteen or nineteen-twenty, I think.   I was about two.

L: 'How old were you when the family moved?'

Between two and three.

L: 'Did your grandfather die after you moved?'

When we moved there my grandfather was dead, because when we lived on F———— Street I didn't see my grandfather around there. The only time I remember seeing him was when he was in his coffin, in the same house where my grandmother lived.   I think the reason we moved from P———— was that my grandfather died and my mother wanted to be near her mother.

L: 'This grandfather was your mother's father?'
Yes.
L: Now, Harold, we have reached a place where it is quite important that we do nothing for a short period. We have been striking a lot of resistance. . . . '

> The resistance, as illustrated in the dream and behavior of the patient, was so strong that it was considered best to terminate the analysis for a period.

Yes; I can't seem to remember anything.
L: 'Therefore I don't want to see you again until a week from this coming Monday.'

The Twenty-eighth Hour

Well; I had only one dream that I remember. It happened a week ago last Friday, after the day you told me to hold off for a while. This was the dream: I had a secret, some kind of a secret. I guess it was an airplane motor. I had the secret about this motor and somebody tried to get it away from me. It was a man with a mustache, so of course I thought it was you. I remember I was locked in my cell and he was threatening me with everything if I didn't come through with the secret. I remember the small windows in my cell and how I started to take a swing at the person. I started thinking about it afterwards and of course I placed it. The man had a mustache so of course it represented you, and the secret is the information you want, we want. All I remember is that I knew the secret but I wasn't going to tell anybody. I guess I do know it but not so's I can tell it.
L: 'Well, Harold, the significance of that dream is of course perfectly clear to you. It shows, doesn't it, the tremendous amount of resistance that was there. I guess it was a good thing that we broke it off for a week.'
Yes; yes.
L: 'After all, you do know a secret; and we are both striving to get at it.'
I spent a lot of time studying this week. O, I wasn't doing much but I really believe I studied more this week than maybe in two or three years in school on the outside. School was detestable. I see now all I missed. It's going to take a long time catching up. I used to play hookey a lot and go swimming and things like that. I'd take every Friday afternoon off and go down to the Bay, even when the weather was cold. I'd go swimming sometimes even in February.

We'd make a bonfire and stand around it and warm ourselves and then dive into the water. I don't remember many of the kids that went with me to the seventh and eighth grade then. I don't know what happened to them; I guess some are in jail. I played truant a lot when I was going to St. A————'s too. I think I remember one time when my uncle saw me and he knew I was playing hookey but he didn't say anything to my mother or father: he just talked to me and told me to be careful and not to run around with boys who stayed away from school. I always liked him after that. I remember there was a bunch of kids who thought they were tough and we used to break into stores and lunch-wagons. I stole a lot of cigarettes and gave them to this uncle. Once in a while he'd ask me where I got them but I never told. I'd get drunk a lot with him but I don't think he's the one who taught me to drink. He always wanted to get drunk. He'd work for a few months, then he would quit and drink for a few months, and then he'd go back to work again. I don't think he cared about anything. He had a wife but was separated from her. I saw her several times; she didn't impress me.

My other uncle, he had a broken forehead. It was all dented in from a train wreck. *He* really drinks a lot, but he's a little different from my other uncle. My other uncle wasn't interested in anything: the one with the broken forehead, he was interested in baseball and other sports. He would get me in a corner and tell me everything about baseball and football. I didn't like to listen because I was never interested in that stuff. We always got along alright though.

Once in a while I would work for my grandmother in her garden. I would help her fix flowers when I really wanted to go swimming. I didn't like it but once in a while I couldn't get out of doing it. . . .

I had a lot of trouble with Perry this week. He seems to be changing. He didn't speak to me, he didn't eat with me, he didn't say anything to me. Every time he'd see me he'd put his head down and act as if he didn't want to speak. . . .

My cousin Riggs used to have a lot of friends. I'd hang around with him and his friends and we'd play cards or pool together. We'd cut a lot of classes, not do anything except go to the show or play pool or just hang around. Riggs wasn't a very clever fellow: he was cunning. I know I felt like fighting or hitting him many times. Maybe I was afraid to hit him. He's heavier than I am but I don't feel afraid of him.

When I lived on S——— Street we used to have snowball fights. When I was about twelve there was a fellow who was sneaking around the car behind me and he hit me on the head with a stick. So I turned around and went after him and I hit him so hard he didn't know what happened to him. His mother always gave me dirty looks when she saw me after that. I used to have a lot of fights when I was that age. They were mostly at nights because I hung out then with a gang of kids who prowled around only at night. We were a bunch of kids that wanted to break everything. We'd throw buckets of water from the railroad bridge on to the street where people were passing: we'd put rocks on the street-car tracks and on the railroad tracks and bullets, anything that would make a noise: we'd throw stones and handfuls of dirt at the trains going by and into open windows. The railroad detective got to know all of us by our first names. He was a grey-haired man of about fifty named Nelson. He couldn't run very fast and we knew it. In the summertime we'd get a long string with a hook on it and when the fellows that worked on the bread-wagons or the big bakery near where we lived would put their lunch-boxes in a cool place, we'd pull up these guys' lunches through a grating and tie them so that they'd have to get a ladder to reach them. Sometimes we'd get rolls of film, light them then extinguish the flames and throw them around the classrooms. They wouldn't burn anything but they made one godawful stink. I remember one time when we lived on B——— Street and I was around eight I tried to steal some ice from an ice-truck that was going by and the driver saw me and stopped the truck and grabbed me. I was so scared I leaked in my pants. I told him I just wanted a piece of ice. He figured I was try-ing to steal his pick. That's the only time I ever did anything like that and was caught. I mean that's the only time I ever leaked when I was caught doing something.

I think I wore glasses when I want to St. A———'s School. I used to catch hitches on trolley cars and trucks and break them. I must have broken fifty pairs that way. I didn't like to wear them; they were a bother to me; they didn't do me any good. I'd put them in my pockets and every once in a while I would sit on them and break them that way. I remember I used to like to take a small pair of binoculars with me to school. I'd sit in the back of the room with a friend of mine who was a Boy Scout with me, and when the sister would write something on the board I'd look at it through these glasses and it would be real close, otherwise I'd have a hard time seeing the board.

I went to the hospital to have my tonsils out once. I was there for about three days or so. When I went home on the bus I got sick and dizzy. I guess it must have been the gasoline, the carbon monoxide, that was making me sick. I always thought it was the ether or the hospital smell or something. I remember when I was getting to smell the ether I saw rings, small rings getting larger and larger all the time, and then disappearing sort of. I told the nurse about it and she said it was my eyes. She didn't believe things were like that with me but I actually saw those rings get bigger and bigger and bigger. She kept telling me to blow on those rings and I did, but that didn't make them go away. When I was on the bus I got sick. I figure it was car-sickness. I didn't go to school for about a week after that. I don't remember much about that hospital. I was in the ward with three other kids and the kid next to me got a visit every day. I only had two visits there in the three or four days; and I remember I expected a visit and didn't get any, so I put my head under the covers and cried. This kid next to me felt sorry for me and he gave me some oranges and apples.

When I ride somewhere in a car I get sick. Riding with my uncle once I got the carbon monoxide right up in the cab, so I kept the window open with my arms hanging outside. My eyes felt funny, as if they were dropping right out of my head and if I pulled my eyelids back they would fall in my lap. I had an earache too.

My aunt Louise, she always kept after the three of us, Riggs, Tony and me and our sisters, in fact all the kids in the family. She wanted us to go to High School and finish. She said that she would present the first one of us who graduated from High with a wrist watch. I guess I am the only one who will finish, and I have to do it in jail....

THE TWENTY-NINTH HOUR

I was telling you I had some trouble with Perry last week. I haven't really had trouble with him, we can get along alright. We get into arguments once in a while. He keeps impressing on me that I am stupid, so when we get into an argument he walks away and waves his hands in the air over his head; then he comes back and we start in where we left off.

One day last week I came up and looked around in my cell for some things then I went to the washroom to take a shower, and when I came back I found a note on my locker that he would never speak to me again. I went down to his cell and tried to find out. I showed him the note and asked him what was the matter but he wouldn't say anything; so he wouldn't speak to me for a few days and wouldn't eat with me or look at me; he just kept away. About two days later I went right up to the cell where he lived and started talking to him. He seemed pretty cheerful and ever since then we are talking together again. He told me why he did that. I guess he thinks that I like him very much but when he gets into one of his sieges he wants to find out what I really think of him, whether when he gives me a note like that I would ever attempt to speak to him again. It seems to me that he doesn't go with many people, that he doesn't want their good will or friendship. He can have all the friends he wants, and as far as sex is concerned he can have all of that he wants too. But he just isn't interested: he wants something finer than that. He told me he doesn't want friendship and he doesn't want sex; just love, just love. I don't know whether or not he thinks I am in love with him. He says he's in love with me; maybe he is in his way; I don't know. I like him a lot; like to associate with him. If I wasn't coming over here to you maybe I'd be in love with him; but while I am coming over here I'd be tempted to tell you everything. I never told him

Note the accurate gauge to the transference and the progress of the analysis which the homosexual attachment provides. It is a cardinal principle of this type of therapy that extant situations, no matter what the content, be utilized to the full.

that I am telling you. I guess he has an idea I am. He just doesn't care about people to be his friends: he just wants someone to love him. He would sacrifice a hundred friendships for just one person who loves him. He says that the trouble with people is they're too sex-minded. He illustrated that statement with Ruby, saying he isn't so constructed that he could fall in love with him except for sexual purposes. He says love should not only be sexual but mental too. I guess I keep quiet a lot and when I do talk I talk sort of softly he imagines that I am in love with him. We get along alright. I manage to stall him off and quiet things for a while, then they start again. Someday

I'll hit on a plan that will stop him for a good long time. I guess in his way he *is* in love with me but it seems rather funny. I guess he really believes I am in love with him or else I wouldn't hang around. He hasn't tried to lure me into his cell again. I like him because he gives me ideas and information.

I don't believe I was ever in love with anybody. I don't know what the word means. There was a girl who always said she was in love with me. She'd cry when I'd chase her away. That was Lila. But she was unstable: she went with anyone who wanted her, she didn't care who. After I came back fom my aunt's place she was going around with some fellow who had the clap so I didn't associate with her anymore. She was sort of timid and shy; she didn't bother anybody. In a way she reminds me of Perry. I don't see how it could be but here are two entirely different people, a girl and a man, and they are both in love with me and both are feminine. Perry says he is feminine. You know, I figure that if he really should stop talking to me I would have to tell him that—that I'm in love with him, just to keep him around and stall off on any sexual activities. But I guess I would have to tell him that if that is the only thing he's interested in ... There really isn't anything between us, Doc. If there was I'd be tempted to tell you. One way to stop him might be to tell him to wait until this is over.

He reads a lot of books and then starts arguing where they are wrong, and he finds mistakes in encyclopedias and atlases and wants me to figure out what they mean. Maybe he's insinuating I am stupid. All in all, though, I really get along with him better than with my mother or my sister. I always hoped my sister would be something like—tall, well-built, intelligent, quiet—like what Perry is.

I never had a person like Perry fall in love with me. I know several people in here who are like Perry but he impresses me as one of the finest people I have ever known.

I don't remember anything about people being bi-sexual. I didn't know people were really like that until I was fifteen or sixteen years old. Everything I learned about sex I learned in the crudest manner, on the street corners, in poolrooms. I seldom tried to teach myself things like that. When I was reading a book and I'd come to a word I didn't know I would skip it. I'd skip a lot of words. I know now how wrong that is. I missed the most important part of everything. Maybe I am missing something about Perry? Maybe I haven't put myself in a position where I can understand him. He just impresses me as if he was a girl and I think of him just like I think of a girl. There was a fellow talking to me about him and I was using the word 'she' in the third person when I was referring to Perry. I wasn't conscious of myself when I was talking like that but much later I realized what I'd said.

There is nothing dirty about Perry. Everything about him is fine and clean. I don't know why he picks on me. Why should he pick on me? tell me that he is in love with me?

L: '*Harold, do you think it is possible that, rather than Perry having picked on you, you really picked on him? wanted him to make love to you?*'

I have always pictured my sister as something dark-haired, quiet, intelligent, like he is; but my sister isn't like that.

L: '*What you want to do then is to find a suitable substitute, an ideal?*' Yes; yes.

L: '*And of all the people you know, whom does this ideal most closely resemble, aside from Perry?*'

Why; my mother is dark-haired: my father has black hair but he is quick-tempered. Maybe my father, but I don't think so. I never thought of anything like that. I always figured that I would like my sister to be like that, neat, clean, dark-haired.

L: '*But she isn't like that?*'

No. She has brown hair and she's quick-tempered: she's like a dizzy chorus girl. My mother is short and a little stout. There was that girl Amy I was telling you about: she has black hair and is almost as big as Perry is.

L: '*Can you name anyone else among all the people you know who would come near, would resemble this ideal?*'

My aunt Vanya is most like Perry with the exception that she has a quick temper. When she doesn't want to speak to anyone she just doesn't speak. She combs her hair back too. She resembles Perry more than anyone else. I haven't seen her in a long time. She's about twenty-eight now. She wasn't exactly beautiful; her nose is straight, not as flat as Perry's, and she's older. Sometimes her husband doesn't speak to her; he also gets into moods when he doesn't want to talk to anyone. She works hard. She treated me fine and

I know she always treated my sisters fine when they had diphtheria. She bought the first radio for us we ever had. I don't know why she left my grandmother's home to come and live with us. She used to sleep with my sisters. But she hit me a lot too. One time she clipped me right in the head: that was the time her sister-in-law said something to me about my eyes and I answered fresh. After she hit me she started thinking about why I said that to her sister-in-law and then she apologized and said I should have told her. But I don't explain things to people. Why should I make a long story out of something? I'm not afraid of getting hit in the head.

One time when we lived on S———— Street I went to a Boy Scout meeting and came back late at night, about eleven-thirty. The door was always left open, so she called me into the room where they were sleeping, she and my sister. She told me not to go back to where I was supposed to sleep because there had been an argument with my father about my sleeping there. So I undressed and got in bed with her, and several times during the night I woke up and found her hand on my penis. I didn't see anything so I made believe I was sleeping and tried to turn over. In the morning she didn't say anything. I don't think I ever said anything to her either, and I know I never slept with her again. After that morning I asked my mother what the argument with my father was about. She said it was about my being in the Boy Scouts; just a few words were said, there was nothing to it.

I didn't like my aunt Vanya very much. She seemed tough; she wanted to hit people.

I remember now the only time that I slept in the same bed with my other aunt, Louise. I was about twelve then. This was when my mother and my father and my two sisters went to my cousin's out at L———— for the week-end. They went away on a Friday night and I was supposed to stay with my grandmother. I know that on Friday night the man who married my aunt came around looking for us and he came into a lot where me and my two cousins and about six other kids were trying to break into a lunch wagon, and he told me my aunt wanted me to come home. It was about eleven-thirty at night (I always used to stay out late at night when my mother and father were away). So I went to my grandmother's house and my aunt Louise was alone. She wanted me to give water to the canaries— they had about ten or more of them. Then this fellow went home and my aunt started fixing me something to eat, some cake and some milk, and then we went to bed. My aunt was afraid to sleep alone, she was used to sleeping with my other aunt, and I remember I put my pajamas on and went to bed with her. She put her arms around me and kissed me once or twice. When I woke up in the morning my pajamas were all open. I don't know whether I opened them or not. I slept all night like a log. When I woke up it was about six or seven in the morning. Nobody was with me, my aunt got up early, and my pajamas were all crinkly around me, and when I straightened them out they were open. So I went back to sleep and when I got up my aunt called me in just when I was getting dressed. I don't recall whether I looked my aunt right in the eye when I came down. She seemed cheerful, nothing was said about it. That afternoon she was in another room taking a nap and she called me. When I came in her dress was about three inches above her knees. I guess I was looking at her thighs and she must have been sensitive because she pulled her dress down. I don't know what she called me for, what she wanted; I guess it was to fix the shades on the window or something. She was always kind to me, she always told me that if I ever needed money to ask her for it. Even when I was arrested this time she said she would give me the money to get away from this part of the country. . . .

I had a dream last night. I guess I took some money from my mother, a five-dollar bill or a ten-dollar bill, and I went out and bought a gun, some kind of a revolver. It seemed like the room in my house was just like a cell here. I dug a hole in the side of the wall of the cell and I had a little box and I wrapped cotton around the gun to keep it from getting rusty, keep it nice and clean. I dug a sort of square hole, about three inches square and I don't know how deep. Then I hung a mirror over it. The mirror was broken in two places. When I looked at the cell door I could see across the corridor, about two or three cells down, and saw my father shaving. I've seen my father shave many times and one time I did have a gun hidden away in a wall. There was a board on the side of the wall in my room and one time I ripped it off and drilled a hole in the wall, about two by six inches, and I had a little box that just fitted in there. I wrapped the gun in cotton and put the gun in the box and the box in the wall. Then I put a stick right against the wall to keep anybody from seeing

it and to keep it from falling out.   But somebody found it I guess:
when I looked for it one time it was gone and I couldn't find it.   I
never said anything to anybody but I think my father took it.

   *L: 'Now let's go back to the dream, Harold.   I want you to associate
to any of the items or events in it.'*

   Well; I remember that over the hole in the wall I hung a mirror to
keep people from seeing it.   The mirror was about fifteen by twelve
and I hung it the long way, leftwise, not up and down.   And on top
of the mirror in the exact center of it a piece was broken off and the
cracked-off pieces were missing and there were two cracks; from the
center, one crack ran to one side and the other to the other side.

   L: 'So that the mirror was divided into three parts?'

   Yes; the two parts broken off on the sides were very small.   In the
center the piece broken off was about two inches and there was a
slight crack to either side.

   L: 'Yes, I understand.   What is a mirror used for, Harold?'

   For looking into.

   L: 'Yes, of course, but what do you think it signifies?'

   It was just like curtains on a window.   You couldn't see things
where two pieces were missing.

   *L: 'If two pieces were missing and you looked into it, what is the
answer?   What do you see?'*

   Yourself.   O, O, the broken pieces indicate that they need to be
fitted in, replaced.

   L: 'Now let's get to the gun.'

   The gun was just like any other ordinary gun.   I don't know if I
ever owned one just like it.

   L: 'What kind of a feeling does the possession of a gun give you?'

   It—it gives me courage: it's something to—to back me up: I don't
have to fall back on anyone.   I get a real feeling of—of manliness.

   L: 'And what about this gun in the dream?'

   The gun I used to hide in the wall was an automatic: the one in the
dream was a revolver.

   L: 'What's the difference between the two?'

   Why; an automatic is just straight and flat.   This one in the dream
had a round cylinder, right on the end of the barrel.

   *L: 'Harold, what is a gun most like?   You know that any instrument,
such as a gun may represent an extension of our functions.   For instance,*

when men pick up, let us say, a club or a stone, they extend their functions. Do they not?'

I give myself a bigger reach: shooting at a distance, it brings the subject nearer to me. And the shape of the gun . . . It might be called an extension: it might be a—the phallus. And the hole in the wall that I put the gun in, that might be the woman's vagina. And three doors down I saw my father shaving; when I looked out the door I could see him.

L: 'Now, Harold, you said that in the earlier situation when you were at home, you had put the gun in the box and the box in the hole in the wall. When you looked for the gun later it was missing. Now who was most likely to have taken it?'

The most likely one was my father. I know if my mother had found it she would have said something to me about it: she would probably have hollered at me or even hit me over the head with it.

L: 'That wasn't your father's way?'

No. He would probably just take it and say nothing.

L: 'But you think it was your father who found it? That he stole your gun?'

Yes. I searched the garage where he usually keeps such things. I searched and searched, went through all his things I could find but didn't discover it.

L: 'Let me recapitulate, Harold. You had a gun, and you say it represents a phallus. You put this away, you bury it somewhere and your father discovers it. Your next act, your next move, was to take a mirror and place it over the hole where you buried the gun; but the mirror was broken, something was missing. Therefore, when you looked in the mirror a part of what you saw was missing. Is that right? What do you make of it?'

I make of it this. The gun was my phallus and I wanted to hide it because my father would steal it like he stole the other gun when I was home. He had the razor in his hand and he was shaving so maybe he was going to cut it off, take it away from me that way. The broken mirror shows that something of me was missing, I guess, because when I would look in it I would see part of myself missing. That part is the gun, I mean the phallus. But maybe there is another interpretation.

L: 'Go right ahead.'

My father has black hair and so does Perry.   Maybe it represents a secret desire to have intercourse with Perry.   It isn't clear how and I think the first one is better but I just thought of this.   Sometime ago I told Perry that I woke up in the morning with my hands around my pillow, that I had a wonderful dream.   He begged me to tell him what it was.   I guess he thought I dreamed about him.   It seems strange: a hole in the concrete wall.   You know them, those concrete blocks that cells are built with.

L: 'It was a difficult job to get into them?'

I don't remember.   I recall laying it in there, not in the box or wrapped in cotton; I just laid it in there and then hung the mirror right over the hole.

Anytime I was with Perry or am with him now it stimulates me. I try to run away from him when it comes to a point where I can't control myself.   I don't try to force myself on him.   It wouldn't be difficult for me to—to have intercourse with him.   He seems to think that everything I do is planned out; that I only talk to him when somebody is likely to interrupt us.   I would say that I don't know whether it was or was not difficult for me, all I'd have to tell him would be that I am in love with him.   He tells me that he watches my actions.   When I say something he doesn't pay any attention to what I am saying but how I say things, the muscles of my face and neck, and how I use my hands. . . .

THE THIRTIETH HOUR

I didn't get along well with many of the kids in the school.   A lot of them would laugh at me: they seemed to squint their eyes when they looked at me, so I wouldn't say anything, just turn and walk away.

In H———— Street school especially I didn't like to sit in the sunlight.   There was a fellow that sat with me way back in the classroom in the arithmetic class and when I couldn't see the blackboard he'd give me the examples and I'd do the work.   When I was at St. A————'s in the fifth grade another fellow that sat with me would copy everything from the board and give me the problems.   I never did any copying from the board there.   I'd make believe I was writing when really I was drawing pictures or scribbling, and once in a while the sister would catch me and I'd get punished.   It always seemed to me that the sister was picking on me.   Sometimes when I knew something was going to happen, when I didn't have my lessons or something like that, I'd play truant; I just wouldn't go to school. One time when I was playing hookey my mother was walking down the street and she saw me. She didn't call to me or anything: she waited until after I came home from school and then she gave me a licking. At that time I had the habit of shielding my eyes against the sun by holding my hand to my forehead. My mother made me break that habit: I guess it made her feel uneasy when I did that. . . .

All that I can remember about living in P———— is that my father had a business of—O—re-treading tires. I don't know much about it. He had a truck, just a small truck, and he used to go around and come home with a truckload of tires, all used. He'd put them on a machine that used to—go around and round and round and make new tires of them. I don't know why we moved from P———— because we had a—well, it wasn't exactly a house, it was by itself but it had glass windows on it. It was on the side of a road. There were a lot of other houses around there. They all seem away from ours. Our house looks like—like a store. It must have been in a small town somewhere. The truck was in the back of the house. The machine was in the store where he fixed the tires. I don't know how it worked out, but when we were moving back we took the machine with us. My father was going to start a business where we went but I don't recall that he did. When we got there he got a job as a truck driver. I think we moved after my grandfather's death. I remember once when I looked up at the third story of a house I saw somebody at the window and someone told me it was my grandmother.

> *During the recounting of the history from this point to the end of the hour there was evident distinct physical struggle to recall. Harold's face and neck became flushed, his fists were clenched and unclenched with spasm-like consistency, he moaned and made inarticulate sounds and stirred on the couch as if in pain. These memories were undoubtedly painful to him.*

My aunts weren't very big then, one was about fourteen, one about ten or eleven. They were both going to school, a Catholic school, St. C————'s. My aunt Louise once took me, long before I started school myself; she took me to the Polish school where she was going and I sat between her and the girl she was sitting with. I remember I started playing with the inkwell, banging the little steel flap on it, and the sister hollered that I was making too much noise and I hid underneath the bench. The sister was in black and she had one of those white things around her head. When I first came in the sister wanted to hear me pray and I couldn't even speak Polish. I could understand it a little because my father used to speak it. My aunt was sitting not very far back, about four seats back, with another girl. She was fatter than my aunt was but I don't know what color her hair was. My aunt was on the left side of me, the other girl on the right. I know when she was writing I pushed her arm and I started playing with the inkwell and the sister started hollering at me that I was making too much noise and I hid underneath the bench. I know that. I can't remember if there was anybody else in the room but it seems to me there were around twenty boys and girls. This was long before I started school. I know it was one afternoon and I still remember my aunt asking my mother if she could take me. My own sister was a little baby then and my mother wanted to go to the movies so my aunt volunteered to take me to school with her. I remember I got tired walking: it was too far away; I didn't want to go and I told her that I was tired walking. I don't think I slept in the school. I was watching everybody. After the sister hollered at me I got my head up again from under the bench and looked around. I even looked out of the window for a time. The sister was interested whether I could pray or not and I hid behind my aunt. I know I used to be able to pray. My mother taught me. I remember when I was about ten my sister got a licking for laughing about something, I don't remember what it was, when my mother was teaching us how to pray. I wanted to laugh too sometimes but I saw my sister get a licking and so I thought better of it. The classroom that my aunt was in had big double seats, two in a seat. My aunt Louise liked me a lot, even when I was that small. She used to take me out to the park near home and when she wanted to give me a drink of water she'd hold me up. You know, I must have been about two or three when my aunt took me to school. I'm sure I wasn't very much older than that anyway.

I know my mother went to the movies a lot. She used to hold my sister when she was a baby yet. I was I guess about three or four and I used to cry I wanted to go home, to go out of there; it always scared me.

When I lived on S———— Street we had a porch that was elevated from the ground about two feet. We had a clubhouse there and we kept milk bottles and soda bottles that we could get a nickel on there. We had everything in that clubhouse, dirt, junk, an old car seat, parts of bicycles, things like that. We stole much of that stuff. Sometimes we would break into a lunch wagon. It was easy. You take hold of the lock and you put a spike about eight inches long inside and you press down on the lock and the lock snaps open. Then we'd steal maybe ten bottles of soda, then close the lock and everything would be o.k. One time when I was about thirteen my father gave me a beating and I ran out of the house and didn't go home that night. I got hungry and came back to the lunch wagon to steal something to eat, a bottle of soda, a couple of cans of milk. When coming through the lot I saw my uncle and he started chasing me. I ran. I jumped over some fences and ran as fast as I could, but he must have been just as fast as I was. He caught me and took me home. So I got another beating and went to bed.

I never liked my father much. If I cared to say something to him and he didn't understand me he gave me a dirty look. If I played truant my mother would give me a beating and tell my father about it and he would holler at me, call me a bum. Sometimes I would lie to him and he'd find out I lied and call me a liar. So I found that the best thing I could do was just to keep quiet, say as little as possible to my father, never go into details about anything. I seldom saw him: I seldom spoke to him. When I was older I used to see him maybe once a week on Sunday mornings. Now I can remember that every once in a while I would catch my mother and him arguing about me but I would say nothing to him. Everytime I went out of the house I didn't care what happened. I'd got so I'd go to a poolroom or something like that, get drunk. I was so sick of everything I didn't care whether I had a job or even looked for one. . . .

My cousin Emma, she was about five years older than I am, she was Riggs' sister, used to mind us when we were kids. I was about twelve then I guess, but she was really there to watch my sister Anna. I remember I used to sit in a place where I could look up her dress. She knew it too, and I knew she knew it, but she didn't seem to mind much. She'd see me look at her like that and she didn't care. I didn't get very far with her. She was older than me and she treated me like a kid.   She had straw hair and bowlegs; not very nice.   One time I wrote a dirty note to her and asked her to come under the porch with me and I'd lay her.   My uncle found the note.   It had my name on it.   I denied it but I got a beating anyway.   But everything was forgotten in three or four days.   I said to her I knew who wrote it and I told her some guy's name.   I didn't even know any fellow by such a name . . . .

The Thirty-first Hour

Lately my eyes feel sort of heavy; they feel like they burn, they burn in the sunlight.   I never liked to go out in the sun.   I always kept them sort of closed during the daytime.   I liked to go out at night when they'd stay open all the time and they wouldn't burn like they do in the daytime.   But whenever I went out during the day I liked to go out by myself and not bother with anybody.   That's why when I went out at night it was different.   I hung out with a gang of fellows from P——— Street or went to a poolroom.   I liked to stay on the river most of the day, go in with one or two other fellows swimming or boating all day.   It just seemed that I didn't want any people around me, didn't care for their company; they were boring.   I didn't like to ride in a car either.   It would make me sick.   Whenever I went anywhere I hitched with Riggs.   One time we went all the way to P——— and back.   Sometimes when I was playing truant from school I'd get a hitch over to N———, hang around the docks all day and come back by night.   One time I had a pair of glasses on—I was about twelve then—and I was running on the street after the truck and Riggs was with me.   He got ahold of it and jumped on, and I remember the truck stopped real sudden and I ran right into it and I broke the glasses.   The guy must have seen me trying to get the hitch through his mirror.

My cousin Riggs and myself and three other guys were planning one time to get a hitch on a freight train.   The other fellows went; I didn't.   They came back two days later.   I didn't feel like going on a freight car.   I don't think I ever rode on one for more than three miles.   We'd get hitches on the railroad from one town to another, about three miles.   The whole gang would ride back and forth.   Sometimes when I'd get sick of staying home, or of school, I'd leave for a couple days or a week, but I never got any hitches on freight trains. I guess I was afraid of them: they were so dirty, filthy, and a lot of bums hang out on them. I got all my hitching done on trucks. One time I went hitching out to my aunt's place and that's more than eighty miles from home. I got back two days later. I remember I stopped off on the side of the highway and there was a roadside stand. It was closed so I broke in and got something to eat. Then I took my clothes off and went swimming in a little lake nearby. I liked to go off like that once in a while. I enjoyed myself. If I wanted to go swimming I went swimming: if I wanted to hitch I'd hitch. I didn't care anything about money, whether I had any or not, or about eating. Sometimes I'd get so hungry I'd eat anything.

The first time I left home I guess I was about nine or ten. My cousin Benny and me left home together. He had about two dollars and we went to a show that night and then just hung around. We didn't go back to the house until our people found us and took us home.

Every once in a while when I was home I got the feeling that I didn't want to stay there; I wanted to be by myself. My mother used to worry about me. She'd cry. I guess all mothers worry about their sons.

I didn't get along with my father. Sometimes I wouldn't talk to my sisters or my mother for three or four days. I felt out of place, so I would put on my hat and coat and go out. I didn't care where I went. I walked out on the street and if I turned one way I kept on going that way. That's the way it was. I guess when I was between fourteen and eighteen I left home most: I'd leave every three or four months.

I remember my uncle was going to take me down to South America when I was around seventeen. He was going to collect his bonus, about a thousand dollars, and he told me he was going to take me to South America. But he was going to get his bonus in June and the February before that he got killed. So we didn't go. He always tried to keep me away from kids he didn't like. He knew I'd get in a lot of trouble with them. He told me to leave guns alone, that I'd get in trouble with them, and that I shouldn't steal things. I thought more of him than anyone else. He would hold up for me when my mother hollered and when she gave me a beating. He always had lots of arguments with my father about things. We'd drink together.

All I know is that sometimes he got so drunk that he couldn't stand on his feet and I had to take him home. He'd get so drunk I'd take him down the cellar where there was an old bed and he'd sleep it off there. My mother always fixed him up so when he'd go home my grandmother wouldn't notice anything. He didn't care about anything. He was married about ten years but separated from his wife for a long time. He just didn't give one damn about a thing. When he was working and he wanted to quit he'd quit. Then he'd drink and quit everything but drinking.

I used to play with a kid named Rickert. He seemed to me like a sissy, not like a tough kid. I guess he was the smartest one in the classroom. He would always sit up near the front. Sometimes I'd be sitting near the center. In the English class he was the smartest one, all the girls were around him. Sometimes when the teacher would want to punish somebody she'd put them in a seat where he was surrounded by all the little girls. That was the punishment for them. I got punished sometimes like that and I didn't like it. I didn't like to sit with girls all around and on every side of me.

When I lived on F———— Street I must have been three or four. I don't remember much about my father then. I know my mother was younger looking. She wasn't so stout as she is now. My sister used to be in the cradle and sometimes I would touch her or something and my mother would holler at me for touching her, bothering her while she was asleep.

When we were living in P———— I know the house————to me it was like a two-story house. I don't know how many rooms there were. I know it looked like a store in front. On the first floor there were the windows and there used to be the machine that my father worked on automobile tires with, and in the back there was a room with a lot of tools in it.

Sometimes I used to see—my mother—feeding my sister—from—her—breasts. I guess my sister was just a little baby. My mother—used to feed her—through her—breasts—and—and I— used to—watch. I don't know how long we were living there. I guess my sister was about five months old then; younger than that, maybe three months. She was born in B————. I remember now that my father had a relative in P————. I guess that's why we moved there and—and he couldn't speak English very well. I know sometimes my mother used to argue with my father because she had to talk for this relative.

This entire section was delivered haltingly and with apparent strain.

My mother used to tell me that when they were first married my father beat her and she left him.   The first time was when she took us, my sister and myself, to my grandmother's house.   That was when we were living on B————— Street.   I was about four then and my sister was about two.   She separated from him but my grandmother made her go back.

When we lived in P————— my father had a truck.   He'd go out and buy a lot of old tires and I'd see all different kinds and sizes and shapes, big and small.   Once he made me sit in one and turned me around and I fell out.   He told me to hold on when he turned me upside down.   I was alright but when going over again I fell out.   I can hear—I can hear him say something—something—I can't make it out.   He said something like "bad kid . . . crying."   And sometimes he'd holler at my mother in front of me.   All I know is I used to wear a dress then and stay close to my mother.   My mother—was a beautiful—she was a beautiful woman then.

I know I didn't like to go in the storeroom, the room with the big windows in it, because the light was—shining there.   I didn't like the sunlight.   I didn't like to look in the sunlight, everything was so bright and shiny.   I just didn't like it.   I'd stay out of there.   My father chased me out of there a lot.

My sister used to sleep in a baby carriage and I slept—slept—in the—cradle.   My mother and father slept together in a big bed in one room.   I think the carriage was the one I had.   The cradle had a box-like shape, with wooden spokes on it.   There was a dresser in the bedroom and a big mirror on it.   I don't remember what was on the bureau: it wasn't high, about three feet.   It had a round mirror suspended on the wall above it.   Sometimes my mother would—pick —me up and—sit me on it and I'd—I'd look in the mirror.

I don't know if my father made any money out of his business.   He would chase me out of the store when I got in there.   He'd holler at my mother for leaving me in there.   He said that—he said—I—was —was—blind; that I'd get hurt.

One time I stepped on a nail.   I remember I walked over a pile of boards that had nails in them and I had sneakers on and one of the nails stuck through. My aunt Vanya called me a blind dog—a blind dog—in Polish. I didn't want to stay around there after that so I fixed my leg up. It was swelling but I wanted to go home right away. My grandmother made me stay, but I got away as soon as I could. A blind dog . . .

L: *'Now, Harold, I want you to think carefully. Why should your father have said that you were blind at that time? If it is true that he said you were blind at that time, then your grandfather's funeral must have been before that time; because you remember you distinctly recalled that your eyes were open at your grandfather's funeral.'*

My grandfathers funeral was just about that time. I remember we came from P———— to see my grandfather when he was dead, maybe a couple of months afterwards.

L: *'You're sure it was from P———— you came?'*

I—I used to go to the storeroom. The sun was shining and I'd block my eyes, hold my hands up to them. He used to push—push me—push me out.

L: *'How old were you at that time?'*

I don't know.

L: *'Tell me; about how old?'*

About two and a half or three. I couldn't walk so well. I—used to wear—skirts. My sister was about five or six months old so I must have been about two and a half or three.

L: *'It was about the time of your grandfather's funeral that you came to P———— from B————?'*

Yes—yes. I don't remember much about coming to P———— from B————, but in P———— the house we lived in was different from the one we lived in in B————. We had a nice house in B————. Everything looked bright, painted up, cheerful. We had about six rooms and a big sunporch in the back. The rooms were cheerful, big. I know we had a big square gramaphone, the same we had when we lived on B———— Street. I guess my father must have been making quite a bit of money when we had such a fine place in B————. Wait! I think I know how it was. He lost his job or something and we went to P———— only for a few months. Maybe that's why the house wasn't so nice. In B———— it was bright and cheerful. I—I'm seeing parts of it. There is a table and a highchair for me. I have a lot of toys, rubber toys, dolls, things like that. I must have been about—O, about a year and a half. I don't remember my sister there. My aunts used to come over. My aunt Louise used to feed me. She'd make me eat spinach. I hated it. I know my mother used to pick me up then. She looks like—like my sister does now. I don't think she was more than eighteen or nineteen. There was a sun-porch. The sun used to be there in the morning. There was a yard in the back. Kids used to play there. My father was different then. He wasn't so small as he is now, not so broadshouldered. He had—had all his—hair.

There used to be—little bars—with—beans on my high chair. I remember I used to hit them with my spoon. They'd rattle. They'd buzz . . .

I know we didn't have a store or anything like that in B————, and I don't think we owned a car. The furniture looked different, funny, all changed. The dining room, there were candles in it, and a big chandelier over the table, with glass hanging over it. It would shine and sparkle. It was a small dining room. There was old-fashioned furniture in the parlor. We had wall paper on the walls, with flowers on it. All the rooms seemed to have wall paper in them. I don't know . . .

The Thirty-second Hour

Because the writer's presence was required elsewhere at the usual after-noon hour, Harold was asked to come in the morning of this day. As it developed, this change in the routine had a marked effect on the opening minutes of the hour. Clinicians should be wary of disrupting the therapeutic routine in any way.

Yesterday we were talking about different things we liked to do. Some like to hunt and fish. I haven't done much of it, only when I was living with my aunt and uncle. Even when I was ten or twelve I liked to fish and hunt. Sometimes I was just, well, just lazy. I just liked to lie around and do nothing . . .

L: 'It seems a little difficult, doesn't it, for you to come in at this hour, Harold.'

Yes. It's so—different. I don't know; there are a million things going through my head at once. Maybe it's because I usually study in the morning. I am trying to force it out of my mind.

L: 'Instead of forcing it out, just pick any one topic—no matter what it is—anything, and start with that.'

Anything that goes through my mind?

L: 'Yes; go ahead.'

I don't know what makes me think of the girl I used to go with, Lila. She knew sometimes when I was flat broke, broke as anything, and she offered me money, tried to force money on me. I wouldn't take it. She was a funny sort of girl. Lila was straw-haired and she had freckles on her face. Sometimes we used to spend a day or two together. But—I—she—I had a funny dream about two nights ago. I tried to tell myself to forget about it and not to tell you. It was a dirty, filthy thing.

I was dreaming I was buying a car off a person, buying it off a man —he looked like my father—buying it I guess off my father. He wanted to sell me a car. It looked like the old car we had when we were living on B——— Street. It seemed like I was older than I was then, though. Anyway, I was sitting on something, I guess the running board of another car or on the grass, and I was looking up at the car. He wanted forty-eight hundred sixty-nine dollars for it but all I wanted to give him was two thousand dollars. Then this man, whoever he was, probably my father, he started playing with my peter, started committing fellatio on me. I don't know why I dreamed a thing like that; I never had a dream like that before.

L: 'Is that all there was, Harold?'

That's all there was to the dream. That's all there was to it. I don't know why I dreamed it. I didn't try to associate it with anything or anybody. I figured I'd tell you.

I know my father had that car from 1926 to about the end of 1934, then he bought himself a new car. I never drove the '26. One time my mother was coaxing him to teach me to drive so I could get my license but he said no. I can't figure the money angle on it. I don't know about this—this other business. It seems so funny.

L: 'Suppose you start with buying a car from your father. Just say whatever comes to you in that connection.'

Buying a car? I asked him once to teach me: he said no. I never asked him again. I don't like to ask people more than once for anything; if they say no the first time I never ask them again. Maybe that's the reason I didn't get along very well with my father, because I wouldn't keep on asking him for things.

L: 'Why should your father try to sell you a car?'

I don't know; I can't understand. Why should he want twice the price I wanted to pay for it? That's a large amount of money.

L: 'Did you think it was worth it?'

I don't think so, not four thousand. I was going to give him two thousand for it.

L: 'Was there anything else you can think of?'

No. I was sitting in the grass looking up at the car. I saw the front, the fenders and the windows. It reminded me of the old car we used to have. I don't know why. I took it out once in a while when he was out working somewhere. I guess I was about sixteen or seventeen when I used to take it out. I don't think he ever knew about it.

L: 'You don't know why your father should try to sell you a car?'

No; I don't.

L: 'Well, what would be one obvious reason?'

I don't know. It might be that he had something he was trying to sell me. Maybe I'd have some money and I could buy it, or maybe he could borrow money from me.

L: 'Well, Harold, isn't it obvious that one reason he was selling you a car is that you apparently didn't have one and he thought you wanted one?'

Yes; but he wanted four thousand dollars, I could buy it from someone else cheaper. It might be he wanted money from me. I was a prospect for buying a car from him and he would be receiving some money for it, so it would do him some good.

L: 'He offered you the car for exactly four thousand eight hundred and sixty-nine dollars?'

Yes. Why just that sum? I don't know.

L: 'That's quite an amount of money. You only offered him two thousand?'

Two thousand. I figured the car was not worth that much to me, it was an old car, run down. I don't know why I offered him two thousand when the car was probably worth less than two hundred. Perhaps I wanted to give him some money.

L: 'Now, two thousand dollars is a round figure; four thousand eight hundred and sixty-nine is a complex figure. Is there any significance in that?'

It might be that the smaller amount represented me, as the smaller person, less of a person, placing less value on me; and probably the larger amount represents a more complex, greater, stronger . . . Still and all, why should the numbers be as they are? One is twice as great as the other, the father twice as great as the son.

L: *'Well, what does that mean for you?'*

I—can't think—unless it's because I was—jealous? I envied his big strength. My father is strong, very very strong. He has big strong arms, a big chest. He used to pick me up and let me drop, let me drop on the floor from about four or five feet. I probably only weighed about a hundred and ten pounds then, but he picked me up like nothing. I hated him for dropping me like that. I fell right on the floor and sometimes when I was down he would take a kick at me. I hated him, hated him for that. I figured nobody has a right to do anything like that even if he was my father. But maybe I wasn't exactly envious; maybe I just recognized the fact that he was stronger. I guess I put more value on myself than on him. I guess two thousand is a larger amount than four thousand eight hundred and sixty-nine . . .

L: *'Why?'*

It represents myself. The smaller amount is greater than the four thousand; O, not as a measurement but as a bundle, something all in one.

L: *'Actually, he was giving you something at a larger price than you were prepared to pay for it?'*

I don't know. It all goes back, O, everything. He wanted me to work and keep looking for a job, and I got sick of looking for work and I didn't want to work; so I used to stay out at nights and I'd see him only once a week, probably only Sunday mornings.

L: *'You offered him a round sum and he offered to sell for a complex, larger sum. Is there any meaning for you in this?'*

I—don't know—unless the round sum, the two thousand, represented the—the female—genitals. Could that be? And the complex number the male genitals? Well, here we have a round number; that might represent the female; and the complex number, the small appendages, of course might indicate the male genitals. The figure '8' might represent the testes . . .

I guess I was always sort of timid and shy with my father. That's why I kept away from him. He was more—manlier than I—manlier; a man. He was greater in his physical strength than I was. But I don't seem to measure anything by physical strength or by people's bodies. I think a fellow is a fine person if he has a good mind, regardless of his body.

L: 'Now let's go to the other part of your dream. Recall as much of that as you can.'

Well, it seems that I was lying on the grass or sitting on the running board of another car. I could see the car he wanted to sell me. The man I was with looked like my father. He started playing with my penis, then later on he—he did fellatio on me. I—there was a—a discharge, I remember, and that's when I woke up. Just about the time I woke up I can remember I was putting my penis in my trousers again and buttoning them up. I don't want my father around me so why should I want him to do anything like that?

L: 'Do you see any reason now why you should have dreamed that?'

Even dreaming about it makes me feel ashamed of myself. I don't know why but—well—well—it might be—it might represent that I was—changing this—man for Perry.

I don't know why I should dream a thing like that. It was distasteful to me. I didn't get along very well with my father all the way back through the years, even when I was a baby. My mother told me things. He didn't like to hold me, even when I was a baby. That's what used to prey on my mind. Perhaps the reason why I dislike him is his physical appearance. He is bald-headed and slightly bow-legged, like a gorilla, big-chested, big, powerful arms. He didn't have well-developed legs though. When we were young he sometimes twisted our arms to show us how strong he was. When I got older I didn't want to be around home, to be near him. I didn't care if he *was* my father; I didn't want him around me.

L: 'What did your mother tell you about him?'

My mother told me that when I was a few months old she wanted him to hold me and things like that: she wanted my father at least to hold his own baby once in a while. He never seemed to want to. Now my younger sister, he always wanted to pet my younger sister. He spoiled her: he petted her too much. It seems he likes my sisters more than me. Every time he looked at me I'd get a funny feeling. I didn't want him to look at me. When we had the dog, a female dog, she was a pal of mine, so sometimes he would lock her up in the garage and wouldn't let her out. So I used to sit around the garage and wait until he let her out. That may be another reason why I dislike him.

He always seemed to like my sister. I remember when she was in second or third grade in school she'd sit on his knees and recite nursery rhymes. I never did that. One time he wanted me to recite my ABCs and I wouldn't do it. I said I forgot, so he started calling me a dummy. He couldn't speak English very well: when he pronounced some words he said them in a low pitch and some other words in a high pitch. It never all seemed to be in one tone; and that's another thing that used to prey on my mind.

I remember when I was about eight my mother and father were sitting in the kitchen, my sister was sleeping—it was about ten at night—and he wanted me to recite a poem I was going to give in a school play. I told him that I had forgotten most of it. I remember he wanted me to stand in the center of the room and recite this poem. I recited one verse and told him I forgot the rest; so he started calling me names like dummy.

I guess that's one reason I didn't like to go out with him, go anywhere with him, in the car. When my mother and sister wanted to go I'd make some excuse and stay at home. Sometimes I'd sit in the back seat and not say a word to anyone, make believe that I was reading the newspaper. Then the car started to bounce up and down and I couldn't read and I'd get sick. I never did enjoy anything with him. He just didn't seem like the right sort of a man anyone would have for a friend; he was hard to everybody but himself. He wasn't a good business man. He was always doing favors for his friends, doing something for somebody; and when something went wrong he'd come home and curse and swear and start an argument with my mother. My mother wouldn't say anything. She'd just cry.

Before he got the Buick he had an Overland, and one time I threw dirt—dirt all over his car. O, I remember: there was a dog underneath the car and I was trying to get him out so I threw some dirt at him and some of the dirt got all over the car. He came out and looked at it and wanted to know if I threw the dirt; then he hit me, hit me right in the side of the head. Later he told my mother about it. She started telling me why did I do things like that? "bad boy." I guess I wasn't paying attention to her very much.

When he used to hit me I could—I imagined I could—hear people singing. It would agitate me more. It seemed to me that people or somebody was singing. It was pleasant to hear, and yet—I know I was crying. I don't know whether it stopped me from crying.

L: 'Do you recall—now think carefully, Harold—the same singing when your mother hit you?'

When my mother hit me—yes—I heard it too, but it was a different kind of singing when my mother hit me. When I was about fourteen I heard it once. It was a popular song, very fast, not jazz; it went smoothly. But when we were living on B———— Street one time my father hit me. It sounded like a choir: it seemed more like women singing, choir, a group of women singing when my father hit me. It sounded so soft and sweet, the music was smooth and pleasant to hear. I always used to hear some kind of singing, sometimes it sounded like singing accompanied by music, sometimes like singing alone, but never music alone. The time when I broke his razor I heard sweet music. I remember that time. I don't know what they were singing but they were singing something sweet. It reminded me of angels singing. Three days later I wanted to cry again so I could hear it again, but I couldn't force it in my mind: I couldn't hear it. Soft music and singing. Something used to agitate me so I would cry more. Sometimes I would forget about crying and just listen to the music. Sometimes I'd just sit in the corner and cry, just sit there and hear something. Sometimes I would forget about crying and I'd hear it for as long as fifteen minutes, sometimes as long as an hour, as long as no one disturbed me or I didn't fall asleep. Sometimes I would sit on the floor and fall asleep and my mother would come and wake me up, call me for supper and dinner, and would destroy everything.

I don't cry much. When I was eighteen and my father hit me I didn't cry. Sometimes he would say something to me and I'd go away somewhere. Usually when I'd cry I'd go in a dark room where the light wasn't strong and everything was soft. That way I would hear something.

When I was about three or four, when we lived on F———— Street, I know my mother used to play the victrola a lot. It was about four feet high. She would play mostly Polish records. Some sounded very nice to me. I think Polish is the first language I understood. I understand it and speak it fairly well now. I guess I know it for one reason, that I listened to my father. My mother used to make us pray in Polish. I've forgotten how to pray.

My sister used to like to listen to the victrola. She used to sit in the cradle when she was about one or two and sometimes I would look at her and she would smile sort of funny. I used to have the same cradle. I guess my mother didn't want me to be around my sister very much—because—I used to pat her on the head—and—one time I put my finger in her eye.

This type of aggression and its significance is clear to the analytical observer.

L: 'When did you put your finger in her eye?'

When she was in the cradle. She was about a year and a half old and I was standing by the cradle patting her on the head and the cheek and I guess I must have put my finger in her eye. She started crying and my mother came and told me to keep away from her. She hollered at me because I made my sister cry.

L: 'When that occurred, Harold, do you remember whether your eyes were open?'

I don't know. This was when I was three or four and my mother tells me that my eyes were closed when I was about two. But I know that when we lived in P——— the house—the store—the machine. I remember when the sun was shining I put up my arm. I couldn't see through the sun. Now I can see a little bit but then I couldn't see anything.

L: 'Since when can you see through the sun?'

When we lived in P———, when I was about two, I used to stand in the sunlight and I couldn't see anything, the same as it is occasionally now. I can't see very far. The snow reflects the sunlight right in my eyes. I can see alright when I look down to watch which way I am going . . .

Immediately following upon this hour, the patient was placed in a deep hypnotic trance in order to facilitate the recovery of subliminal memorial material. It was evident from the foregoing that, although quite early memories were recovered, the nature of further repressed material forbade their expression under routine conditions. Accordingly, Harold was placed in a deep sleep, and after ascertaining the depth of the hypnosis by the usual techniques, the recovery of early memories continued as follows:

The Thirty-third Hour

L: '*I want you to listen very carefully to what I am going to say. We are going back through the years. We are going back first to yesterday. Do you remember yesterday? Where were you at fifteen minutes after two yesterday afternoon?*'

In the Hospital . . .

L: '*Where in the Hospital?*'

In the Psychology Clinic, talking to C————.

L: '*Now we are going back further. We are going back to when you were in L———— with your cousin, sitting on the lawn, looking up at the stars. Do you remember that?*'

Ye—yes.

L: '*Do you see the stars? Describe them to me.*'

They look like—stones—on velvet—glass, glass on velvet cloth. The light—is shining on them. They're reflecting the light. There are hundreds of them, reflecting the light. They seem to be reflecting the light. They look like glass stones on velvet cloth.

L: '*Now you are getting smaller, much smaller, younger, much younger. Your hands are smaller, your feet are smaller, your whole body is smaller. You are going back to the time when you were quite young; the time you and Benny went to the movies and Benny dropped his knife. Do you remember that?*'

Yes—yes.

L: '*Now listen carefully. Do you remember the name of the moving picture you saw at that time? Do you remember?*'

It was about boats, war-boats, warships. It had an *Our Gang* comedy and there was some vaudeville. The other picture was about wars, about church-steeples falling down and everything being shot-up. The picture was—was *Man's Enemies.* There also was—it was—the name was *U-Boat 11* or *15*—no *11.* It was the story about a German submarine. They went after the submarine in an old schooner. The submarine captain, he was a German, he went up to see some old friends of his at the front. They were shooting—shooting everything. The U-Boat . . .

L: '*How old were you then?*'

I was nine—nine.

L: '*Now I want you to go back to a time earlier than that. You are getting smaller and younger. You must listen carefully to what I tell you. You are a little child now. We are back to the time when your aunt Louise took you to school with her. Do you remember that?'*

Yes—yes.

L: 'Now listen to me. Remember now when your aunt Louise took you to school with her. How were you dressed? How was she dressed?'

It was in the summer. She had on a light-colored dress.

L: 'What color?'

I can see her. I can see her. What color? It looks like yellow. No; it's pink, pink . . .

L: 'What were you wearing?'

I have a pair of shorts on—and a shirt—with a white collar on it.

L: 'How old were you then, exactly?'

Four. I was four years and—and . . .

L: 'We are going back to an earlier time now. You are very small now, a very small baby. You are in your mother's arms now . . .

'That's a nice feeling, isn't it? Your mother is holding you. Your mother is young. She is holding you. She is standing, holding you, in a very bright room. This is in B———. Do you remember?'

> Here the subject evidenced profound pleasure, a beatific smile appearing slowly.

Yes—yes.

L: 'What room is she standing in?'

The sun is shining. It's the sun porch—the sun porch.

L: 'What is your mother saying? Your mother is talking. What is she saying?'

She is saying that I got measles. I got measles—and she doesn't know what they are,—doesn't know what they are. She is looking at my face. She is saying, "Poor little baby!" She must be saying she is going to see a doctor—about the sores in my face. I've got measles. She doesn't know what they are.

L: 'Now, Harold; you are in your mother's arms. She is holding you. You have the measles. There are spots on your hands. Are your eyes open?'

Yes—no—no. They are blinking. The sun is too strong. I have to blink. The sun is too strong. It's hot—everything is hot. My clothes on—my blankets make it too hot. The sun is hot—the sun is—shining, and the walls are bright, everything is bright. Bright. I can't look at it for a long time. I have to blink my eyes.

*Here perspiration accumulated on Harold's face and he lifted his hands
to pull his clothing away from his body.*

L: '*Now you are even younger, Harold, smaller. You are very small,
just a little baby. You are sitting in your high-chair. You have a spoon
in your hand. What are you doing with the spoon?*'

I am hitting something with the spoon . . .

L: '*What are you hitting?*'

I'm hitting—a bowl—with—the cereal I'm eating—in the highchair. I'm hitting—some—beads—beads, colored beads—on the
high-chair.

*Here Harold's hands beat convulsively in the manner of a child pounding
with a spoon.*

L: '*Are your eyes open? Look carefully. Are your eyes open or are
they blinking?*'

The sun is coming in. They are blinking . . .

L: '*Are you sure?*'

When I look at anything steady. When I look at the ceiling—or
the floor. Everything—is—coming up from the—floor. It makes
my eyes blink. I can see it. It's coming up from the floor. It sort
of gives me—my eyes hurt. It hurts me. There. It comes up.
I hit it with the spoon. It's still coming up from the floor—but—
the windows are in back of me. I am sitting with my back toward
the windows—at the table. It has a white table cloth on it—and a
lot of dishes and things. Everything is so bright. It is early in the
morning. The sun is shining in . . .

L: '*Now listen to me, Harold. I am going to ask you a question.
Listen carefully. Why did you first start to blink your eyes? What
made you blink your eyes the first time? Now you are very small, very
small. This is very long ago, when you were in the cradle.*'

I am in the cradle, right next to my father's bed. I see him. I
see—I can see—it—way up. My mother—I see my father on top
of her. I'm in the cradle—and I see him. I—it is early in the
morning—not very dark—not light—and—I'm in—the cradle. My
mother's nightgown is—up—over her hips, and—she—is on her back.
My father is on her—and they—Oooo—the . . . He gets off her—
and I—see—his—I see my—mother. The light is coming in. The

*Harold was extremely agitated throughout this period. He moaned
continually and tossed himself about. His breath came fast and his whis-
pered words came from between dry lips.*

shades on the windows are drawn. I can see plain—the covers are off. My mother's nightgown is over her hips. I can see the—thing—all the way up. My father—is on her. I can see—see—his—penis. I can see—my mother's—vagina. There is—hair—hair—all over her . . . I'm lying in the cradle. I cry. My mother—I can see—my father up. She takes her nightgown and—puts—it down—over her knees. My father puts the covers—over his—himself. She starts over to the cradle. She is talking to me, tickling me under the chin. I just woke up. It's hot. Then I'm playing in my bed—with my hands . . . . I'm moving them—up and down—like they . . . My mother is talking to me. She's—saying—something. I—I—don't I don't understand her. I'm crying. I'm putting my fingers—up in my—mouth. In a little while my mother gets up. She gets up—her knees—I see them. She stands up and the nightgown falls—falls down to her ankles. She picks me up from the cradle—and—is—kissing me. She takes me into another room. It's the kitchen. She lights the stove, the gas stove, and puts the coffee pot on. She puts me in the high-chair. She must be fixing breakfast. She calls my father. I know—my father—father. . . . Mother is—she's hollering. Get off—her. Don't be so rough . . .

L: *'Now, Harold, listen. You saw your mother and father having intercourse when you were a little baby. How old were you then?'*

I am about a—year—old.

L: *'And until then your eyes were wide open? That experience was something you wanted to forget?'*

O yes—yes.

L: *'Is that the secret you are hiding? Is that why your eyes are closed?'*

I—My mother tells me—it's from the—measles. I don't know. Ooooo, I don't know. The sun—the sun is too—bright.

Here the evidence of intense suffering increased.

L: *'Was it bright when your mother lifted you from the cradle? What do you hear?'*

Here Harold seemed to be straining to hear something.

I can hear you talking and —I—O—I can hear a lot of talking. I can hear *them* talking. My mother is telling him I think—my mother is telling my father—he is hurting—hurting her—get off. O, the sun is so bright!

L: 'Now listen very carefully, Harold.   I am going to ask you to do something.   I want you to forget everything that happened since you fell asleep.   You can't remember.   Just forget . . .'

The Thirty-fourth Hour

It was obvious when Harold entered the room that he was very upset.

Doctor, I have something on my mind that I've got to tell you. You told me when we first started, you told me that I would have to tell you everything, if I wanted to get straightened around.   But— I can't tell you everything.   There is something on my mind that I can't tell anyone who is living, even if he *is* a psychologist. . . .

When I was about eighteen years old I—I killed a man.

I can't tell anybody about it.   I should have told you a long time ago.   I didn't think it would matter much.   Nobody knows about it except myself and—you.

> *For many and obvious reasons, prolonged consideration had to be given to the question as to whether it was justifiable to include this matter in the manuscript.   On the one hand, there were of course ethical and professional scruples arguing for its elimination; on the other hand, it was recognized that scientific integrity categorically demanded its inclusion.   The factors which proved decisive as well as important are set forth in the note on page 284.*

I don't know.   I feel—like—uncomfortable—about telling you. It's a funny place about telling you something like that.   I trust you more than anybody else in the world, still—the idea—a man is a man regardless how he is, and I want—to live, live outside these walls someday.   I can't tell you anything about it.   I should have told you in the beginning.

Nothing ever happened to me like that and nothing ever will. Nobody else knows I . . .

You see, I don't know whether I should have . . . I have been thinking for about three weeks about explaining—telling you.   I couldn't bring myself to do it.   You see, I have the feeling that if I want to be fixed I've got to tell you everything—and somehow—it feels as if we are right on the verge of—fixing my eyes . . . I don't know. What do you think?

L: 'Well, Harold, let us see.   You feel that we are on the verge of something and any information you withhold from me would damage what we have done. And in the second place, you are not quite sure that you can depend on me.'

I trust you more than anyone else in the world, more than any other human being. But you—you have a position, you have a duty to perform.

L: 'Now we might as well have an understanding about this. I am not going to make any protestations or promises to you. Let it be this way: if you wish to tell me, you can be sure I won't betray you; if you don't want to tell me about it, if that is your preference, we'll just forget about it.'

I would rather not say anything. Believe me there is nothing else in my life that I wouldn't tell you about. This was—we were in a poolroom, and he called me a dirty lying mother—f——r. I agitated myself for about two weeks—and—one day—I—I got him alone.

I was scared. I didn't want to do any time. I was afraid of time, that's why I didn't care when I went out on hold-ups if I got shot up. . . .

I thought that if anything went wrong with this experiment, with this treatment, it might be caused by the fact that I didn't tell you. But I can't tell you all, even if you would want to stop the experiment. I'm in a spot. I don't know what to say. I'm in the penitentiary and I can't : . . I trust you more than anyone else in the world, but I can't say anything.

L: 'Harold, as I have already told you, if you don't want to tell me, it will not matter.'

When I was about ten or eleven I played cowboys and Indians a lot. I'd get real fun out of playing cops and robbers too. All the money that I could get I spent right away. I didn't care very much about money: I'd get rid of it, get rid of everything around me. Sometimes when we played cards or shot craps my cousin Riggs would ask me for money: if I felt in the mood I gave it to him and never asked it back. When I was younger, my cousin Riggs and I tried to steal a car one time. We got in and started the car and it went backwards and it piled up on the car behind it, so we never tried to steal a car again. We would do a lot of things that didn't matter very much. We'd steal bread and cakes from the lunch-wagons and once in a while we'd soak the breads in water and drop them on people from the bridge. This was when we were around twelve or thirteen.

When I was twelve I belonged to the Boy Scouts. My cousin

didn't belong there. I had a lot of fun with those kids: they were honest and fine. They really had this daily good deed business at heart. I guess they're all grown up now. When I broke away from the Scouts I started hanging around with those kids from S——— Street and getting into a lot of trouble. I wasn't as closely watched around home as I was before twelve. Before that I had to be home every night at nine but after I was twelve or thirteen I'd sneak out of the house at night, sneak out and steal all kinds of things.

The whole scenery around the house and the whole neighborhood seem changed. Buildings are going up. They are going forward. It doesn't remind me of the place it used to be ten years ago.

I don't remember much about my grandmother and my aunts. My aunt Louise wanted me to go to school and study real hard and be something. She promised that she'd get me a job where she worked. I never finished High School on the outside. I just was running here and running there, doing this and doing that. I didn't care whether I finished school, whether I'd have anything to eat or clothes to wear. I used to leave home every two or three months. I never went hitching in any freight cars. I was afraid of them. I remember the kid that got his leg cut off when I was about fifteen. I saw a big crowd of kids on the railroad and I saw the train coming, and suddenly the train stopped. When I got up there the kids were all crowded around, and I saw the kid and saw his leg lying five or six feet away. A cop picked it up. I saw him. It was nauseating. I couldn't stand it, picking up a leg like that. I knew the kid; he was about ten or eleven; he was in the same gang with me. He got hurt somehow or other. I didn't get hurt.

Even when I was twelve sometimes I didn't go to school. I played truant all by myself. I would stay away for two or three days and then stay away from home too. When I got hungry and tired I'd go home and then I'd get a beating, so I'd get it all at once. But I hated my father to give me a beating.

Before I was eleven I didn't like to read books or do anything like that. When I belonged to the Boy Scouts I used to read a few books on sports, then I got interested and switched from sports to detective stories and crime stories and things like that. I used to think of myself as a brave criminal, a smart man, hard with everybody.

I was never interested in stealing anything before I was twelve years old; O, I guess I stole a few pennies. When my mother sent me out to get something I told her that the price was higher than it was, so I'd buy a few candies or something.

I don't remember if I got into any fights at H———— Street school. I was a pretty quiet kid; I didn't bother anybody. I didn't think I knew very much. I used to sit in the back of the class, away from the teacher and everything that was going on.

I can't seem to remember very much. Everything seems as if I've told you already. . . .

L: 'You see, Harold, the only reason it seems to you that you have told me all of this, is that you have developed guilt feelings about not having told me.'

A feeling of guilt?

L: 'Yes. You feel just a little bit sorry that you did tell me as much as you did as well. Now let me put you at ease by considering with you my own position, the position you placed me in by telling me what you did. You can see, if you think a little, that your telling me is a potential source of danger to me—not only to you, but to me. Now that I am possessed of this information, if it ever got out you would naturally think I did it. No don't interrupt me! You must realize that it constitutes a potential source of danger to me. We both understand those things. Now the reason you feel that there is something standing in the way of your telling me things, that you have told me all this before, is merely a manifestation of that resistance. You are sure you see that?'

Yes; I am.

L: 'Well, what do you think of it?'

I should have never said anything . . .

L: 'Why not?'

I don't know. I know there's nothing you can do about it. There is no way the courts could convict me or anything.

L: 'There is no way that anybody could harm you?'

No; even if you did say anything I could still deny it. I am not afraid of you or anyone else saying anything, but it's . . .

L: 'What are you afraid of?'

I don't know. I don't know. It's just somebody else knowing this, that's what it is I guess.

L: 'You think somebody else knowing it might worry you?'

No: I don't think so . . .

L: '*Well, then, what special feature bothers you?*'

I don't know. I—I even had the feeling that—if I said anything to anybody else . . . I firmly believed that I would never say anything to anybody about it. I don't mind you knowing it; knowing it you might be able to form a—more definite conclusion about me. And even knowing it, you can't do anything about it.

L: '*Let's put it this way: perhaps you are sorry you told, perhaps you regret telling me, because it might make some difference in my attitude toward you?*'

Yes. That's it!

L: '*Now let's look at it closely. What is the relationship between us?*'

Psychologist and patient . . .

L: '*And what else?*'

Well, I guess a slight friendship.

L: '*Is there anything more than that?*'

Well, more than just a slight friendship . . .

L: '*Yes. You see, Harold; there is and there has to be complete trust between us; my trust in you, which helps me to do my job, and your trust in me. And, you see, there can't be any question about a change in my attitude first because, as you have rightly said, there is no danger to you in what I now know. It can't be proved. It happened many years ago. Right?*'

Yes; that's right.

L: '*And secondly; even if I did say anything about it, there would be a tremendous difficulty about producing even a shred of evidence.*'

Yes.

L: '*And thirdly there can't be any change in attitude on my part because, to me, what you have told me is the same thing, in the same category, as what you told me about putting your finger in your sister's eye. Do you see that?*'

I understand what you mean, Doc . . .

L: I want you to understand the basic mechanism of this .hing. There is one process with which you are already familiar; resistance. I have explained that to you. Now there is another process which is not quite as familiar to you; the process we call transference. That is the name for the "more than friendship" relation which we have. It means that because of mutual respect and confidence, we can depend upon each other, we feel warmly about each other. Now when one of us resents the other, mistrusts him, or dislikes him, that state is called negative transference. We must try to preserve the positive type of transference, because with this type of accord our work here becomes easier. Since you told me about that incident, you have been in a state of negative transference, resentful, suspicious, mistrustful. I am trying to make you understand what happened to you. Now if you understand, you may go on.'

I made a lot of mistakes in my life but the greatest mistake I ever made, I feel now, was reading the wrong material, the wrong books, things that have no value. O, I can catch up on those years: I have to catch up. All I was thinking about was getting drunk and laying around; all I wanted to do was drink. When I had no money I'd go out and steal some. In the beginning when I'd steal I'd feel nervous, but after a while I'd cool down and everything began to seem natural. Even when I pulled my first hold-up I almost shot the person, I was so nervous. I had an old gun, and somehow it went off, right through the windshield. I was so afraid I didn't know what to do, drop the gun and run away or what. Finally I managed to stay. They didn't have any money. After that everything was more natural. I held up a few insurance salesmen. I felt right at home with it: it seemed right in its place.

I never want to pick up a gun or any other weapon again. I never want to look at any.

Somebody shot at me one time. I don't know whether the bullet went over a house or where it went. I know I lost my wrist-watch that time and it had my fingerprints on it, but I was never accused of that crime.

I had several guns in my time. They weren't really good guns, they were cheap. I had a lot of brass knuckles, blackjacks and so on. My mother found a blackjack one time that belonged to me.

My mother would search for things all over the house. It finally got so I had to put my gun in back of a bureau and fasten it to the wall with adhesive tape. She never looked back there. Whenever I had money she accused me of stealing it. I'd tell her I won it in a crap game or a card game. She didn't believe me.

Everything seemed unimportant to me. Everything seemed to vary, seemed to cover up for something else. I'd stay out of the house so I didn't have to listen to my father. I guess he didn't like me very much. I used to get drunk and he'd see me drunk once in a while. It made him mad so I would stay away two or three weeks. That way it would agitate him more.

When I was broke it was hard for me to ask my mother for money. So I'd steal it, in any way, just to get it. People used to say, 'Gold is where you find it,' even if you find it in other peoples' pockets, so I'd steal the gold. I pulled quite a few hold-ups and burglaries; that's the only thing I ever did, I mean in that way, of course. I tried my best to curb my desire to get money. Only a small amount should be sufficient for anybody. I just want to fish, and write. That's all the things I want to do. I don't want any money, I mean accumulate money in a bank, in stocks or bonds.

I don't know: when I look back everything seems all kind of funny. I can't really believe it. I know its going to be the exact opposite from what it has been in the past. It was really bad but I can't change it now. Just let it go by and forget about everything, pass everything up. I don't want to bother much with making money when I get out. I don't want to tie myself down in one place. I didn't like it when I was a kid and I don't like it now that I am a man. I always liked boats. I used to have a lot of fun when I stayed out at L————, just sailing around the bay. There are a lot of islands with cabins on them and I slept in a different one every night. There were no fish to speak of but there were a lot of crabs and we went crabbing a lot too. I didn't wear many clothes, just a pair of shorts through the day. When I look back . . . I should have stayed like that.

When I was about eighteen or nineteen I used to like to leave home when it was raining and walk around, stay out about four or five hours and then go home and go to bed. I didn't like to say anything to anybody. The next morning my suit would be all wrinkled up and I'd have to press my pants. I used to press my pants almost every day, just to have something to do I guess. I'd go over to the park to see if there were any girls I knew, see if I could have a little fun. I dressed up as best I could. My clothes were always neat. They weren't good clothes, but they were always neat and very clean . . .

THE THIRTY-FIFTH HOUR

I notice my eyes are open a little more than they used to be. Sometimes the sun is too bright and then I can't see very far.

Before I can remember they used to remain open all the time, and when they were open in the sunlight I couldn't see anything: I had to close them.   I couldn't even see my hand in front of me.   Now I can see a good deal more clearly, even when they are open in the sunlight. I can't see very clearly yet, but in the future I'll be able to see more distinctly.

One time I ran right into a pole.   I didn't see it.   The sun was shining right in my eyes, everything was so hot, shiny; the street was reflecting the sunlight right into my eyes.   I was running across the street and I hit my head right into the pole.   I learned a lesson then: that I shouldn't run, walk slowly, watch all around me and see that no cars are coming.   I really hurt my head then.   I was about ten and I was coming back from my grandmother's house.

I know the sun was always too bright for me and I never liked to go out in it.   When there was some place to walk besides in the sunlight I would walk there.   I prefer the night to the day.

I think my vision is improving since I began to come to you.   I don't know if there was anything wrong with my eyes in the first place, but I can say that my vision is really improving.

When I was younger everybody used to feel sorry for me because my eyes were that way.   My aunts, my grandmother, everybody. My grandmother never said anything about it, neither did my aunt Louise, but my aunt Vanya did.   When I was younger everybody used to pet me too.   My aunt Louise, I think she liked me most. When we lived on B——— Street she would bring toys home for me, and when I was at her house she always had some cake.   I used to eat a lot of cake when I was out.   My grandmother always treated me fine too.

I don't think we lived in P——— very long.   I was still small when we moved.   My father had a brother or a cousin or some sort of relative there, and I guess that's one reason we went there.   He was in the business of reconditioning tires.   This was about twenty years ago.   I don't know what happened.   He didn't like me in the shop where he was working because I used to get in his way.   The sun was shining through the big windows and I'd walk in the sunlight and I couldn't see anything.   When I was in the sunlight I'd cover my eyes and then bang into something or other and he'd get angry with me. At that age my sister was very young and my mother was still nursing

her, nursing her at the breast. My sister had the measles when we
were living at F——— Street.   I can remember that because the
doctor—he was a tall, thin doctor and he wore a dark suit—he said
that I wouldn't get them because I'd had them once. My sister
was only about three or four months old when we lived in P———.
She was born when we lived in B———.   We lived in a two-story
house with another family. They had two children, the girl about
four and the boy around two, a little older than me. They had a
little wagon or something and they were aways arguing about it.   I
was about two when my sister was born and I don't remember much
about it.   I know we had a big—a big sunporch, and the sun used to
shine. There was linoleum on the floor, of a real light color, and the
sun would reflect off that. When I'd sit in my highchair the sun
seemed to come up right in my eyes. The windows on the side had
shades on them and sometimes my mother would draw the shades.

We didn't have a car then, but I know my father must have had a
good job because he would need a pretty good income to afford the
home like we had. Something must have happened; he must have
lost his job. This was in nineteen-twenty or twenty-one.

L: 'Harold, where did you sleep?'

I don't know. I—I—only remember the—highchair—the highchair. There were—big windows and when I had the measles I
used to sit out on the porch to have my meals there. I know we had
a large pantry off the kitchen right next to the porch. O, I don't
know: I can't seem to remember.

L: 'Do you remember where you slept?'

I guess I had a cradle. I slept in a cradle with squared wooden
bars on it. On one side of it was my mother's bed, on the other side
was a big bureau. There were wheels on the cradle, and sometimes
my mother would push it over to open a drawer in the bureau when
she wanted something. A big mirror. We had a gas stove. It was
real light in color; it looked like yellow, real light. We had a kitchen
and a bedroom where my mother and my father and I slept, and
dining room. There was a big funny-like chandelier, with glass on it.
It used to shine when the lights were on, and tinkle when the wind
blew through the rooms. And in the parlor we had funny furniture,
old, very old-fashioned. The dining room—there were I guess eight
chairs in the dining room, and a big table in the center of the room.

The chandelier hung right above the table.   In my mother's bedroom there was the bed and the cradle was between the bed and the bureau, and there were two other bureaus in the room and a closet.

L: 'On whose side of the bed was the cradle placed?'

On my mother's side.   O . . . I used to sleep on my mother's right. My father on the left.   Sometimes I would sleep in the bed; they would have me in when I couldn't sleep or something was bothering me.   Sometimes when I would cry or something my mother would—reach—out through the bars and—pat me and quiet me.   And often, in the morning, when my father would leave for work, I would be sleeping and—she—would take me out of the cradle and put me in the —bed—with her.   There were two big windows in the room, both with curtains and shades.   Every morning, around mid-morning, the sun would come in and shine on the linoleum on the floor.   The linoleum was real shiny.   Sometimes when the shades were drawn it seemed as if the sun still was coming in, but most of the time they were up.   O, we lived on the second story—because—when you looked out the window—there—wasn't anything for a long way, and then there was another house. . . .

L: 'Do you remember anything that happened when you were in the cradle next to the bed?'

I know—my father used to holler at my mother when I cried—when I couldn't sleep or something.   It makes me feel as if I—can still hear—it makes me—feel as though he—was—always hollering at me—when he—something—when he was saying something to my mother about me crying.   I can't remember much about it.   The beads on the highchair always seem to come up.   I spent a lot of time in that highchair.

L: 'Do you remember anything that happened, early in the morning, when you were in the cradle? . . .   It was a little dark, the sun was just coming up, and you were in the cradle?'

It seems to me that I was old enough to—stand up—in the cradle and—hold on—to the sides.   When I looked—in the mirror—on the floor—the sun seemed to shine from the windows and everything seemed to be coming—right—into my eyes.   They always got up about the same time, and every time they'd get up the room filled with sunlight.   The sun seemed to be glancing off the walls, the floor, everything. . . .

There was one time, I guess I woke up around the regular hour. Every time I woke up I'd look at my mother's bed—to—see—if they —if she—was in bed. I'd never see my father in bed with her because he already went to work. Either my mother was in the kitchen or in bed, and as soon as I woke up I'd look over there to see her. I guess I just got into the habit to just wake up and look right over there.

The recall of this episode was accompanied by much overt expression of pain and suffering.

I—I—remember my father . . . I know—at night—sometimes he would—holler at my mother—I guess to quiet me when I was crying and—he wanted to—sleep.

I saw him in bed—one morning—I woke up—and—I saw something. I saw my—mother and father—in bed. I guess I must have been looking at them for about a minute there. My mother—looked —naked—to me; my father had his—underwear—or something—on him. I saw—I saw—them—having—having intercourse. It was a Sunday morning, I guess, because he never used to be in bed in the morning—and—one morning—he was there. Then—they were having—intercourse—and my mother was—I remember—my mother saw my—saw me looking at them. She was saying something to my father—and then—she—turned around. I guess my father was— on top—of her, and he—I don't know—I . . . When my mother saw me looking at them she—must have—told my father—and my father looked at me. I got scared—but—when he picked himself up—I—I saw—his genitals—and—I saw my—Oooo . . . But I know—my mother—she pulled the nightgown down over her knees and she got up and started talking to me. She went in the kitchen—and sat me in the high-chair and started to make breakfast for my father. I was sitting in the highchair playing with the beads. My mother was talking to me. I don't know what she was saying. She was fixing the table. Then she called my father and he came out and got dressed and sat down at the table. I don't know . . . I—he—started talking to me I guess. I don't know what he said. I don't know. I don't know. Everything seems blurred to me. . . .

L: 'Try to go back to that scene and reconstruct it as fully as you can.' I know I used to wake up every morning and the sun was shining

in the room, and I never used to see my father in bed. I usually
could see my mother. Every day when I got up I'd look at my
mother's bed to see if she was up. If she was in—bed—I'd make—
a noise so she'd hear me and talk to me. One time I woke up—and—I
looked—at the bed. I saw my mother. I could see all the ways up
to her hips. She was naked. I could see—my father—on top of her
—my—father—on top. They were—having intercourse. I—they
—were saying something, I didn't understand what. I looked at it
for a little while. It seemed like a year. Then I guess my mother
looked over at me. She pushed my father and—and I guess she said
I was up. He—picked himself up. When he did I—saw—his—
genitals—and my mother's. My father's genitals were—big, so big.
I don't know. I don't know. I—I was frightened. He just looked
at me. I was scared of him when I saw his genitals. My mother . . .
I was scared of something. My mother jumped out of bed. My
father put his back towards us. My mother pulled down her nightgown. She came and picked me up and took me to the other room.
My father pulled the covers over him. I—I—it—seemed queer to
me. The sun was shining—shining into the room.

   L: 'You were afraid?'

I was afraid of my father. I—he always hollered when I cried.
He was angry at my mother. I used to hear him. When he was
sitting at the table talking to me I was afraid of him. I don't know.
I guess I was always afraid—that he'd do something—hit me or—
something. I was just sitting there. He was asking me what was
the matter. I don't know. I can't . . . I guess I was afraid, seeing
—seeing his—genitals. They seemed so big and so . . . It seemed
as if they—were—going to—hurt me. They were something—like—
like a strong animal to me, not like a dog you could pet and play with
and that wouldn't bite you. This was going to hurt me or—somehow
it was going to do something. I don't know. It all seems so blurred.

   L: 'Did you think he was going to hurt your mother?'

I don't know. I was afraid he would hurt *me*. I was afraid seeing
my father's genitals. They looked like a new, different animal, a
vicious animal, a dog. I heard my mother say something to him. I
know she said, "He is looking," or something like that. I—it seemed
she was saying . . . She was crying. She seemed to be saying that
he—should—stop it. She—I—she was telling him not to do it

because—it hurts. I can hear it. My father always seemed rough. He always hollered at me. I guess I must have thought he might hurt my mother. I guess I was afraid of him. I always thought he would hit me or something, that he might hurt me . . .

L: 'With his genitals?'

It seemed like that. I guess I was afraid of him because his genitals seemed like something that would—that would—hurt instead of . . . I just looked at them, for a long time, a minute or so. When he picked himself up I saw his genitals then . . . I don't know. I was afraid of them . . . . So big and—so—vicious-looking—so—brutal. They . . . I saw my mother all the way up, all the—hair and—every-thing, her—genitals. He seemed to be saying she should lie still and that he is not hurting her or anything. He said it in a way . . . I guess he must have been hurting her. It seemed he didn't care about anything. She was saying he was hurting her, he should stop it. When she looked over at me I could see her eyes. I guess I was afraid, looking at her. When my father looked over at me and saw I was awake, he jumped up then. When he did, I saw his genitals—so I got more afraid—that he'd be coming over to me and—hurting—me with—his genitals. I—I—my father was hurting her. She was hollering he should stop it. He was talking—if—in such a tone that he didn't care whether he was hurting her or not. When my mother picked me up, everything seemed all right again. She held me real close to her. It made me—feel—safe. Then when I was in the high-chair and my father came in again I was scared of him. I was afraid of my father, not my mother. I could see when she had her night-gown way up over her hips her—genitals—very hairy and—black. It was something different, something I—never saw before. I just felt that—it—felt like a carpet or . . . I can't seem to remember. I didn't want to look at it. It looked ugly. I guess I wasn't afraid of it. I was—afraid—afraid of—his. Her—it might have reminded me of a—a—a cat—that might—scratch you. I know it was some-thing I didn't—want—to—touch or—see, because it was as if . . . I was not afraid of it. I was afraid of my father's.

L: 'You were afraid of his . . . Harold, tell me something. Did you ever read any books on abnormal psychology, or psychoanalysis? Have you ever heard anything about psychoanalysis?'

No. I've never read anything. I heard only about Freud.

L: 'What have you heard about Freud?   Did you ever read a book by Freud?'

No; I never read any book.

L: 'Where did you learn the term 'phallus'?'

I don't know.   Phallus?   O, I remember.   When I worked at the greenhouse—I worked there for quite a long time—there was a fellow working with me.   He used to be a Wall Street broker.   He was a fine man: he used to help me increase my vocabulary.   Every time a new word would come along he would tell me about it.   That's the way it was with this word.

L: 'Have you ever discussed any of these things with Perry?   Have you ever told him what we are doing, what we are talking about here?'

No—no . . .

THE THIRTY-SIXTH HOUR

Well, Doctor, I really feel some improvement in my eyes.   I don't know; it's a funny sort of feeling.   It feels as if my eyes were bulging out, as if the muscles were tightening.

L: 'Well, Harold, that's fine.   I'm glad to hear it.   Now, have you anything special to say to me today?'

No, I don't think so except . . .

L: 'Except what?'

Except that Perry has been talking to me again.   You know, I told you a long time ago that he asked me if I was telling you everything; so he asked me if I was telling you everything; so he asked me again if I was telling you everything that come into my mind.   I told him no, I wasn't; that there are only three or four things that I can think of at one time and that's all I'm telling you; the other things I'm forgetting about.   So he thinks it will be a complete failure.

L: 'You told him that you didn't tell me everything?'

I told him I couldn't tell you everything.   I don't worry about him.

L: 'That's cheerful news about your eyes today.'

It feels sometimes as if my eyelids were holding themselves up; the eyes seem to be bulging out.   Yesterday C———— said that the little thing, the lens in the pupil, contracted to a pin-point; that he had never seen it so small.   I feel my eyes bulging out.   You know, Doc, when you made my eyes stay open after you put me to sleep here; well, when I went into the sun my eyes would stay open.   I could feel

it but I couldn't see anything. But on Saturday I could see a little
bit right in the sun. I suppose I will have to get used to it and then
the eyes will absorb most of the light , . .

> *Here Harold was placed into a deep hypnotic sleep and again the classical
> tests for determining depth of trance were made. The treatment then con-
> tinued.*

L: '*I want you to listen only to my voice. Listen very carefully and
do exactly as I tell you to do. You will say things to me that you wouldn't
say if you were awake. You will tell me things that you wouldn't tell
if you were awake. You really want to tell me; but there are things you
somehow can't seem to tell when you are awake.*

*Now, Harold, when I say 'ready' you will start talking, saying any-
thing that comes to you. You will just talk. You will find that you are
telling things you did not tell when you were awake. You really wanted
to tell but you just couldn't bring yourself to do it. There are such things,
are there not?*'

Yes; there are . . .

L: '*Now. Ready.*'

I—there's . . . I stabbed him in the neck—several times, and in the
chest—and way down. I guess I lost my head. I agitated myself.
I hated him. I hated him. He was older than I. He was a tough
guy. I don't know what it was all about, but I hated him for calling
me a lying mother—f——r. I promised myself I'd get even with him.
I was afraid for a long time afterward. I was afraid everytime I
went out. I was afraid, so afraid I started stealing everything, holding up everyone. I left home and I stayed at my aunt's for a couple
months. Then I went back and I stayed home all winter.

> *The commission of a crime as a reaction to fear supports the view that
> many psychopathic manifestations have as their aim the restoration of a
> disturbed balance: it seeks to relieve the tension by a discharge in another
> direction.*

And when I needed money I went out and stole. I couldn't get
enough. I wanted to get enough money together to get away somewhere, and then I found I couldn't get enough for that. So I wanted
to kill myself. I was going to go in my father's garage and start the
motor running and sit in the car and go asleep but I got afraid. I
just wanted to go to jail, to get away from everything. So I went to

jail and stayed there. I never figured I would go to jail when I was young. I always thought I would be dead by the time I was twenty-one. Ever since I was ten years old I thought I would die before I got to be twenty-one. But I am still alive. I don't know why. I guess I didn't have the nerve enough to get in the car and start the motor.

The 'need for punishment,' so often pointed out by orthodox analysts, is clearly shown here, as well as the striving toward 'Thanatos,' or annihilation.

I used to go with that girl Lila. She used to beg me. She said she wished I would kill her. She would cry and cry and get on her knees and say she loved me. She couldn't resist men. I used to hit her once in a while and she'd cry and cry and cry.

I thought of a lot of ways to get a little money, steal it, hold up banks. I was getting ready with those other fellows to hold up a bank when I got arrested. I'm glad I'm here now. I am glad. I don't know why I wanted to hurt this fellow. I just hated him, just like I used to hate everybody. I hate my . . . Every time somebody says something about my eyes I boil all over. Sometimes people are waving their hands in front of them. I can see their hands moving in front of them. I hate them. I hate my friend Dobriski because of that. I hate him, hate him . . . hate him because one time he held up his hand to his face waving it. I want nobody around me. I want to be alone. People bother me. I guess I'm different from everybody else. I can't see as good as others. I—I guess I'm—blind. I hide in my books all day now. I like them. They are better friends than anybody could be. I study all day now. Some-day I might do something if I can work hard enough. I don't want money. My aunt owes me some money. I don't want it. I know how tough it is with her. I had an argument with her one time when I left home. I remember she was waiting for me when I was going home. I was working for her and we had an argument. My uncle always used to look grouchy at me. One time I stepped on a nail and she cursed me out. I got sick of it and left. But my other aunt was always good to me. I used to dream about her. She was so nice and pretty and everything. I never thought that I—would—want to hold her, hold her real tight,—tight. She's married and got three kids now. She's a fine lady.

When I was about ten . . . I see a couple of kids playing. They've got a three-wheeled bicycle. One of them is riding it, riding around in a circle. He tipped over and fell in the street. He hurt his shoulder. He is crying. He is riding around a circle, fast. He fell. He's crying . . .

My father always used to holler at me. I guess he was a good father and everything but I hated him. He'd curse me out for not having a job. I guess he was good to my sisters and my mother, but for some reason or other I hated him. I guess I hate him more than anybody else in the world. One time he got in an argument with my mother and he—he hit her. There was a long iron poker. I lost my head. I grabbed it and I might have hit him if he hit my mother again. From then on he hated me even more; didn't want me around. I didn't care. I was in another room and when I came in my mother was lying on the floor. He said he just pushed my mother. I couldn't see anything but him and the poker. My sister took it off me.

One time he almost hit me with a hammer for calling him to supper. He wanted to hit me with the hammer. I don't know what I said to him. He wanted to hit me. Why did he want to hit me? What did he want to hit me for? I didn't say nothing. He always wanted me to go to school and learn. When I quit school he wanted me to work. When I couldn't find a job I started to stay out most of the night. It got him madder and madder. One time he picked me up and—and dropped me on the floor.

At this point, additional tests were made to determine the depth of sleep.

I—I feel—as if there are—other things. My father and mother . . . I can't seem to get what they are. They—they are coming now . . . I hated to listen to my mother and father when—when—they were in—bed. I used to sleep in the room next to theirs and pull the covers over my head so I wouldn't hear anything, or make a song go through my head so I couldn't hear them. I could hear them talk about things and people. One time I heard my father tell my mother to— move over and—pick up—her leg. Then after a while he asked her, "Is it in?" And she said, "No." Then he asked her again, "Is it in?" She said, "Yes." I hated to listen to them. I don't know why I used to. I couldn't help hearing what they were talking about.

My father for some reason or other would always holler at my mother. He hit her. I never saw him hit her. He pushed her and she fell down. One time when we were living on F———— Street—I was four and my sister, she was two—we went down to where my grandmother bought a new house, and we were going to live there. I know, because my mother said she was not going to live with my father anymore. They must have had an argument. But the next day we were back home on F———— Street. He just kept looking at her and hollering, "Why don't you stay away if you want to?" I remember she had my sister in her arms and she was just sitting in a chair and he kept hollering at her, hollering, "Go away. Stay away."

When we were in P————, when my mother would say something to my father's cousin—he used to sleep in our house and my mother didn't like him—he told her to shut up, never to say anything against him, not to interfere with his business. He blamed my mother that he couldn't make a go of it. He blamed her for failing. When we were on the truck, when we were moving from P————, we left the machine in some farmer's house. We went to the place on F———— Street and we moved all our furniture on the second floor. We had three rooms, three rooms. I slept in the cradle. I slept next to my mother's bed, my sister along side of me, my sister next to my mother and then my father. Sometimes I used to stroke my sister's hand. She was a little baby then. Just stroked her hand so I shouldn't hurt her. One time I hurt her. I put my finger in her eye. I know I slept in the cradle and my father would say to my mother that she should turn over and look at him once in a while, not to pay so much attention to the children: and my mother would say, "Don't bother me;" and he would say, "Turn over, you bitch:" and then my mother would go away and take my sister away and sit in the kitchen maybe for two or three hours and then go back to sleep. In the morning my father would be mad. He was always telling my mother why don't she go away? He would always tell her why did he marry her for? The only reason was to lay in bed.

When we were living in B———— there were windows, big windows, with light shades. The sunlight would get in, almost halfway in the room. One time I saw mother and my father, my father on top of my mother. He was laying her. He must have been telling her not to move. She—she must be saying not to—hurt—not to hurt her. My mother looked at me. Her eyes were real big. She showed my father that I was looking at her. He looked at me. He looked so mad. He was mad because I was looking. When he got off I could see—everything. I was afraid of him. My mother jumped up and picked me up and held me close. When I was sitting in my highchair and he came in he looked mad. He looked as if he was going to hit me—with—something—big and—long and round like his hand and arm, maybe his—penis. She was right there and she was talking to my father. I guess she quieted everything down. I was afraid that morning. O, he looked mad! His black eyes were shining. I guess he wanted to hit me. When I saw him get off my mother he looked like an animal. I thought his penis might bite me. I—I was afraid of him. But his eyes looked—funny. They were—shining. He was young. He talked in Polish to me all the time.

Sometimes, when my mother put me on her lap, he'd hold me for a minute or two and then he'd say to her (if she was busy or not), "Here; take him. I don't want him." He never wanted me around.

I always used to sleep close to my mother. I wasn't afraid of my mother. I was always afraid of my father. He was so—strong. I always was afraid of him. When I saw his penis it was so—big, so big—like an arm—big—and round—and long, like a crowbar or a stick. I guess I was afraid of getting a beating with it, hit over the head with it. I don't know. I used to get spankings for crying.

I used to sit in my highchair, with the spoon . . . I could see his face. It looks like the lines were cut deep in his cheek and the eyes so shiny. I was afraid. He is talking to me. I can see he . . . I don't understand what he is saying. I'm afraid of him. His hair is funny. It is slicked down on his head. And his eyes, they look all lit up. And the cuts in his cheek, his nose sticks way out, and his ears are funny. I don't know what he is saying. I'm afraid of him. My mother is standing right there. I can't see anything but him. He is talking to me but I can't understand what he is saying. My mother is standing right there, working at the stove. She is cooking something. I'm afraid. My mother . . . My mother is looking at me. She looks nice. She hasn't got cuts in her cheek. She is talking to me. I understand her, not her words, but what she means. She is saying, "My little baby." I'm afraid of my father. My mother is afraid of him too. She is standing there. Nothing is happening to her.

She told him to stop bothering me. He just sits in his chair. She is bringing him a cup. He is starting to eat. He stops bothering me. He gives me a piece of bread. He holds his hand up to give me a piece of bread. I don't want it from him. I don't want to take it from him. I push it back with my hand. The light seems to be gone. It is getting dim. The cuts on his cheeks are smoothing out. His face seems to be getting straighter. There are little bits of lights in his eyes, a little ray of light. My mother, she is walking around. Everything looks alright. She is not saying anything to him. He don't offer me anything to eat no more. My mother is standing up at the stove. She is making something. They're flat and round. I guess they are pancakes. She is frying more. She is sitting down at the table opposite him, right next to me. She is giving me some—milk or something to drink in a cup. It looks white—white. I'm afraid now to take it from my mother. But my mother feels alright; there is nothing wrong with her. She seems alright. So I take it. I don't know; everything is ... I don't know what's the matter. ⸱ I can see my father. There is still a light in his eyes. It is coming right at

This whole episode was delivered in a loud, shrill and hysterical voice.

me, two little darts coming right at me. Before they were bright, now they are smaller. My mother—there are no lights in my mother. It's—my mother's eyes look as if there were holes in them. For some reason the light is going through the holes in my mothers eyes. It seems to fit in there, the light—in my mother's eyes. My eyes are open. I don't know if there are holes in them or not. It looks to me ... The light goes right in my mother's eyes, from my father to my mother. The lights start getting bigger. I guess that's what ... The light goes to my mother's eyes. He—he's—hurting my mother. I see my father's face getting cut up again. The lines are getting deeper, the nose is sticking out. Then he—my mother is talking to him. He is talking with her. Everything seems alright. I imagine I'm not afraid. The light is going. I can see my father's eyes, both of them. The light is coming at me now. It's going at my mother. It's cut off. My mother is sitting there. The light is going right in her. I don't know what's the trouble. She looks at me. She gives me something to eat. I can't ... She is trying to force my mouth open to eat. My father looks at me. I can't get out of the way. He turns back to my mother. He says something like, "Don't give him nothing to eat." My mother says, "Keep quiet." I can see the cuts on his face, cut up like a *dog's* face. He is looking at my mother. I guess he is hurting my mother. I don't know. The lights seem to be going in one ear and one eye—but—I don't know—what that is. I can't see anything else. O, O, everything else is disappearing. It looks like something . . . Everything is black, blacker. The lights are moving in two rays. They're missing me. They're in front of me. I want—I want to go to her. It's black: I see nothing. I see only the highchair I'm sitting in . . . the top of it and the flat table, the beads and these two lights. Everything else is black—black. The lights are shining over on me, on my mother. I don't know what

During the description of the lights, Harold's head jerked from side to side as if he were actually avoiding brilliant shafts of light.

they are. They turned that time, straight at me. I missed one that time. I can't miss both of them. They're shining brightly. I can't get out of the way. They're standing steady, pointing at me. I don't know what they are. They're coming from where my father is sitting. Everything is black, only the two lights. They're like the headlights on an automobile, like two spotlights, like pin points, like flashlights, small rays projecting through the darkness. They're coming right at me. I can duck one, but one—it hits me. I don't know if it hurts or not. I—I'm afraid of it. I'm—holding my— hand up to my eyes. I'm holding my hand up to my face. I—I don't know what that light is. When I hold my head down one light only touches me a little bit. It seems to be right on my head. It seems to be coming right out of the darkness. I can't see anything. I don't know why everything is black, everything is black. I can't see my father: I can't see anything. I'm reaching, reaching. I'm afraid of that light. I don't know what it is. I can't even see my mother but—I—the lights—the lights—I can't seem to get out of the way. They shine right on me. I can't cut them off no way. I think they're from my father's eyes. It was not dark before. It's dark. I see the—like something coming right at you. Once in a while they just flash on. It hurts. I can feel it in the back of my brain, like somebody sticking a knife in my eye.

L: 'Harold; look carefully. Is the light coming from your father?'

It's all black.   Only the two lights coming from where my father is sitting.   There's something . . . His penis . . .

L: 'What is the source of the lights?'

They're coming out of his eyes.

L: 'Why are they coming from his eyes?'

When I was lying in the cradle . . . My father was on top of her. My mother looked at me and my father—looked at me.   My mother's eyes were so pitiful and—soft.   Then I looked at my father.   His eyes were so hard, like bright lights.   I saw the whites, the whites, looking right into my eyes, shining.   I don't know whether I am afraid of his eyes or his penis more.   They're mixed up.   His eyes— his penis.   Once in a while he catches my left eye.   He don't catch my right eye.   The left eye on the side toward the bed . . .

> *Once again routine tests were made to discover whether there had been any alteration in the depth of sleep.   It was found that Harold was still in a profound trance.   Additional instruction regarding the exclusion of extraneous noises was given before going further.*

L: 'Now, Harold, you can remember before that.   You are going back before that time.   You are a little baby.   You remember clearly.   What do you remember?'

I remember—about eight—no—six months old maybe.

> *The persistence of memories from the age of six or eight months is of course open to question.   It is controversial whether the neural organization is adequate to the retention of events.*
>
> *In hypnoanalysis the clinican can often utilize the motor behavior of his patient as a time-line and frame an approximation of the sequence of events in his patient's life by comparing motor behavior during a recital with motor norms such as Gesell has provided.   Harold performed—motorially— as one would expect an infant of almost one year to behave.   His movements were most unrefined, gross, and lacking in coordination.*
>
> *The writer personally believes that the events which Harold is describing took place during the first year of life.   He thinks that an event of enough significance and portent can be preserved memorially but not necessarily comprehended.   Harold is not telling us that he understood what was happening at the time.   He is telling us that he saw something which evoked in him a reaction of fear.*
>
> *Accumulated resistance to awareness of having witnessed the so-called primal scene must be quantitatively tremendous: but hypnoanalysis appears to be a weapon keen enough to penetrate to the core by sloughing off the accretions of years of eventful living as well as neutralizing the tenaciousness of an ego bent upon preserving the psychological status quo.*

There are also at least two additional considerations. Primary in importance is the fact that Harold believed these events to have transpired at this age: and, indeed, they could not have occurred very much later if the relationships of all other events in this recounting are to remain undisturbed. Finally, it must be recognized that language—after all—is the missing element. We do not doubt that a child of 6 or 8 months can see an action; we do not doubt that it can experience fear; and if the items with which we are dealing are as primitive, crucial and fundamental as modern dynamic psychology proclaims, we cannot deny some dim and tenuous apprehension—even to an infant—without holding up to question the entire scientific structure.

A very little baby. I have a bottle with a nipple on it. I was . . . Yes. My mother giving me one. My father is sitting there. His eyes have green in them but they are not shining. Six or seven months old. Old enough to hold a spoon. My mother feeding me. I'm all sloppy, all slopped up. I like spilling everything all around, get a kick out of getting all dirty, everything smeared all over my face. She . . . Then I am looking at the sky. The sun is shining. There is nothing wrong with me. The wind is blowing. I feel myself moving, moving. I guess somebody is pushing me. Once in a while I look at—wires or something. They must be wires to telephone poles. There is a little jar—and a bump—bump. It feels nice. Things are rolling by. I'm not watching anything in particular. I know! I'm in the carriage. Sometimes I can see—people, looking over the carriage, looking at me. I can't make them out. The sky is all lit up. The people looking at me and the sky bright behind them. I can see the shape of their heads and their hats but I can't make them out. They seem different. I'm on my back looking up at them, that's why I can't make them out. They're not clear. They're all blurred up, far away. A woman's hat . . . A man's hat . . . I can't see their faces; can't tell who they are. They're looking at me.

L: '*Harold; look closely. Is there anything wrong with your eyes?*'

People seem—seem blurred to me. It's my—my—belt, the belt that holds me in the carriage . . .

L: '*Are your eyes winking?*'

I—don't know whether they are blinking. I can't feel that they are . . . I don't know. I see the wires.

L: '*Did this happen before or after you saw your parents having intercourse?*'

It happened after . . . because I can still remember about my—father. I could still remember. I can still remember. I can still . . .

L: 'Can you remember anything that happened before you saw your parents having intercourse?'

I can see something—but . . . I guess I'm sitting on my mother's lap—and I'm looking out the window. There are two—cars—in the street. They hit each other. They make a big pile on top of each other. People are all around. They hit like that. I was sitting on my mother's lap in the window there, looking out of the window.

L: 'Are your eyes winking?'

No. No! the winking came after. It came after they were—that morning—bed—they—my father—on top . . .

L: 'Harold, listen to what I ask you, then answer. Have you always been afraid of your father's penis? Have you been afraid since that morning?'

Yes. I—Yes. I see—him when he gets up from my mother. I am afraid. Oooo, I am afraid. When he gets off my mother she comes and picks me up. I can still see him. I—when he gets off my mother—I don't want to look at it. It's big—big. Something forces me to look at him. I can see it. I'm afraid . . .

L: 'Do you remember when you had intercourse with your sister? Do you remember that?'

Yes. We were living on B——— Street. We were sleeping in the same cradle together. My sister slept in the cradle and I slept in the parlor on a small bed. In the afternoons we took our naps and I slept in the cradle with her. We wanted to be together. Sometimes we'd get in the big bed and have pillow fights. My mother would holler at us and put us in the cradle. We were close together. I played with her, put my arms around her. She played—with—my peter. We had—intercourse. I—we—were too big to fit in the cradle. It was so small. We were so close together—like that—and we had intercourse and then we'd go to sleep . . .

L: 'Did your mother ever find you having intercourse with your sister?'

No; she never caught us.

L: 'Did your father?'

No . . .

L: 'Do you remember when your father threatened to have Nellie bite your penis off?'

Yes. He brought the dog home. A good pet. I didn't want to

eat. We had some green stuff and I didn't like it. He said, "If you don't watch out I'll have the dog bite your penis off."

L: 'What is the Polish word he used for penis?

Pipsha . . .

L: 'Do you remember the man who called you a lying mother—f——r?'

Yes . . .

L: 'Why did you wish to hurt him?'

If I had him again, I'd do it again. I'd stab him again. He called me a lot of names, lying mother—f——r, c——s——, names like that.

L: 'Why, Harold?'

We were playing pool. He was at the next table. When I pulled the stick back to make a shot I hit him on the elbow. I hit him real hard. He looked at me. Everything was real dark in the poolroom, except for the lights above the table. Then he said, "Why don't you watch what you're doing?" And then he called me lots of dirty names. I said I was sorry when I hit him. I guess I spoiled his shot. They said he was a tough guy. He's not any more. I didn't pay any attention to what names he called me until I got home. I started to think, why did he have to call me the things he did? He thought he was tough. He could call me all the names he wanted to and get away with it. I started agitating myself. I never had anything to do like that with my mother. I can't even think about a thing like that. I slept with my mother a lot, even when I was fifteen, but I never had anything to do with her. I would never even touch her. I don't know why he said that. I was—in a daze for about a week. Then I was going to show him that he wasn't going to call me that again. He'd never call anybody that again. He was tough. He had a gun on him. We used to play cards and he'd cheat. Sometimes he'd cheat me. He was tough alright. He spent a lot of time in the jail house. I guess he was tough, tough. He—wasn't—very tough. One day I caught him on the street. I pulled a hunting knife that I stole from my father and stabbed him, stuck him with the knife. He fell. I ran. I didn't look back. I was scared a long time after that. I kept running away from myself. Every time somebody would go past I would be scared.

L: 'Harold. Did this man resemble anyone you know now or knew then?'

He looked—more like—my father—than anyone else. He was strong. He had a big chest. He was tough. He could have picked me up and dropped me on the floor. I guess when he called me a mother—f——r there was nothing to it. He was tough. I guess he was going to show everybody how tough he was.

L: *'When you did that, Harold, with whom were you getting even?'*

Getting even? I guess maybe I was getting even with my father, in a way. I agitated myself for about two weeks. I was like in a daze. When I came home at nights my father would be arguing with my mother and calling her names. Calling her names. It agitated me more. Yes; I was getting even with my father. One time when he pushed my mother down I grabbed the poker. I didn't see anything in the room but him . . .

L: *'Now, Harold, I want you just to sleep, sleep deeply, a deep refreshing sleep. When you awaken you will have forgotten all the things you have told me; forgotten everything. You are forgetting now. You have forgotten already. Have you told me anything, Harold?'*

Tell you—I . . . Why, no—I don't—I forget—I . . .

L: *'That's right. You have forgotten. And when you wake up you will tell me that you have had a good rest, that you are feeling fine for having had a good sleep. You will not recall that you have told me anything at all. Now you will awaken. One—two—three . . .'*

O, I must have . . . I've been asleep. I had a good sleep . . .

The Thirty-seventh Hour

L: *'Harold, what do you remember about yesterday?'*

I don't know. All I know is you burned my hand. Here. I know I didn't have that yesterday when I came here, and I know you've burned my hand before, so you get the blame for this too.

> *The burning of the dorsal surface of the hand was one of the routine tests for depth of trance. It was done with a live cigarette.*

L: *'Does it hurt?'*

O, no . . .

L: *'Is there anything else you remember?'*

About yesterday? All I remember is looking at your ring. I fell asleep. You put me to sleep. All I could see was the R. L. on the ring.

L: 'All right, Harold. Let us go ahead as usual.'

Everything seems so black. I can't see anything. Let's see. It's a little blurred. I spent three years up at my aunt's place, but only in the summer time. I don't remember much about it. I guess I went fishing and I'd go up in the woods and stay there all day. When I got back sometimes I'd get hell for not working. When I wanted to go away I just went away. I didn't care if anybody liked it; I didn't care whether I asked permission. I just went. I thought I didn't have to ask permission. I thought I was old enough to think for myself. I did everything because I wanted to do it. When I wanted to go out at night sometimes I would ask my mother, but if she wouldn't let me I'd go anyway. So when I'd come home she'd be waiting for me and I'd get a bawling out. "Wait until the morning and I'll talk to you then." But when the morning came she'd wake me up and tell me, "Don't do it again;" and she'd scold me a bit. I didn't pay much attention to her. Sometimes she'd beg me to stay in at least once a week anyway but I just couldn't stay around. I'd read trash most of the day and at night I wanted to go out.

We used to be just a gang of mischievous kids when I was around thirteen or fourteen. Some nights when we had nothing to do we would cut clothes-lines that people had in back of their houses, and then in the daytime we'd go around to hear the women curse. I used to get a kick out of that. We'd steal everything, clothes-lines, newspapers, magazines. We'd go with our bicycles to the paper mills and steal magazines there. I would take them home and read them. Those I took home were mostly detective magazines and crime stories. Once we broke into a butcher store. We took everything out of that store, everything but the cash register and the scales. I got caught— there were three or four other fellows with me—and we went up in front of the Judge. He gave me three years probation. The other kids got one year. The reason I got more was my trying to escape. We went to see a probation officer or someone and they took us in a car, three of us in one car and three in another. When we got there another fellow and myself went to the toilet and we opened the window and jumped out on the roof of another building and I jumped down to the ground, into a yard. I thought the other fellow was following behind me, but for some reason he didn't come along. I jumped over a fence and started running through an alley. There was a big dog there and he started barking after me: he wanted to bite me.   So I jumped over another fence and into another alley and kept going until I came to the street.   I don't remember clearly what happened.   I had my prison clothing on and so I got picked up by a cop.   He took me back.   I got me a year for that.

I never stole a car in my life but I rode in a lot of them.   I mean actually take one from the street and drive it away.   We drove them until they were out of gas, until the gas tank was empty, then we'd leave it where it stopped.   One time I left a car, a stolen car, near my cousin Joe's house.   I told him I left the car there and he didn't like the idea of my putting a stolen car right in front of his house because he had been in the reformatory and different prisons and he thought the police might make some connection.   When I came here he was doing time for holding up a truck with hardware.   I guess the whole load must have been worth between a thousand and two thousand dollars.   He got caught but the other fellows with him got away. Joe, he always seemed broke, but I always had a feeling that he had money hidden away.   I remember one time he pulled a roll out of his pocket.   It was about one inch in diameter and there was a twenty-dollar bill on top.   I guess he stole it somewhere.   He'd gamble a lot, gamble and let his wife and kid go hungry, gamble everything away.

We played pool a lot, and cards when we didn't have anything to do.   When we had no money and wanted to buy whiskey or go to the show we'd get in a card game and cheat if necessary.   That way we'd get five or six dollars and then we'd get drunk.   Riggs would do the cheating most of the time.   One time I actually caught him cheating. We were playing pinochle and he cheated me out of a dollar or so. But that was nothing.

O, I don't know . . . I used to get so sick of everything when I was on the outside.   I'd leave home whenever I felt like it, then I'd come back.   I didn't like to ride freight trains though.   Too dirty, too many bums on them.   I'd go hitch-hiking or catch a hitch on a truck.

L: 'Harold, if you had caught your cousin cheating, what would you have done?'

O, the gun was just to scare him.   I don't think I would have shot; there were too many people around.   The other fellows, the fellows we were playing with, they had guns on them and they didn't like the idea of my putting my gun on the table. I just wanted to show him that he couldn't cheat. I wouldn't have shot him in front of everybody. I guess he was alright but I should have known better, even when I was going to High School, than to hang around with him. One time I broke into a house and stole six dollars and I told him about it. We had a good time for about two weeks on it and I had one dollar left, so I hid it away. When I came afterwards to look for it, it was gone. He was the only one who knew about it. I always felt that he had stole it from me. I never had any direct proof that he did steal it; he never admitted it to me. He repaid me that dollar many times over, though, in giving me money when we went to the show. When I had money I would take him, and when he had money he would buy.

A kid named Skinny hung around with us. One time when I was going with Lila he wanted me to bring her around. Whenever one of those guys wanted her and when I didn't want to, he said, "That's right; keep it all to yourself." If I had gotten into a fight with him I would have killed him.

L: 'Why?'

I hate to fight with people. I hate to get hurt. I like to get them on the floor and hit their head on the floor. I don't hate them enough so I would purposely kill them; I just think I want to save myself. I'm not afraid if I know there's trouble and that I have to fight. It just comes if it comes. I hate to get the worst of it and I never got the worst of it. When I was about sixteen or seventeen I got in a fight with a big kid. He weighed about fifty pounds more than I did. And I was really afraid of him. The reason was that he said something about my sister so I went to pick a fight with him and when I started to fight I was afraid of him. I bumped into him; we both fell down; he grabbed me around the neck and I turned and he fell and hit the steps of the porch with his head. I just forgot everything until somebody pulled us apart. I started cursing him. I wanted to get him off from where we were fighting so I cursed him out and told him to get off the property. When we went off I was afraid and so I sic-ed the dog on him. He called me a yellow bastard. I put my hands down and ran right into him and hit him in the chest with my shoulder. I was standing on the porch talking to this kid that told me what he had said about my sister; so he denied saying anything about my sister. I was on the porch steps about one step higher than he was, and when he denied that he said it and the kid said it was true that he did say it, I just forgot everything.

L: 'What did he say about your sister?'

He said that she was in bed with a kid named Fred. It wasn't true. Fred was such a shy and bashful kid. My sister used to tease him, put her arms around him and kiss him. Whether it was true or not he had no business telling it. Why should it come back to me? Why should he say it to people that know me and bring it back to me? Besides, he was trying to make my girl, and that was another reason.

L: 'Each time you went up to your aunt's place, isn't it true that you went there to run away from yourself?'

I was up there three years. When I quit school, that was my excuse and all winter I hung around and didn't do anything. I went up again the next year. I was doing nothing but drink, drink, drink. I got sick of it, sick of everything; so I went up there and stayed all summer. When I got back I was just hanging around and—so—I went up again. I went up there and stayed a couple months. When I came back I guess I didn't know what to do. I did six months for something and I came out of the jail in April. I stayed around for a few months. I was doing alright. I got a little money but I had to go away, go up there, to get away from everything. I wanted to get away. It got so—monotonous. I went up there and stayed until January. When I came back things went wrong for about a year. I just got a little money here and there and for about a year everything went from bad to worse, bad then good again and bad once more. I didn't care what happened. I got sick of everything, just sick of living. When I was up there I was looking for a few places in S——; some places we might hold up in that town. I got two fellows from around home that were going to do the jobs with me. I went up to S—— alone and stopped at the R—— Hotel and after three days I sent a telegram to these fellows to come up. I got sick of just sitting around drinking and I tried to read, read anything; but I'd always see this gun that I laid on the dresser, and something kept telling me to shoot myself . . .

L: 'Was this after or before . . . '

It was after my little—accident . . .

L: 'After your accident? As a matter of fact, Harold, that was why you went to your aunt's place, was it not?'

I guess so. I guess so. I just wanted to get away from people, or maybe better to get away from me, from Harold, because every place I went I found myself there. I always seemed to be with myself. I couldn't get away from myself. When I'd look in the mirror I'd see myself, I mean really see myself—not just what was looking back at me. After three or four months up there I guess everything started to go better and things began to smooth out. So I started casing for some places where I could get some money. I went to different places and wound up at S——— in that hotel.

I saw the gun. I kept seeing that gun on the bureau for about three days. I couldn't . . . I bought some whiskey but I couldn't even drink it. Everytime I was reading the newspapers, reading the funnies, it would be there. I don't know why I didn't hide it. It always seemed to be staring me in the face and something kept telling me, "Shoot yourself! Shoot yourself!" I'd try to fight these thoughts, but I know if I'd stayed there a little longer I would have shot myself.

Then one time somebody knocked on the door. It was the maid. She was coming in to change the towels and she saw the gun on the dresser. I tried to pick it up and put it in my pocket, real quick. I checked out of the hotel right away. She didn't say anything, but I know she saw it. I went to the railroad station and took the first train out of there. I went about four stations then stopped and got off the train. Then I waited about two or three hours for another train. Before I got to the train the second time I threw the gun away. It was so heavy in my pocket. I wanted to pull it out and shoot all the bullets out of it but I threw it away. I didn't want it anymore. I went back on the train. Both of the other fellows went up there the next day. When they came back they wanted to know what was the matter. I just told them something went wrong. I didn't tell them that I threw the gun away, that I was afraid of it. I stopped at this town, about four stations below S———, and got off the train. I was afraid maybe the maid told the cops something. I passed three stations and got off. I left my suitcase in the station and walked around the town. It was January and there was snow on the ground. I walked along this country road. The gun was in my left-hand hip pocket. It was so heavy, heavy, heavy. I walked about three or four miles. I finally woke up. I didn't know where I was but I knew which way I was walking. I was afraid. It was so heavy. I wanted to pull it out and shoot all the bullets out of it. I threw it away and walked back to the railroad station. . . .

When I was hanging around for a year after that I pulled a few hold-ups and got some money. I carried a gun then but I never had the feeling I wanted to shoot myself again. I used to think about it and when I'd think about it I'd force the thoughts out of my mind. I'd say to myself I was crazy.

L: 'Is that the only time you ever thought of committing suicide?'

No. It wasn't. The other time . . . About a month or so before I was arrested on this charge I was thinking that everything was going wrong and I had no money, so I started talking to some of the guys I was hanging around with and we pulled some hold-ups together. But, I don't know; one was married, the other two didn't like the idea, and so the whole thing fell through.

Once in a while, when I was carrying a gun, I would think of that time up in S———, in the hotel, and I'd try to force it out of my mind. I figured I didn't want to shoot myself. If I was going to die, I'd die an easier way. If somebody would shoot me, o.k. But I felt that I wanted to go to sleep and never wake up. I kept thinking about my father's garage. I was going to go in there and close the doors from the inside and start the motor; make sure that there was enough gas in the tank for running it about five or six hours. I don't know why I didn't want to do it. I just never got around to it, I guess. Things started popping. Some guy made a connection to buy a machine gun and there was a chance to hold up a bank and get enough money to leave the country. One day I wanted to go in the garage and start the car, then I'd set the date ahead to the next Tuesday. Tuesday would come and something would happen. One time about eight in the morning a fellow came over and told my mother he wanted to see me. I guess my mother figured it was about a job or something. This fellow, I guess he felt bad, so we went out and got drunk; so I didn't do it then. I was going to wait until Thursday that time, but when Thursday came I had to do something around the house. I never got around to it. Then I was figuring maybe I'd get that machine gun and we'd hold up a bank or maybe a couple armed guards on those armored trucks. I always wanted to do that. They have guns but you can't see them, you know what they got, and you see the bags of money. It seemed easy. Sometimes they'd walk forty or fifty feet from the truck, and you know they wouldn't do anything with a machine gun pointed at them, even if they had guns. But I always thought about going into the garage. I knew the carbon monoxide would kill me. I'd set it a day ahead and then when the time come I'd change it. I'd say to myself, "Wait a few days more, something will happen." And when the next day came I'd want to wait a few more days.

I was in the garage one time to get a file or a hacksaw to cut a shotgun barrel and the car was standing there. Everything was so quiet; it didn't make any noise. The door was shut. I got afraid when I was in there so I just left the hacksaw and ran out and closed the door with a bang. I know one thing: I ran out of there so fast that I slammed the lock on the door. I put the keys in my pocket and I looked back. I was afraid of staying in there. You see, I always felt that something would happen, something would come up, and I'd get a few thousand dollars, enough to leave. I never got the few thousand. I don't know why I was afraid of that car when I went in there. My father had a bench at one end of the garage and the car was at the other end. I started looking around the bench. He had a small mirror there and I didn't like to look at the mirror. I don't know whether I looked in it or not. Then I turned around and saw the car. Everything was so quiet. I became conscious of the car. Everything was so quiet and peaceful. It wasn't very dark, a little light was coming in through the door. I looked at the car and ran out and closed the door real fast, slamming the lock. I didn't want to go back there anymore. I don't think I've been in the garage since then. I'm afraid of the car. It seemed to me like a monster then.

I don't know what to say. It seems—every day—I just pushed the day away. That's the only two times I ever wanted to kill myself. I was afraid both times. I believe in my own mind that someday I might die by my own hands. I might live long—but—when I die— I think—I'll kill myself. That's the way I'll die, or at least I imagine that's the way I'll die.

I tried to read a newspaper and everything but I couldn't get interested. I couldn't even read the funnies. I couldn't drink the whiskey. I always saw that gun. If the maid hadn't come in I might have shot myself. It was a small gun. It wouldn't have hurt me much: I wouldn't have felt it much. A small gun. I could almost hide it in the palm of my hand. It would fit in my vest pocket. It was just a little gun. I paid ten dollars for it. It wouldn't have hurt me if I didn't want it to. When I was walking on that road it felt so heavy, heavy, heavy: it felt as if it weighed ten pounds in my pocket. I—it was cold. I didn't feel the cold. I guess there was snow in my shoes—but—I—I—my feet felt as if they were on a hot plate. The cold must have been stinging them. When I was walking along—walking—walking—walking—the gun—so heavy—so heavy. I stopped. I—I didn't know—what—what was going on. I was afraid of the gun. I didn't know what to do. I wanted to give away all the bullets in the gun. I took it out of my pocket and flung it away. I don't know where it landed. It landed in the snow some-where. I knew what I was doing then. I threw the gun away. Then I started walking fast. I walked for an hour, an hour or more, and when I got back to the station I took my shoes off and shook the snow out of them and got on the train and went home . . .

I knew how cold it was; but when I was walking away from the station I didn't feel the cold. Only when I was coming back. Only when I was coming back . . .

The Thirty-eighth Hour

It's pretty hard for me to think of a lot of the things I have missed. There's a lot of things I forgot completely. Yesterday was one of those times. You make me talk about things I forgot I even knew. My mind seems up against a stone wall. It's hard for me to put my-self in a position in the past: like walking along the road and throwing the gun away. I guess I forgot about that almost completely. That's a long time ago. . . .

I had a funny dream yesterday. I dreamed my sister married to some fellow, he was one of these jitterbugs, always dancing and sing-ing. He was supposed to go to Hollywood and get a job as a music director in the movies, and he couldn't make the choice between going to Hollywood or marrying my sister. My sister looked differ-ent, older. This fellow—I can't seem to place him anywhere—this fellow seemed torn between my sister and going to Hollywood for this job. He didn't know which to take. The meaning of this is do what you want to do. Or it may mean something else . . .

L: *'Whom would this person represent?'*

He was a good-looking fellow. Well-built. His clothes were the typical jitterbug type. I was trying to talk him into writing some music instead of trying to be a music director or orchestra leader. That way he could do the thing he wanted to do and marry my sister too. I can't place the fellow. The way I wanted it he could stay married to my sister. I—O—I see. The fellow represents me. My sister—that's this treatment. He wanted—I wanted to give it up, but there is a way of doing both. Or maybe my sister, she represents what's wrong with me and I don't want to know it? I kept impressing on this fellow to stay where he was. He could still write music. I think I see. It was what you said was a resistance dream? Here I am in a position where I am going under treatment and something interferes with my treatment. For the last few times I have been in that position. Now I have to make up my mind whether I am going to continue under conditions where that—that incident—that accident will be talked about. Does that seem right? Are you willing to accept that interpretation, Doc?

L: 'Alright, Harold. Go ahead.'

Well, the girl in the dream seemed so different. She looked the same as my sister but she acted different. My sister is kind of dizzy: this girl was older and my sister doesn't act like that, so serious. O, she is a very fine girl; very pretty, about twenty now and working, making about thirty dollars a week. I think she is doing all right. She never said anything about getting married to anyone when she saw me. She doesn't go out with anyone steadily. We always got along. Of course we had some fights when we were small. One time I brought Lila to the house. I met Lila on the street and took her home. When I opened the door I left the key in the lock. We came in and I closed the door. We were in there about an hour. We got some beer out of the icebox and I guess we were making love. My sister came home and she found the key in the door. She couldn't open the door so she got mad. After about an hour I opened the door and let her in. She saw Lila there and she was real mad. "After all, what is the idea of locking me out? I've got some rights here: I live here, don't I?" We didn't argue about it but she sure kidded me. She used to say that I was picking the ugliest girls. She liked me though. We'd go to shows together and some nights we'd go out. Many times when I needed a little money she'd loan me a dollar or two. She'd give it to me and never ask it back. She never got it back. When I was about twelve or thirteen I used to have a lot of blank checks and dice and things like that in my drawer. She'd search for these things and give them to my mother. I got a lot of beatings for it, so finally I started hiding things, scattering them all around so she couldn't find them altogether. But she'd search everything. She didn't want me to keep it. She'd tell my mother if I went in swimming when I wasn't supposed to. I couldn't keep her quiet on anything. She'd just run and tell my mother. I know she's a good girl all the way through. I remember all the ways back when she started to walk. She looked funny. I tried to help her but she'd sit on the floor and cry when I bothered her too much. My father used to pet her a lot when she was young. She was just like a little wild cat: she'd scratch and pull out everybody's hair. Later she didn't like the idea of my going with girls. She had a girl friend she wanted me to go out with but I never liked her girl friends. She always insinuated that her girl friends were better than anyone I could find. She liked this girl Amy, the one up at my aunt's place. My mother liked her a lot too.

When I was younger I used to get in different moods. I'm not that way anymore; at least since I started this treatment. When I got in that kind of mood I didn't want to talk to anybody, sometimes maybe for a week. I'd agitate myself and keep in that mood. I wouldn't even talk to my mother or my sister, and when she'd say something to me I'd just ignore her. Then she'd get mad and remind me of my mood.

One time I went away and stayed away for about three weeks. When I came back one night I didn't go home. I went to my grandmother's and slept there. I didn't want my father to see me coming home so I waited here until he went to work. Then I left my grandmother's house and met my sister on the street. She was waiting for a bus and she gave me hell right in front of everybody. She was hollering at me for staying away. I didn't say much to her. I just asked her if my mother was well and if everything was good at home. When my father came home that night he gave me such a look ... I didn't like that look. I just didn't like to be around my father. He works so hard. I guess I don't blame him. If a man works hard and has a son old enough to work who doesn't want to work ... He didn't even like for my sister to buy clothes for herself. If she bought a dress or so for ten or fifteen dollars he was mad if she told him the right amount. If she said it cost two or three dollars then it was o.k. They always had to lie to him. My mother always lied to him. When she bought something she always said that it was cheaper than the real price she paid for it to avoid arguments. Sometimes he'd find the sales-slip with the price marked on it. Then he'd really holler! Why did she have to lie to him? and things like that. . . .

L: 'Harold do you feel that your father's attitude was the same to the rest of the family as it was toward you?'

He used to talk to everyone else more than to me. I didn't see him much the last few years. Every time my little sister Anna came home from school she'd play on the street and she'd wait for my father to come home from work. Then he'd play with her all night. My oldest sister didn't pay any attention to him. She told him a number of times to shut up.

L: 'Did you ever say that to him?'

No, sir! O, no. I never said that to him. He'd really kill me then.

L: 'Did you ever steal anything from your father?'

Only a pen knife, I think. That's the only thing I can remember.

L: 'A pen knife?'

Yes. He had three or four pen knives in the garage. He used to keep them in the garage where he had a big bunch of tools. The pen knives were lying around there so I took one of them. He knew it was missing so, if I remember this right, he looked through my drawers and found it, and he started hollering at me, "Why the hell don't you leave your hands off my things?"

L: 'Was there any special reason why you wanted to take a pen knife from your father?'

No. There were three or four of them there. I—I wanted—I wanted it to cut some wood . . .

L: 'One time you took his razor, did you not?'

Yes. He really gave me a beating that time.

L: 'Did you ever steal any money from your father?'

No; but I used to steal quite a bit from my mother. Sometimes when I was broke I'd steal maybe as much as five dollars. My mother wouldn't say anything. I'd give it back to her. I only owe my mother about twenty dollars altogether. I wouldn't care if it was my mother's last five dollars; I'd steal it all when I wanted to get away, even her last dollar.

L: 'Did you ever take money from your mother and use it to buy a gun?'

Yes. One time I took eight dollars from her and bought a gun. Three days later I put it back. I guess she was madder when I put it back than when I took it in the first place, because she thought I must have stolen it.

L: 'In that accident of yours, Harold, did you use a gun or a knife?'

A gun would have made too much noise. I don't know—why I was . . . I used the knife. It's quick and just as effective as a gun. It didn't make too much noise—and—well . . . I didn't use my gun.

L: 'Where did you get the knife?'

It was a hunting knife. I'd had it for a long time. I guess I stole it from my father. I remember one time I stole a lot of stuff from the garage and somehow or other this hunting knife was among them. I liked it: it had a leather sheath. It cost only a dollar or so. I kept it and when I'd go up to my aunt's house I'd take it out there with me. I'd practice to throw it, make it stick in a tree. It was a good knife, healthy, well put together, sturdy. I didn't want to use the gun. The gun would have made too much noise. I didn't like to make too much noise. It had nothing to do with my taking his pen knife. He always had them around. He used to cut leather patches with it, patches for his tubes and tires and things. I just took one. I took the best one I guess. He was sore about it. I remember when I took his razor blade. It was a straight razor. I wanted to find out how sharp it was. I was about eight or nine. I remember it as if it was yesterday.

L: 'Harold; now think carefully. This hunting knife, when you got it did you ever intend to use it for anything? Did you ever make any particular plans for its use?'

No, I didn't. It—I took it when I was about thirteen and I kept it around the house. When I left school and went up to my aunt's house I took some things that might come handy on the farm.

L: 'And you never planned to use the knife on anyone?'

No; I never did. No. No. I don't think I would ever use it on my father. I don't think so. I wouldn't have done a thing like that. That way the whole responsibility of the family would fall on me.

L: 'Did you ever think about that?'

Maybe I did, and maybe I didn't. I guess—I guess—I planned—one time—I planned on getting rid of my father, but I couldn't bring myself to do it. I was thinking of my mother and my sisters. I would have done it without their knowing it but I didn't want the responsibility of the whole family falling on me. Even if *I* didn't like him, my mother must have for some reason or she wouldn't have lived with him. She intended leaving him several times and taking us kids with her. But I couldn't bring myself to do anything to interfere with the security of my mother and sisters.

L: 'What was your plan, Harold?'

I was going to buy a big rifle with a telescope sight and a silencer on it—that would run to about fifty or sixty bucks—and go somewhere out of the city. I'd get out in one of the suburbs somewhere and fix this gun up and then shoot one or two people: first I was going to shoot one in one part of the city, and then another one in another part, an entirely different part. I'd shoot several people, and the third person I'd shoot would be my father. In that way I'd cover myself up so that nobody would know. I'd file the barrel out—you have to file the barrel out—so that nobody would be able to tell that the bullet came from it . . . .

L: 'Who were the other two people to be?'

O, just anybody . . . Just to cover up, you see.

L: 'How would that cover it up?'

Well, when somebody would get shot, and then somebody else, there would be no connection between the three of them; there would be no connection between me and the other two, and no connection with my father. He wouldn't know these people and nobody would tell why; they wouldn't even know themselves.

L: 'When did you think about it?'

I was about seventeen or eighteen then. I just couldn't do it, even if he was mean to me. That was nothing. I didn't care. He kept my mother and my sisters . . . This is not a pleasant thing to tell you. I wouldn't hurt my father now.

L: 'Was this plan inspired by any special or particular occasion?'

I don't remember much about it. I don't know whether my father disliked me more, or whether I disliked him more. I just couldn't stand being in the same house with him. That was one reason why

I'd leave home and do a lot of things to get away from everything. But I don't know . . . When I got arrested for stealing once it got into the newspapers and my mother destroyed the page it was on so he wouldn't see it. Somebody stopped my father on the street and told him about it. When he came home he talked about it with my mother and she said she knew nothing of it. She said she thought it was just that I had by some way violated a probation. He really gave me a beating that time. When I came out of jail after eight months and came home he gave me another beating for going around and stealing things. He was mad. He hollered at me, "Get a job or get the hell out of the house!" So I went up to my aunt's.

L: 'Was that when you conceived the plan of doing away with your father?'

Yes. I forgot. I even forgot about this plan. I don't even know how old I was when I had it. It was the time after I got out of a jail and got a beating for it. I stayed around home for a while and then went up to my aunt's place.

L: 'That must have been around the time your accident occurred.'

Yes. I guess it was about that time. I don't know . . . About two weeks after I got out of jail that time everything was upside down. I didn't know why I was there, what I was doing there, at home, in the whole world, everywhere. Everything was wrong. To please my mother—she was asking me to stay at home nights—I stayed at home. My father was home and he saw me. And he'd blame her, start a lot of those arguments. Two weeks after I got out I thought I just couldn't stand it. I couldn't control myself. I hated him. I wanted to get rid of him. Then I started thinking, after all he . . . I hated him enough to get rid of him, still I liked my mother and my sisters. My sister was working but the little one was going to school. Even though he picked on me . . . The reason he picked on me was that I didn't want to work. I started stealing things. But I don't know . . . If he was somebody else then maybe I would have carried out my plan . . .

L: 'As a matter of fact, Harold, you did carry out your plan, didn't you?'

Nooo . . . My father is still living. I never shot anybody with a rifle. I don't know what . . . I—then—I—started drinking. I—I forgot everything. He—he called me a—a lying mother-f——r.

For no reason. I started to agitate myself. It agitated me, but I could have stopped it if I wanted to. It just—just happened. I didn't see . . .

L: 'Why should what the man called you have agitated you so much?'

Why—I—told you. You have me in a funny position here. I—I don't know what to say.

L: 'Why?'

I don't know . . . I—I—why—when I was outside sometimes when I used to feel like I do now I would want to forget about everything so I'd go away for two or three weeks—but—here—I can't go away from here. I have to stay here. I—I feel—so—uncomfortable. I guess I am afraid.

L: 'Afraid of what?'

I don't know. Afraid of myself I guess. You can say anything you want to. I'm more afraid of you than you are . . . O, I won't hurt you. I'll never tell anybody. I'll never even admit to myself that I told you this. I wanted to change something and I changed it: I went away. Here I can't change it. I was going to forget about it as quickly as possible. But now I'll go through with it. This fellow, I guess I hit him accidently, with a cue stick. We were playing pool and I drew the stick back real quick and hit him in the elbow. He turned around and started cursing me. I said I was sorry. There was no reason for cursing me. I didn't pay much attention to it at the time. Then I got started thinking about it. My father used to curse me out; even when I said I was sorry when I did something he'd still curse me. Maybe he appeared to me—O—O . . . Yes; the fellow reminded me of my father in many ways. Yes; he did. I see . . . If he said what he said and then told me he was sorry I wouldn't have . . . My father did things like that. One time I called him to eat. He wanted to hit me with a hammer. I don't know what I said to make him mad. I said I was sorry. He started cursing me. I didn't know what to do. I just went away. He went home and told my mother about it. He told her something or other—and—when this fellow—he . . . When this fellow started cursing me I imagined that it was like when my father . . . I don't blame my father for this. If he had stopped when I said I was sorry . . . If my father hadn't . . . It would have been all right. He cursed me even after I said I was sorry. My father used to jump on me that way because I didn't have a job.   "Get work, you bum!"   He would call me a blind bum and a liar.   I don't know why I did it.   I couldn't help myself I guess.   I had forgotten about this plan.   The plan came back to me . . .

L: 'To dispose of this fellow in the same way?'

I came in here and I settled down and everything quieted down. I seemed to forget everything, even in here.   I know you would never say anything to anybody without consulting me, Doc.   If something happened to you . . .

L: 'Do you want something to happen to me?'

No.   No; but I'm worrying what's going to happen to you.

L: 'Now, Harold; you have already demonstrated to yourself how, in disposing of this man, you were in reality doing away with your father. The name he called you; why should it have made you feel that way? The reason, Harold, is the same reason why you hate your father.   And why did you hate your father?   Let us go back to B————.   What was the origin of your hate for your father?'

I—I . . . You know.   That—what—I saw . . . My mother and my father . . . He was—hurting—her.

L: 'You saw him having intercourse with your mother.   He was hurting your mother.   You knew he was hurting your mother.   Now this man was accusing you of doing the same thing your father had done, of hurting your mother, accusing you of wanting your mother.   The man reminded you of your father, whom you wished to get rid of, put out of the way, so that you could have your mother to yourself.   Even his looks reminded you of your father.   Is the picture beginning to clear?'

Yes; it is.   I see now . . .

L: 'I think you will find that this theme has been running through everything you have ever done, through your whole life.'

I see it does.   I can't say anything . . . I want to do—something I haven't done for a long time—and that's—cry.   I—I—don't know —why . . .

> *Here Harold began to cry and sob and for a period of ten minutes or so was incoherent.*

L: 'Do you feel better now?'

I feel like a better person.   I know so, in fact.   I really don't hate my father now.   Maybe I still dislike him, but I understand the whole thing. I love my mother. That's one reason why I didn't carry out my plan. And I didn't want the responsibility of supporting my mother and my sisters. If I carried out my plan I would have to do that. I used to tell myself that there were cases in the world where the son killed the father. I cared too much for my mother and I disliked my father. This is the first time I—I faced the facts; the first time in my life. It's true. It goes all the way back . . .

L: *'We are going to go on facing facts, facing them!'*

You know, Doc . . . This is the first time in a long time, in a long time, since the accident happened, that I feel relieved. My shoulders are not so heavy: my arms are lighter. Maybe I just imagine they are . . . but they feel lots lighter . . .

THE THIRTY-NINTH HOUR

L: *'I think we have now reached a place where I can explain to you the meanings of all the things you have told me, as well as the things you tell me, as they come up. You will tell me, for instance, of the dreams you may have or, in fact, anything that comes into your head, and at the proper place I'll give you the necessary explanations. By the way, I am very well pleased with the improved condition of your eyes.'*

Yes. That's true. When I look at a book I still have to hold it close to my eyes sometimes. I guess it must be a habit, because the other day when I was sitting down with a book I held it about ten or more inches away from my eyes, and I could read fine. But after a while it started to swing back: it started swinging back to my eyes, close to my face.

L: *'You mean your arms swung the book back, don't you?'*

Yes; yes . . .

L: *'That is because over many years you have formed the habit of holding books and anything you wish to look at close to your eyes. Now you must break that habit. There is a simple way to start breaking it. Do you usually read in bed?'*

Yes. A good deal of the time I lie on my back in bed and hold the book.

L: *'Well, one good way of starting to break that habit is this; if you are reading in bed, prop the book up on the pillow. In that way the book remains fixed. You see, your hands have developed the habit, they are used to bringing the reading material close to your eyes. These habits of manipulation go along with seeing. Holding your books close to your eyes was all right when your eyes were very bad. Now that they are somewhat better you'll want to change your habits.*

Yesterday something hit me. Last night, I mean. I haven't had a feeling like that for more than two years. It's something like a mood. I used to get them on the outside. I remember back when I was twelve or thirteen when I was in one of these moods I'd run away from home, see? To illustrate—the one I had yesterday ... I was walking in the mess hall and the sun was shining in through the windows, and the sunlight, it started to move or something, move from one place to another; and I knew I was going to have a—a spell. I didn't eat nothing. I just sat at the table and I closed my eyes because they were burning. And then I had like a day dream. I imagined that I was in a big room, with about three or four hundred people. They were all in the room. They all had tin cans or something and they were making a lot of noise. Some of them seemed to be jumping up and down, and some of them were sitting at the tables, a few at each table. They were the kind of tables people have in homes, round tables, with only four people sitting at each one; and on one table, the one where I was sitting, there were only three people. I was sweating all over, just sweating.

L: 'Was there anything more?'

Once in a while I imagine different things. Sometimes I imagine I'm watching a big cage of monkeys, and I get madder and madder, because they make an awful clatter and noise, and I feel like throwing my food at them.

L: 'Now let's look at all this closely. First of all you saw lights shifting. We'll start with that, when the sun came through the windows.'

Yes; the sun came in through the windows, shifting.

L: 'And you immediately began to feel frustrated, to have that feeling of frustration. Do you remember now an incident in your life, when practically the same thing happened? Do you remember one morning when you saw your father and your mother having intercourse?'

That—was—a long time, a long time back ...

L: 'Now then; after that your mother took you into another room and there were three of you sitting at the table. You had just come through an extremely crucial experience. You practically reproduced that incident yesterday.

'*You were afraid of your father, of his penis, and the light in his eyes. You recall the times you moved to get out of the way of the lights in your father's eyes? You recapitulated the same thing again yesterday, the whole incident. Then, after that, you were sitting at the table with two other people, your mother and your father. And you felt this very frustrating experience, the origin of which goes way back to that time. Do you get the connection?*'

Yes; yes. I get it. Everything seemed to be going so fast I couldn't make anything out. I know the floor was rushing by me so fast. I was walking slowly, but the floor was going by like anything, so fast.

L: 'Let's start tracing the pattern of your life, from the earliest memories we have brought up. The first is that of a crucial, bitter experience: A child, waking up in the morning, and seeing his father and mother in the act of having intercourse. Something strange, new. The mother seems to express, by her face, by her eyes, by her general expression, that there is something wrong; something she presumably does not like. She pushed the father away. And how did the child see this? How did he interpret it? He thought the father was hurting the mother, and she pushed him away. And when she did, the child saw his penis. The early memory, then, is not of the sexual act itself, but of the instrument with which it is performed. That was a sight hard to bear. It was not only new and strange. There was something else about it. You yourself, Harold, expressed it. You thought it was an animal. Your mother's eyes, as you said, were soft and (I think you called them) pitiful; almost as if it hurt her. Your father's eyes were hard. And so you, the child, became frightened. You were seeing something hurtful, and something forbidden. Perhaps in you there was something, some dim sense that you were present at some forbidden rite; and all this was coupled naturally with fear, with the fear of your father.

'Now let's get back to the breakfast table. You sat at the breakfast table and your father came in and sat down with you. Your mother was busy. She stood at the stove with her pots and pans. She was rattling them. There is a rattling noise, and she is cooking. You are with your father and your father is offering you some food. You reject it. And the reason you reject it is that you are afraid of your father. You fear that he is intending to harm you. Is that right?'

O, yes; yes . . .

L: 'And you saw the light in his eyes. There may be something else here which we'll get at later. But you were, as you said, afraid of his penis and his eyes, and you had seen something forbidden. This, afterwards, became transposed. It became a feeling of guilt.'

From seeing, watching . . .

L: 'Yes. And it first made you close your eyes, having seen something forbidden. Later this feeling of fear of your father became more and more deeply imbedded as time passed. First because of what had happened, and second because of the intrinsic character of your father, because of the kind of person he was. Now when you got a little older, your father did two things. First he threatened you with the loss of your penis; and secondly he rejected you. He didn't want you around him; he preferred your sister. He himself stated that your sister, a girl, should have been the boy. He even suggested that she should change places with you; and remember, she is a person without a penis. That was a suggestion pretty hard for you to bear up under because he had already threatened to deprive you of your penis. In addition to this, there was a perfectly good reason why you should credit him with the ability to do this to you: that was his business; he made his living changing bodies. Do you understand?'

Yes . . .

L: 'Now we'll go further than that. We are making a big forward jump in order to clear this point. Your father threatened you with castration. You were afraid of him, because of this threat and because of his own big organ. It effected you and led to the intensification of the feelings of guilt and inadequacy; guilt for having seen it, and fear. So you closed your eyes and ran away; not physically, because you couldn't do that, but closing your eyes was your way of running away, was it not?'

That's right. I did run. That was the same thing . . .

L: 'Let us now consider the times when you had intercourse with your sister. Now, in one respect, that was a more or less innocent thing: you were after all just children. But you reacted to it in two ways. Your first reaction was caused by your mother taking you away from your sister, removing you. One reason why you had intercourse with your sister— beyond the curiosity factor—was to prove that you had a penis, was it not?'

I know that's right. I—when my—I know—the—. When I saw my sister naked, when we were sleeping together, I became troubled by my penis. I rubbed my hands all over my penis to prove to myself that I—that—I was—better—better than she was, better than she thought I was.

L: 'More like your father?'

Yes . . .

L: 'All right. Now, as I have said, you reacted in two ways. Your first reaction was a further intensification of guilt. You have carried that feeling of guilt about with you all your life, and you have tried hard to hide it. Have you ever again talked about those occasions with your sister?'

No. I didn't. I tried to forget it.

L: 'A further development of your technique of running away. Now, when your mother removed you from your sister, what happened? She impressed upon you the fact that this thing you possessed, your penis, was a guilty object? Is this true?'

I—Yes. I know, when I was younger . . . You know, young kids, when they have to urinate, they just do it anywhere; and when other kids see you do it they point one finger at you and rub one finger over another. I used to hide behind my mother for fear that somebody would see it. I didn't like anybody to see it.

L: 'Now, secondly, your father rejected you, thereby throwing you more and more closely on your mother. You resented your father, and coupled with this resentment was a resentment against your mother for the reason that she obviously preferred your father to you. Because she was accepting his penis and rejecting yours, you were jealous.'

And I disliked him . . .

L: 'You disliked your father and your mother for almost the same reason; is that right?'

I think so. I think so. I disliked my mother for that; and I know I disliked my father much more.

L: 'As a matter of fact, Harold, is it not true that you wanted to take your father's place with your mother?'

I—she—when my mother got into one of those arguments with my father she would chase my sister or me to sleep with him. She would sleep in another room. I never liked to sleep with him. He didn't like me. He preferred my sister to sleep with him. He liked my sister better. Usually it was only for one night and then she'd go back to sleep with him. My sister slept with him quite a bit when we were young. I always wanted to sleep with my mother. . . .

I—I never thought—I could take—my father's place—with my—mother; but now I see that really was what was in back of it all. When my mother got into one of these arguments with my father she wouldn't talk to him for a while and I'd feel good about it. Then after a few days she'd go back to him and everything would be the same again. I used to think, why do they do that? Why don't they argue? If they go back to each other . . . I never wanted her to hit me. If she hit me I'd go back and tell her I was sorry. . . .

I was always conscious of his big shoulders, his big chest, his big body, everything big. I always thought of myself as a small, skinny kid. Compared to my father in every way I was nothing . . .

L: 'And you were jealous of that? You resented it?'

Yes; I did. I know that I was jealous.

L: 'You resented it so much that when you grew up you liked to play with guns, because only by possessing such a weapon could you be on equal terms with your father.'

Yes. I knew when I had one I didn't care what he said to me. I could always take care of him . . .

L: 'Then a gun was your protection. It was a weapon as powerful as his weapon.'

More powerful; because I could hurt him when he was ten or fifteen feet away from me and not just a few inches.

L: 'In other words, you had a bigger, more powerful penis than he had, wasn't that it?'

Unless the penis is not . . . Unless the pistol is not a symbol for the penis. It's like that.

L: 'Why do you think that the pistol symbolizes the penis?'

Well; it has a protruding end—and—it's really an extension. Therefore, it is a symbol for the penis. And so is a knife.

L: 'Now, you stole a pen knife from your father and once, when you were a child, you stole his razor. But you said you never stole money from him. Money; you stole that from your mother.'

I was—afraid of him . . .

L: 'Why should you have been afraid to steal money from him and not afraid to steal his pen knives?'

The money—the coins—round—maybe for the—the vagina . . . I—that my mother . . .

L: 'When you had possession of a gun you claim you also had a feeling of manliness. You had something your father had, you felt, tried to deny to you. In effect, then, you felt your father had castrated you.'

Yes—yes.

L: 'So that you felt when you had a weapon you were in possession of an instrument that was better than your father's penis. In another sense you stole it from your father. You tried to rob him, symbolically it is true, of his potency.'

Yes. I know that.

L: 'You never stole a knife from your mother; but you used the money you stole from her to buy a gun; not once but more than once. Is that not right?'

Yes; that's right. The whole thing is getting clearer and clearer to me now.

L: 'You wanted, then, to prove to your mother that you were more manly than your father. You wanted to show your mother that you had the same thing as he. As a matter of fact, you wanted to show her you had an even better gun than he had.'

I think I see the whole thing now. What you just said, that's right.

L: 'Now let us go on from there. Some time later in your life—we're jumping over a considerable period now—you planned to do away with your father. And very characteristically, if all that you have said is true, you chose to do away with him by using a big gun. Not only that; but you planned to do two other people, three people in all. Now, why? Why not four people? or half a dozen? Why did you settle on three?'

Well—of course—I didn't want to kill too many.

L: 'Can it be that the number three has a symbolic reference similar to the material we have been discussing? When we were discussing one of your dreams you told me that this number had a decided symbolic significance for you. You said that three represents the penis and testes.

'But let's go further. The reason you didn't do this, kill your father and two other people, was because you realized that you couldn't fill your father's shoes.'

I know. I realized that I—wasn't—as good as my father. I realized I couldn't take care of those women, my mother and sisters.

L: 'Now when you went with girls . . . In the first place, you had a lot of girls, didn't you?'

Yes; I guess I had . . .

L: '*You were trying very hard to prove that you were manly, weren't you?*'

I—yes; I admit that.

L: '*And what did you do when you wanted to impress these girls? You pulled out a gun and showed them that you had a gun, that you carried with you a powerful weapon. Why?*'

I—I wanted to—show them I was—better than most men, that I had great strength and—manliness. I—wanted—to show them—I had a big—a powerful penis . . .

L: '*Now let's get to the other incident. Why should you have wanted, after a time, to kill the man who called you a mother-f——r? It's rather obvious now, isn't it?*'

Yes; I see now . . .

L: '*Try and tell me.*'

Well, it's that he reminded me of my father by his actions and his speech. To prove to my father that I was better than he was, after all.

L: '*But why would you be wanting to kill him? And what for? You were killing for two reasons: first, the whole thing brought up in you the incident of your early childhood, the first thing that made you hate your father; and second, because he reminded you—in an obscure manner— of the one thing you did not want to be reminded of: that throughout your whole life you struggled to get into your father's shoes. By harming this man you were harming your father for having had intercourse with your mother, and hurting her: in the second place, you were asserting your superiority over your father: and in the third place, you have had the obscure feeling, all these years, that you really were trying to take your father's place with your mother. In a word, you really are what he called you.*'

Yes—yes. It all came out when I wanted to get rid of him. But why—why did I change my mind—after nursing it all those years?

L: '*That's a good question, Harold. You changed your mind because you realized that you couldn't, under any circumstances, be as good a man as your father. He convinced you of that.*

'*Now what was the method you used? On the surface you used a knife because it was noiseless. There is, however, more to it than that. There are many reasons why people do things; some are rational, some are disguised to appear rational. You used a weapon which, for you, is a symbolic representation of the penis, and which you had stolen from your father. You actually used the weapon most suited to the working through of your conflict. You used, on the representative of your father, the sub-stitute of the weapon which he had taken from you, and which you now stole from him.*

'So there you are. A child sees something that is forbidden, that he apprehends in some dim way as forbidden, and at the same time he is terribly scared. You, the child, become prey to feelings of guilt, and these are later intensified by feelings of inadequacy. You run away by closing your eyes. That thread runs through your whole life. You are running away. The fear of your father, the knowledge that you are not as good as your father. . . your whole life is a struggle with him and a running away from him and your inadequate self. Finally you commit a symbolic murder to rid yourself of him.

'And the fear of castration that you have always had; it's shown very well by many incidents. You slept with your aunt and you awakened in the morning to find her hand on your penis. She wanted to steal it from you! And you dislike her. One time you slept with this man who was a boarder at your house, and he also slept with his hand on your penis. And, one night, you saw someone who was trying to break into the house, ostensibly to steal. Do you know if that man was really there?'

I'm not sure he was there. I heard—the screen in the window rattling, and I think . . .

L: 'Whether or not he was actually there does not matter. At any rate, it intensified your fear of being robbed of your penis, did it not?'

Yes. It's true. I never felt a great fear consciously. I never felt a great fear, but I was more afraid of my father, that my father would hurt me that way. I was consciously afraid that he would hurt me with his big hands, great big hands, that stuck way out, big, round, muscular. Maybe his hands are symbols for his penis, his hands and his arms. He used to pick me up and just drop me. I ran away from him but he always seemed to be able to catch me some way or other. Mostly his hands; he used mostly his hands, only once in a while a stick. I was afraid of his hands. When he said he'd sic the dog on me to bite my penis off I was afraid of him then. I was small, but he, he looked so—big, so big and brutal. I was afraid of him, his big arms—his big arms and hands, his big, powerful muscles. He had a grip like a vise.

L : 'I see that you realize you did not grow up with a conscious fear of his penis, a verbalized fear. That fear was displaced by fears symbolic of his penis. Let us not forget, moreover, the reason for your eyes behaving as they did.'

I—I know—everytime he tried to slap me in the face I would hold up my hands to protect my eyes. I didn't care about the rest of the face. It was my eyes I was worried about. I tried to hide the sight of him from me too, the sight of his arms and his big hands. When I broke his razor, what was the singing? I heard a singing. When he hit me a lot of times I'd hear singing, and sometimes I'd hear a big noise, a racket.

L: 'Do you remember if, when he hit when you were a small child, the phonograph was playing?'

I don't know. One time I had—I don't know what you would call it—I was imagining something like a big wheel. I've tried to place it. I'd refer it to—the thing—the round disc or wheel they have in a clutch in an automobile, only this was real big. It was kind of greasy, oily. When it would turn it would screech and scratch, kind of rumble. One time I had a feeling like that . . .

L: 'Do you remember . . ? Your father had a machine . . .'

He had a kind of a machine, a sewing machine. He used to cut wood. It had big round wheels, discs, on it. He used to cut the wood for things he wanted to make. It was a real big machine. Sometimes he used a real big blade, three or four feet across. He used to attach it to the truck to run it. That's it! Now I know . . . The singing . . . The truck . . .

L: 'Now I want to make sure, Harold, that you understand all these things we have been talking about.'

I understand alright . . .

And the funny part of it is that it's true. I can remember back—instances, places, just vaguely. But every time you asked whether it was true or not I could remember everything. It's all true. I didn't kill my father because I knew he was better than I was, because I knew that he could care for my mother and my sisters better than I could. I disliked him enough so that I had to kill him though; there was enough behind it so that I had to kill him. I hated my father enough so I killed the other fellow in his place. That did the job. He reminded me of my father . . .

THE FORTIETH HOUR

I have been thinking hard since yesterday and I find that what you have been telling me is true . . .

L: 'I want you to think carefully. Can you remember anything about a light that seemed to come from your father's eyes when you were sitting at the table that morning?'

I—I don't remember—seeing any lights. But now when I picture my father his eyes are shining; they look like lights . . .

L: 'Let's re-trace the scene. Early in the morning you wake up. You are lying in the crib. You look over at your mother's bed. You see your father and your mother; your mother's night gown is drawn up over her hips, your father is in his underwear. He is lying on top of your mother. Your mother looks over at the crib. She sees you watching. She pushes your father away. You look at her. Her eyes are soft and pitiful. And then you look at your father. His eyes are shining brightly; they are hard. As your mother pushes your father away, you see his penis; it is big, fat; it looks like an animal, brutal and vicious. A little while later your mother comes over to the crib; you see her get out of the bed, and you note her nightgown as it falls down over her legs. She takes you in her arms, holds you close. She takes you into the next room and she starts getting breakfast. She places you in your highchair and sits you close to the table. Now you are at the table, your mother close to you on one side, your father on the other side. Now you go ahead!'

My father hands me something to eat. It looks like bread or cake. I don't want to take it. Then my mother starts feeding me, giving me a drink of milk or something but . . . I was sitting closer to my mother than to my father. She is sitting right alongside of me. She is about two feet away; my father, at the other side of the table, is about six feet away. I don't know . . . All of a sudden I see his face change. It changes: it is getting thinner, the nose is bigger, the ears are sticking out, the hair . . . , the eyes get shiny. All of a sudden the light pierces out, sort of jumps out at me, long rays. And, I don't know . . . I—it seemed as if—the way my father kept looking at me— his eyes . . . They don't look like eyes, just like lights, the heads of flashlights, rays of lights coming out of them, coming out at me. He looks at my mother. My mother's eyes have holes in them. The lights—the lights are right on her. They shined right in her eyes, one in each eye. The rays go from one end of the table to the other.

I see the lights in my mother's eyes.   Then my father looked at me.
The light was hurting me.   Then I was—I remember I was trying to
dodge it.   It's funny: everything is black.   I couldn't see my father.
I couldn't see my father.   I couldn't see anything.   I can look down
and see the—the flat board you fit over a baby on a high chair, and
the beads.   I can see the beads on the high chair.   The two lights are
piercing right through the darkness, just like two powerful lights
shining there.   There—they seem to be coming from where my father
is sitting.   I could see them when it wasn't dark, when I could see
everything.   They are right on me all the time.   If I moved my head
a little ways one would catch me in the left eye.   I tried to duck
away, but everywhere I turn there is one on me, one piercing, piercing
at me.   It was all I could see.   From one end of the table to the other
was the light rays shining on . . . But it was dark.   I don't know if
it came from my father.   When it was not dark I could see the lights
going right in my mother's eyes, and they stayed in there.   They
seemed to be going in there from my father right to my mother's
eyes—and stay—inside of her—somewhere.   When he would look
at me both the lights couldn't get at my eyes at the same time.   One
on each eye . . . . One would shine.   I would close my eyes to it but
I'd feel it through my eyelids like a strong and powerful light shining
right through my eyelashes.   I would duck as much as I could.   But
I couldn't dodge; every place I moved one ray would hit me.   I tried
to get in a lot of different positions, close my eyes, move my head, but
I couldn't do it.   It came from where my father was sitting before I
saw his face change.   Then his face became all cut up.   I couldn't
see him because everything was—black—dark.   I couldn't even see
the doorway that led to the other room.   It was like a dark room
with two flashlights almost held together, shining at something . . .

L: 'Why should your father's face be 'cut up'?'

I—I can't seem—to . . .

L: 'Did it remind you of someone? something?'

It—it—it looked like the—picture—of—a devil, or a dog—a dog . . .
His face was thin; the ears were sticking up and out; his hair stuck
up, his eyes were shiny—like—bulbs.   The light came out of them,
piercing the darkness . . .

> *At this point, Harold was placed in a deep hypnotic sleep. Routine
> tests for depth were conducted as usual.*

L: 'Now we are going back to the morning you were telling me about. Do you recall what you were telling me about?'

Yes. About the darkness—and the—lights . . .

L: 'We are going back, going back. You are getting smaller, smaller. You are a little baby. Now you are in your highchair. The board is over you, the beads are in front of you. How many beads are there?'

There is a bunch of them, twenty or thirty of them. They aren't very big, as big as marbles. There is a wire running through them. There are several rows of them. They're a lot of different colors. Each row is one color . . . I hear—a noise—in my right ear. It is coming from where my mother is. She is cooking something. I can hear the gas burning. It smells like—like coffee percolating. My mother is rattling pots and pans. She is stirring something—oatmeal. She is hitting a pot with a spoon, hitting it real hard to get the oatmeal off it. I can hear the water faucet running. My father is saying something to my mother. She is walking over with a cup of something. There is steam coming from the cup. Coffee? My father puts milk in it from a bottle. It looks so—black. My mother walks over: she has a cup too. She sits down and—and puts milk in her cup from the milk bottle; then sugar; then she stirs it. My father gives me something; it's a piece of bread with butter on it. The butter looks greasy and I don't want it. Then my mother gives me something to eat. She pours some—some coffee only lighter—in a saucer and puts it on my board. I have my spoon in my left hand. I can't eat it. My father looks at me. My mother talks to me: I don't know what she is saying; her voice seems far away, far away. Now my father and my mother are talking. It seems far away. I'm looking at my father's face. It starts changing. It gets cut up, like dried up—sunken in. His ears seem to stick way out. Then the lights . . . They're small, dim lights at first. They get bigger and bigger and bigger. His face is changing. His hair is sticking up. It looks real thin. He looks at my mother. I am afraid of him . . .

L: 'Why are you afraid of him?'

I don't know . . . His face, his eyes . . . I am so afraid he might hit me with—with that penis, with his big—hands. They look real vicious. They could pull me apart. He looks so cruel, so mean. His cheeks are cut up: his ears are flopped over now: his chin is—is —O—pointed . . .

L: 'On which side of your father are you sitting?'

I am sitting on my mother's right, almost directly in front of my father. My mother is sitting in front of my father. My mother and I are on one side: my father is on the other side. We are facing him. I am sitting right next to my mother so she can feed me. He looks at my mother. I can see everything getting black, from the corner of the room behind my father to myself. It starts coming in like a cloud. I can't see anything except the beads. The lights are shining in my eyes . . .

L: 'Whom does your father look like?'

I—he looks like—I don't know—he looks like an animal—or—a devil, a dog.

L: 'Does he look like anyone you know? anyone you saw as a baby?'

No . . .

L: 'Do you remember ever seeing him like that before this time?'

No . . .

L: 'Do you recall anything that happened before that morning—way back?'

Before that morning? I see—faces going past me. They don't look like my father's face. All these faces look kind and gentle: they look like they were all smiling. They don't want to hurt me. Only one time—I see my mother—pushing the carriage. My father is on the left side. He is looking at me.

L: 'Is this before or after that morning?'

It is before . . . Because I . . . Oooo, I remember—remember my mother—feeding me with—her—breasts—through—her—breasts . . . Oooo—I—I—can't see much but when I—sometimes . . . Now I see my aunt Louise. She is saying something. I'm in bed, going to sleep. I can't hear it. It seems somebody is standing next to her. A man. I can see right through him. He looks like a—shadow. I can see—he looks like . . . Right through I can see him. He walks around. My aunt goes out of the room with him. When he walks I can see right through him. I'm lying in a bed. It is before that morning. There is a man standing there. It looks like a man. I can't make out the features of his face. I can look right through him. I can't see through my aunt. She is small; only about twelve or thirteen. She went out first, then he went out. She closed the door. I don't know what he is, an outline, a shape. I fell asleep. I had a

dream, I think. Somebody was singing, a person—standing there—
talking to me—singing—real soft. I can see the mirrors in the room,
and the table...The table—something—on it. A basket with
things in it. And I can see right through him and see the table. I
don't know who he is. I can't see his face. I can't see anything
except the outline of his face, his hands, his body. After he goes
out with my aunt I fall asleep. I see him standing there, saying
something. I can see right through him. Then he isn't there. I
think I am falling asleep, falling asleep. Then I heard somebody
rush in, somebody rush, rush in. Somebody opened the door, opened
the door. It was a woman. I don't know who it was. It was a
woman. She had a big bunch of hair, bobbed hair. She is rushing
at me. Her face is funny. She comes running to pick me up. She
comes so fast at me, so fast. Her cheeks are sunken in; her face is
all...She looks like my Aunt Louise. She is reaching at me fast.
Her face looks funny; her nose is big, thin, sticking out. The man
—I can still look through him. I'm afraid of my aunt. When my
aunt comes running I'm crying. My aunt is rushing in the room.
I'm in my—mother's—bed. When my aunt comes rushing in she...
I remember I was crying. He seems to be saying, "Go to sleep, little
baby." I remember...I was crying. When I was crying my aunt
came rushing in. Her hair was kind of—floating behind her. When
she starts to pick me up I see her teeth. Her teeth are funny. Her
mouth is open. She looks as if she is gritting her teeth. She picks
me up. Oooo...I try to push her away. My mother—she comes
in and takes me. She starts rocking me in her arms. I closed my
eyes. I tried to stop seeing this man. He seemed to be there. He
seemed to be just looking at me. He wasn't saying anything. My
mother is singing to me. She wants me to stop crying. Then...
Then—I am in—the kitchen. I am sitting on my mother's lap. She
is sitting in a chair. She starts feeding me...soup—with things in
it. When my mother feeds me she wants my aunt to take me. I
didn't see him that morning. I didn't see him that morning. Only
my—mother and my father—they—in bed...Darkness came over
the lights. I don't know where the darkness came from. O! O!
A tunnel! A small tunnel. I see a man with a black hat on. I see
his face, all chunked in. His eyes are soft and tender though, but he
—his face and cheeks are all...I'm sitting and I see him walking

towards the carriage.   There is nobody there; my mother is not there.
I can feel the belt on me; I can feel the belt holding me down.   It
looks like her . . . It looks like he has a black hat, a felt hat; but his
eyes are soft.   I can see his eyes under the hat; they're soft, tender.
His cheeks and nose are cut like that.   He has a black heavy coat on.
I can't see his hands but I can see every line of his face.   I don't
know who he is.   I don't recognize him.   I just see him for the first
time.   Then my mother comes and starts pushing me.   He was
standing there and then my mother came and started pushing me.   I
don't get frightened of him.   I can see he is not going to hurt me.
My eyes are wide open . . . They are not closing at all, at all.   His
eyes were so soft.   They—like a cat's eyes they were soft.   He has
a black hat—a black hat.   O! O! I see! We're in a movie house!
My mother and my father . . . I'm in my mother's lap.   I'm wrapped
in a blanket.   It's so. hot, hot, hot.   I'm so small . . . I hear—music
playing and I can look up and see—people—talking on the—the
screen.   I don't hear anybody.   Just music.   I see—words—letters.
I don't know what it is.   What does it mean?   I see men in big hats,
big black hats, with guns, shooting.   They have big, shiny guns.   O!
When I look up I can see rays of light from a little opening, a little
opening like an eye.   The rays of light piercing through the darkness,
through the darkness.   In front, when I turn my head, I see big men
with big hats, big hats, and shiny guns, guns with bright handles.   It's
dark.   I can see people in front of me but I can't make them out.
The man with the black hat had kindly eyes.   His face was cut up,
his nose was sticking out, but his eyes were soft.   I don't know who
he was.   I can hear the squeaking, scratching, that the carriage makes
while it rolls, rolls . . .

    *L: 'Harold, you will awaken when I tell you to.   When you awaken
you will remember all you have told me; and when you come tomorrow
you will know more about it.   You will awaken refreshed and remembering all you have said.'*

THE FORTY-FIRST HOUR

    L: 'Harold, you have some things to tell me today, do you not?'
    What I remember from yesterday is all . . . You wanted me to
know—to remember—if I'd seen anyone my father resembled.   I
still don't know who or what.   But I can . . . From what I do remem-

ber I don't know yet who or what my father resembled. I can't seem
to explain myself saying some of the things I said, like about my aunt,
like about the time when my aunt rushed into the room. She seemed
quite agitated and excited. I was crying because I saw a man. I
guess that's why I was afraid. I think he said something to me, whoever it was. I think I saw right through him, the walls of the room
and the small table behind him with the basket on it.

L: '*You were crying then?*'

I know I was crying and my aunt rushed in so fast I was afraid of
her too.

L: '*Do you remember if he touched you?*'

No; he was standing at the foot of the bed. He didn't reach over;
he didn't touch me . . .

L: '*Do you remember what his face was like?*'

I couldn't see his face: I could just see an outline; his face wasn't
on it. Like a shadow, I could see right through him.

L: '*But did you see his outline?*'

An outline, just an outline. It was in the daytime. They must
have put me to sleep early in the afternoon or maybe in the morning.
He wasn't there when I fell asleep; he went out with my aunt before
I slept but he was there when I woke up.

L: '*Do you remember having gone to a moving picture with your mother
and your father? How old were you then?*'

I was real small. I wasn't older than six or eight months.

L: '*Do you remember what you saw?*'

Men—with big hats—real big hats, cowboys. It was a cowboy
picture I think. I think it was the first show I ever went to.

L: '*Tell what you remember about it.*'

It's hard to think. All I remember about it . . . In the show it was
dark. I could see the bright rays of light coming from the projector
room flashing on the screen. It was a cowboy picture, big hats, guns.
O, I know! It was dark. The rays from the projector room—they—
—were—the lights that—that—I saw coming from my father's eyes!
When we went to the show I wasn't even sitting in my mother's lap,
just sort of lying in—her—arms, half-lying, half-sitting; and I remember the rays of light going to the screen. My father . . . Whether I
imagine the man who was—when I was in the baby carriage, I don't
know. I—I thought I saw a man—with a black hat and a dark

overcoat. His face was sunken in and dried up. His eyes were soft. I wasn't crying, just looking at him, looking at him—and he looked at me too, for a moment or so. But I don't know why when I was sitting in my high chair with my father and mother at the table, why it started getting dark all of a sudden. I can't explain that. I remember my father's face looking at me, then changing, the lights getting brighter and brighter, the rays seeming to shoot from his eyes; then it started getting dark, but it didn't just get real dark, everything at once. It was like a cloud of—smoke—or gas, so I couldn't see; like real black smoke coming rolling in, covering everything, filling in all the air around . . .

L: 'Now continue from where you saw your father's eyes shining.'

I could see the sunlight, the daylight, in the next room next to the kitchen where I was sitting. The darkness just seems to vanish into the floor. The lights are still there. I can feel them on me. My mother—she seems to be eating. The lights are still there and he looks at my mother. It's hard to see the lights because there is day-light in the room, but I can make them out a little bit; they haven't disappeared. I guess he is paying no attention to me. I was crying then. My mother and father seemed to be talking. The lights are between my mother and my father, between them, in the center. They are disappearing, going into daylight. They disappear. There's just beams of light. My father's eyes seem to be getting smaller, smaller. They seem to be going away. The blackness is coming, blackness with a very small bit of light in the middle. I guess that's his eyes. There is a very small light, then it goes away. It goes away. I see a saucer on my board, a spoon in it; a saucer on the board that folds over the highchair. I don't remember seeing it there before. I don't know where—how the saucer got there, how the spoon and the saucer got there. There is some liquid in the saucer, the spoon is turned toward my left hand, as if I was going to pick it up with my left hand. I don't remember seeing the saucer before. I see the sun in the other room, the rays coming in, coming in at an angle; and the sun on the floor seems to be just splattered all over. I can't see the window, just the floor. I'm afraid to look at him. I'm afraid to see that light. I'm not eating. The saucer has a spoon in it and there is a liquid in it. I don't look at my father; I'm afraid of his eyes. He's got black eyes, like coal. I—I know—

I must have been seven or eight months old. I couldn't feed myself. I could just about sit up. I can see the saucer and the spoon because that's in the liquid and all I can see is the handle of the spoon sticking out of the saucer. There—there seems to be a calendar over my father's head. A calendar is there, with a picture of a—a big ship on it. I can see over his head but I am afraid to look at him because when I look at him I see the lights. I'm just looking at the steamship. It seems to be coming towards me. It's a front view. I can't see the numbers on the calendar: it's all jumbled up, the months, all jumbled and mixed. It's a big calendar. The numbers are big. I can see my mother now. I can see all the dishes, the cups in front of her, and her hair . . . I know she is staring at me but her eyes are not cruel. When I can look quick I see they are soft. I look at the table and see the dishes. I feel that my mother is looking at me. I can see the salt and pepper shakers and they look to me like they're penises, two penises standing up on small round discs, small round glass discs. One is real white and I can see the white stuff in it. The other one is different-colored. I see the tin caps on them, round tin caps. I don't know why they should remind me of penises; but they look like them standing on two discs. These salt and pepper shakers are just standing there. I just can't seem to get them out of my vision. I'm looking at them and they are standing there. They're just standing there. I can't get them out of my mind . . .

THE FORTY-SECOND HOUR

L: 'Harold, today I want you to go back again to the things you were telling me about yesterday. There is no more darkness. You are sitting in your highchair; the spoon in the saucer is immersed in the liquid, its handle pointed toward the left. You are sitting near your mother. As you look into the next room you see the sunlight on the floor, thick, heavy, splattered. Over your father's head you notice a calendar with the picture of a ship on it. Now you continue.'

The handle of the spoon is towards my mother. On the table there are other dishes. I can still see the salt and pepper shakers. They keep reminding me of two penises. I seem to be sitting just a few inches, maybe a foot, above the level of the table. I look down sort of and see the salt and pepper shakers at an angle with the table. I'm not sitting as high as my mother and father. They are sitting higher than I am and their heads are higher. My mother looks at me. She says something but I can't understand. My father is sitting there. Nothing wrong with him. It's light. I can see he's got a white shirt on. There are a lot of dishes on the table. I don't know how they got there or what. The sun is real bright, very bright. It's hitting on the shiny floor; it looks like smeared over the floor. When I was sitting in the show . . . I know . . . My mother is holding me on her lap. I'm held in her right arm. I can look up and back a little bit and I can see flashes of rays from the projecting room. I know when I used to go out in my baby carriage the sun would shine; but my eyes were alright—in the carriage. The sun is shining; nothing seems wrong. I guess I was about six or seven months old then. I know I could sit up just a little bit. I see a lot of different things, housetops, trees, poles and wires. Now I see the baby carriage . . . It—everything—seems—jumbled up . . .

Here Harold was again placed in a deep hypnotic sleep. The following instructions were administered after tests for depth of trance were concluded.

L: 'Now you can remember things very clearly, so clearly that you can act them out. You are going to act just as you did when all this happened. You are getting smaller, smaller. You are a little baby again. You are going to behave just as you behaved when all this happened. Now you are a little baby. You are wrapped in a blanket, all around. You are with your mother and father in a moving picture theatre. Your mother is holding you in her right arm; you are lying in her arm. Now you are going to tell me about it. It's dark. Through the darkness you see the lights from the projector. Now you are going to behave just as you behaved then; and you are going to tell me about it, tell me about it completely. Go ahead!'

I can see the screen—and the big hats on it. I can see a big man. He is laughing. I can see his face a little bit. He turns his head and I can see his hat. He is laughing. I can hear music—soft organ music. It's dark. I can make out figures around me, people's heads and . . . My mother seems to be watching everything. When I touch her she puts my hand down. She seems to be watching the picture closely. In my mother's arms—it's soft—real soft—like . . . I move my feet a little bit. I can hear some music. I can look up and see back a little. I see flashes of light going by. I see the lights from the projector room in the back and—my father—he looks at me . . . He is talking to my mother in whispers. I can see his face.

From here on Harold actually performed as his words suggest, accompanying with gestures, tears, moans and movements of the body the spirit of his utterances.

It's got some light on it. My mother, when I touch her—she pushes my hand down. She is more interested in the picture than in me. I see the picture, people's heads in front and on the side of me. All I see is the shape of the heads. I can't see the features of the faces and the heads, just the shapes. I see the screen lit up. I see a horse. I don't hear the horse. I see it walking by. It looks so soft and smooth. The horse opens its mouth. Its mouth has big teeth in it, big teeth. I see his face. He's all—laughing, laughing at something. Another—fellow—falls off—a horse into the—water. That's what he's laughing at. The screen is moving, it's jumping, jerking, moving . . . I can't see the rays from the projection room very much when they are close to the screen. I see the light where it is real small. It looks almost like a circular light. I can't hear anything much except the music. My father is talking to my mother; they are whispering something. I—I see horses on the screen. No noise. I see—like dust—clouds of dust. It's settling now. There seems to be a noise. I'm in a comfortable position. I want to go to sleep I guess. I don't know what it is that I'm playing with. It's—beads —or . . . It's something circular, rough, big. I put it in my mouth. My mother looks pretty and young: she has long brown hair. My father has black hair. I can see it; it's all lying down on his head real nice. Nothing is wrong with him. He looks well built, not thick, not fat. But far—far off in the back—why—I can look back and see over my mother's shoulder or arm. I see—in the blackness—this light, a lot of rays coming out of it. They all seem to be shooting at me. It—it scares me. I am afraid. I see the lights in my father's face and I am afraid. I remember how we came in. We came in on the—left—side. There was a carriage. It's not a big theatre. We came in and they carried me through the lobby in the back. We went towards the—left side, down the aisle; and we sit on the left side of the screen. When we came to the show it wasn't dark, not dark. It was in the summertime. I can see people running up and

down.   There seem to be—trucks and automobiles.   I can hear the
noise of some truck as it goes by.   It just goes by and . . . We went
across the street in the carriage with my mother.   The noise didn't
bother me very much.   The big truck, it shook me a little bit but
it didn't frighten me.   We're going along the street.   My mother is
pushing the carriage.   My father isn't pushing it.   My father is
walking on the—left side.   The belt feels tight around me.   About
eight months old.   I can sit up in the carriage a little but this belt
is on me all the time.   I can't move past the belt.   I see the tops of
houses and buildings going by.   Once in a while I get a look at some
person, get a look at somebody walking by.   It's daylight but the
sun isn't shining brightly.   It just feels nice to be riding, riding,
except I hate to go over bumps, gutters.   When we walk in the show
my father puts his hand on my chest.   He wants to look at me.   I
don't like him to put his hand on me.   It makes it hard to breathe.
That morning, when I'm sitting in my highchair I see the lights.
Those lights from my father seem to be piercing.   The lights . . .
It's hot.   The lights . . . I remember them from the show.

L: 'Harold, this is the day after you were taken to the show, isn't it?'

I . . . I got up late that morning.   My father and mother were in
bed late.   I never saw them both in bed before.   I guess they . . .
I don't know . . . When I was sitting in my mother's arms in the
show . . . I can still hear the music.

L: 'Did you awaken in the show or when you came out?'

My mother sat up and shook me a little bit.   We went out and she
—put—me in the—carriage.   She covers me up in it.   We start
going home.   There's a—lot—of people in the street.   It's dark when
we are going home.   The stores must have been open late.   I—it—
is—Saturday night . . .

L: 'Harold, the morning of which you have been speaking was a Sunday
morning, was it not?'

Yes.   It was last night.   It was last night when we went to the
show, wasn't it?   My father was never in bed late with my mother
before.   I never saw him before . . .

When I'm sitting in the kitchen, the darkness . . . I see two lights.
They're—together—like in the show.   I—I'm crying when it gets
dark.   She didn't seem to pay much attention to me.   I didn't cry
before it got dark, only when his face started getting all cut up.   I

was afraid of him. I was crying. I know I was afraid of him. I was crying when my aunt rushed into the room. This—man—I could look through ... I could see him standing there. He didn't seem to do anything. When he spoke to me I started crying, yelling. My aunt rushed in. Her face was funny; her head was funny and she was dressed funny. O! O! I see a picture ... It's got an outline of a man, completely black, just a shape, a silhouette, on the screen. That's it! O! O! This is the afternoon, the afternoon after that morning. The shape was in the show last night. That's where I saw the figure. I remember it and it scares me. I'm afraid. I cry. My aunt rushes in ... My aunt's face is funny. My father's face is funny too. I don't know whether ... Before it started to change, before the lights started coming the last time I can remember his face was all—fading out, the darkness coming over it, the whites showing—and—something was wrong. I saw a face like that before. It looked so vicious. It might have been the face of a dog ... O! O! O! I see—a picture—in the movie house! I see the picture of something like a dog, a wolf, something ... A wolf! They show a picture of him. He runs away. His face ... His eyes are shiny, his face looks cut up, sunken in, covered with hair. My father looks like the wolf! His nose got bigger, thinner; it stuck way out; his ears got bigger, pointy just like the wolf ...

I—I—my mother starts feeding me. It tastes like—sour milk—coffee without sugar. I can hear my father talking to my mother. I can't understand what they are saying. My father is talking to her. I don't know what he is saying. I—she—is feeding me and I don't want it. I see my mother take a cup away. She puts it behind me somewhere. The saucer is still in front of me with the spoon in it. My mother sits down. She wants to feed me—whatever it is. I feel—my cheeks—are wet. I don't remember ... I was crying very hard. The knuckles of my hands are wet. I—my father looks alright and he—he hands me something. I don't want it from him. I start to cry again when he hands me something. It looks like a piece of bread. Crying—crying again. She picks me up and holds me in her arms. It's nice. She's patting me on the head. She's holding me. I'm crying. I—she's talking smoothly to me. I just want to forget about everything—about the wolf, the lights, my father in bed—hurting my mother. She is just standing there rocking me in her arms. She's got my head on her shoulders, on her left shoulder. I'm looking at my father. I'm looking at the stove. I can see the stove. It's got four—four fireplaces on it. It looks black. I see a . . . My mother starts walking up and down. I—my head—my head is right in front of her, in front of her, almost to her neck. I'm leaning on my ear, my right ear. Once in a while when she moves I can see the sun in back of her. I can see my father a little bit. I know I'm crying, crying. My hands are all wet . . .

Before Harold was awakened, he was instructed to remember all that he had said during this hour.

The Forty-third Hour

I don't seem to remember much what we were talking about yesterday. O! it's coming back now. I saw yesterday these salt and pepper shakers. I don't remember now seeing any salt and pepper shakers like that in all my life. I don't see how they could be on the breakfast table. I thought I was sitting in the highchair and I thought I saw them. They reminded me of two penises. Just why, I don't know. I don't use much salt in my food and I don't use any pepper at all. Do you think that's perhaps why I don't use any salt or pepper? I don't like pepper now because it burns and makes me sneeze. Even when somebody else at the table is using it I don't like the smell. Yet I use salt occasionally. C——— and I were talking about Dobriski today. He doesn't use salt and pepper either. There was a fellow from Chicago, a tough little kid, who used a lot of pepper. When he threw that pepper around at the table everybody would sneeze. I hated that.

When I was about ten, Benny carried knives. He'd play with them all the time, even worse than me. He'd draw bull's eyes and pictures of animals and throw his knives at them.

When I was twelve or thirteen I used to play cards with the fellows, not for money, for match covers and things like that. One time another fellow and I stole about a thousand of these from a kid. My sister found mine and turned them over to this kid again. When she told my mother that she gave them to this fellow she got a licking. The reason was that she shouldn't have given those things to the kid: she should have turned them over to my mother first.

L: 'Have you ever thought about why you steal?'

When I want something, I take it: I steal it. I never stole any large amount of money—if that's what you mean. I stole a few dollars here and there but I never went into the higher hundreds or thousands. I always seemed to take just a few dollars; enough to get along on was what I wanted. I guess I used to steal to prove to myself that I could do it; to prove to myself that I could do anything I wanted to do. Sometimes when I was in swimming, or when we'd jump off trestles into coal piles on the tracks, I jumped off the highest places. I did it just to show myself and the other fellows that I could do it. I liked to dive into the water, never mind from what height. But when I'd steal something I must admit I was afraid.

L: 'Afraid of what?'

I don't know. I guess I was kind of shaky and nervous. I wasn't cool and calm. But later on I got used to it and didn't mind it very much. I was still a little shaky even after I got the hang of the thing, but not very much.

L: 'What, specifically, were you afraid of?'

I don't know . . .

L: 'Were you afraid of being discovered in the act?'

Yes.

L: 'Or were you more afraid of being punished?'

Well, I don't know what it was. I guess I was afraid of both of those things. I don't know which I was most afraid of most.

L: 'Why were you afraid of both of them?'

Well, if I was discovered in the act I knew I'd be punished . . .

L: 'How would you be punished?'

O, by a prison sentence. And I was afraid I'd get a beating up with a club or a rubber hose down at police headquarters. I was always afraid of that rubber hose. I always used to think that if they got hold of somebody they'd always beat him up—with a rubber hose. I didn't like being hit by a policeman or a detective. I didn't like the idea of their—hurting me. I always thought that policemen were like my father. That's all they do when they got somebody that can't get back at them.

L: 'The same way your father used to beat you?'

I guess so. But I always felt different when I had a gun on me. I never felt afraid of a detective or a policeman then. When I had a gun . . .

L: 'You were just as strong as they were then?'

Yes. And sometimes when we played cards I'd put the gun on the table beside me and it would make me feel stronger.

L: 'And you needed that feeling of strength?'

I did.

L: 'Because without that feeling of strength, you were just . . . Harold?'

Yes. I used to commit other crimes without using my gun. I broke into houses, stores, lunch-wagons . . .

L: 'Let's look at those things more closely to discover if we can see why you did them.'

Well, I always broke into houses myself, always myself. I wanted to do a lot of things myself, that especially, because then I would feel like a real smart person. When I did them myself, then everything was planned and it worked out as I thought it should. I planned it. I thought I could put something over on somebody, completely fool them.

L: 'Put something over on whom?'

My people, my family, somebody I stole things from. It would give me the feeling that I was more intelligent than I was to commit a crime and completely fool everyone else. I wouldn't walk around with my head down when I committed a crime. I'd keep it up.

L: 'You felt even better after you had committed a crime, is that it?'

That's right. When we broke into lunch-wagons some of these fellows used to grab three or four bottles of soda. Me, I'd grab a whole case. I always felt that I was better than the other fellows I hung around with. I felt that I could plan things out more, do things in a way that would be better than what they could do. When I planned something like a hold-up the idea would come quickly to me. Then I'd wait five or ten minutes. I'd get nervous all over, and shaky. Then I'd wait a while until I cooled down a bit before going ahead. When I committed it I'd be afraid for a while but then, about an hour later, I'd feel better.

I used to steal pennies from my mother when I was a, kid. I'm not sure whether I stole anything else before I was ten. O, yes . . . One time we tried to get even with a fellow. He had a clubhouse in his back yard, a big garage where he kept a lot of things, rifles, spears, bows and arrows, a small sailboat, several pairs of dumbbells, boxing gloves and things like that. So once he got in an argument with this gang I hung around with and he stopped travelling with us. I don't know what the argument was about but to get even with him I planned to steal everything out of his clubhouse. So one morning about six o'clock I went inside the clubhouse and took a pair of dumb-bells and the sailboat. I hid them behind the garage. I waited until I was in school and then told several fellows about it. They all seemed proud of me: they patted me on the back and said that was o.k., now we'd steal everything he had out of the clubhouse. But this fellow's mother saw me when I was coming out of that clubhouse. She knew my mother, so she went over and told her about it. My mother called me in and told me to give the stuff to her. I denied everything even though the woman told my mother that she had seen me. I got out of it by saying that I'd look for it, so I went over to the yard and made believe I was looking for the stuff. There was really nothing to it. I made believe I was looking for it and then found it. It was the only time I ever really stole anything up to that time. Then I started hanging around with the kids on S————— Street. I started playing truant, didn't go to church on Sundays. Then I started stealing my school money and going to shows with it. Then it got worse. In the summer we stole cakes out of the bakery. There was a truck that used to come around about nine or ten at night to bring milk to the stores. They'd leave the boxes outside the store and we'd rob stuff from them. Then we really got started stealing. We broke into a lunch-wagon and stole cigarettes and split them with the rest of the gang. About six of us broke into these wagons occa-sionally and we'd make off with a lot of soda. Sometimes we'd find cans of peas and beans. We didn't want them so we'd just open them up and spill the stuff all around the place. The soda, we'd keep most of that for ourselves and just divvy a few bottles with the gang. Then we used to steal keys out of cars. I just stood by those times. I myself didn't do much of the actual work in stealing, except when it came to lunch-wagons and so on. As for milk and things like that, there was another kid named Billie. I don't know if he or I was the leader, but pretty soon both of us were running everything in the gang. We'd go out and see what we could steal. Billie always car-ried a blackjack. He was a kid about twelve and he had a blackjack he stole somewhere, from his brother I think. He and I didn't bother with the little stuff. We'd tell a couple of kids to look inside automobiles and when they'd see a key we told them to get it.   It was somehow more fun to have the kids get the stuff than get it yourself, because then you really did two things instead of one: you told some-one else to get the stuff and you also planned it out.   I remember how we tried to poison all the dogs in the neighborhood.   We didn't like them.   Every time we tried to get through yards and jump over fences they'd bark at us.   So we tried to poison them.

Sometimes when I went away I was afraid to come home and face a beating; but when I got hungry I'd come home.   When I was younger I didn't stay out very long, one or two days and that's all; but when I got to be older I'd stay out longer—two or three weeks, a month, even three months.   Once or twice I went with Riggs but he always seemed like a baby; he seemed to want to cry for leaving home.   So I tried to avoid going with him.   I never liked to be with him anyway.

When we stole something or broke into automobiles or stores I always was the one who figured out and planned how to get into it.   The other fellows didn't seem to be able to think of the ways I could think of.   When we'd get to a locked car they couldn't get it open; but if I was there I'd force the car window open just a bit and put a little wire through the window and pull the door-knob up.   There it was: it came natural to me.   Most of these fellows didn't strike me as naturally born crooks.   I always thought that I must be a natural born crook.   For instance, when we wanted to break a window I got the idea to put some flypaper on that window and then cracking it and pulling it off with the splinters of glass on it.   These fellows didn't know much.   For instance, when you wanted to open a window you'd take a pen knife and stick it between the window and the sill and pull the latch over.   That's the way I'd get into my own house.

We had hundreds of keys, just hundreds.   When I was hanging out with that gang on S——— Street everybody always had a dozen or more keys.   Billie made the other kids carry them in their pockets.   Every once in a while we'd get to a garage door and then everybody would try his keys . . .

Why did I steal?   I guess in a way I wanted to prove to myself that I could do it.   I always wanted to prove to myself that I could steal something and get away with it; that I was a better man than my father thought I was.   I'd think better of myself then.   Even if

I would never use it, even if I would throw it away . . . Every once in a while I would steal a battery all by myself. I'd sell it to a fellow in a garage nearby and he would give me a dollar for it. He knew damn well it was stolen but he didn't mind. I'd keep the dollar all to myself. I needed money then.

L: *'What did you need the money for, Harold?'*

When I got the money I didn't know what to do with it. I'd buy a few ice-cream sodas and go to the show. About forty cents was all I really needed.

L: *'And you could have got that money from your mother, just by asking for it, couldn't you?'*

When my father was home my mother used to give me money to get rid of me, to get me out of the house. I used to wonder why she would do that. Sometimes my mother would come to me and give me a little money to get out of the house. There were many times when she would do that. I'd wonder why my mother gave me money to go to the show without me asking her for it. When my father was home my mother would try to keep me and him separated. It appeared to me that way. When we lived on S——— Street I got into trouble with some other guys when we broke into a store and got caught. I almost cut a fellow with my knife. I would have cut him if he hadn't twisted my arms and taken the knife out of my hand. There were some detectives came down and investigated the store where we broke in. They knew that a lot of kids were hanging around the clubhouse so they started shaking it down. They really shook it down! I was coming along the street and one of them saw me. I don't know whether he was a dick or not. He chased me about six blocks. I was jumping over fences and dodging through alleys but I couldn't lose him. I had a big knife with me, about ten inches long, so when the fellows standing around began to yell and he kept coming right after me I got a funny feeling in me and I just stopped. I stopped and pulled the knife and put my hand back over my shoulder. He came at me and grabbed my arm and twisted it until I dropped the knife. Nothing much happened: I got a year's probation. So I went home and pretty soon I got into some more trouble. During that time my father didn't work much and he was sore because he couldn't find any work. He would work for only two or three days a week. I went to school then, High School, but some days when I was home from school—like Saturdays and Sundays—my mother used to give me twenty-five cents or so and I'd go away and wouldn't come home until supper. She used to tell me, "When you come home you just tell your father you've been at your grandmother's." So she'd fix it up with him and everything would be o.k. I'd go to bed and nothing happened. This didn't happen every week, just some weeks, especially when he was home in the afternoons. It kept on until I was around seventeen and then I started getting into trouble again. I don't know whether she suspected my father didn't like me or what. I often wondered why she gave me the money. I guess I used to think that maybe she liked me better than my sisters.

    L: 'You wanted her to like you more than your sisters?'

    Yes. O, yes! My mother always was good to me. When I'd come home she'd come in the room where I was to see if everything was all right. Yes. I know my father would argue with her about me. When I'd hear it I'd say nothing about it. I'd just go away for a week or so. The last time I heard them arguing about me was before I got that stretch in the jail. I heard them arguing when I was coming up the stairs. I heard my father talking to my mother about me. I guess he was sore because I didn't have no job and my mother was telling him to wait a while. He was saying that it was always the same thing, that I was never going to be any better. I turned around and went out and didn't come back for a couple of days.

    I very seldom used to see my father. I didn't like to see him. My mother always made me go out. When he was coming in the front door I'd go out by the back. A lot of times she handed my coat out to me. Sometimes I'd stand out in the cold and shiver for quite a while, waiting for my coat or sweater. When I got them I'd go to a poolroom and sit around and wait. When I got home late at night he would be sleeping. My mother tried not to agitate him. After the last time I heard them arguing I decided to go away and so I left and stayed away for six months or more.

    The last time I saw my father was in the Judge's chambers. He wanted to shake hands with me. I didn't want to shake hands with him. The marshals pushed me in there. When the Judge gave me **all this time everything got blurry: I couldn't say anything; I couldn't** make him out. I know I was crying because I got so many years. I cried for about an hour and then it was all over. Then the Judge told the marshals to take me to his chambers to see my mother and father; he said my father wanted to shake hands with me. I didn't want to go in so they started to turn me around. When I came in my mother started crying, so I put my arms around her. She fainted afterwards and they brought her to. I was in another room when she fainted. They took me away. I was crying then. I didn't want to shake hands with my father. I don't know whether I blamed him for being sent up or not. If I hadn't heard him arguing with my mother; if he had helped me get a job somewhere . . .

The Forty-fourth Hour

I just feel bad today, I guess.

L: 'Why do you feel that way?'

I don't know. I used to feel like that occasionally on the outside. I know it's just one of those days. I was like that yesterday. I was out in the yard and I had a box of matches in my hands. I tore the cover of it all to bits. Then I spoke to C———— and he said I was just jittery, nervous and jumpy. I'm not angry. I'm not really angry at anybody. I just don't want to talk to anybody. When anybody talks to me I answer them. I just don't want to talk to people first when I feel like this. I can't explain that feeling; but the feeling is—well—it's—I guess it's a feeling of a longing for loneliness. But there is nothing really worrying me, nothing I can think of. I don't worry about many things any more. I feel like laughing now. I can't even read a newspaper. Nothing seems to interest me.

L: 'What do you think would interest you?'

What would interest me? I don't know; dreaming I guess.

L: 'Dreaming about what?'

Riding upstream in a canoe, or something like that: dreaming about plans. I guess it doesn't mean very much. On a day like this I like to be alone, away from everything and everybody. A long, long stream, and going upstream in a canoe that's easy to paddle and would go fast. I get like that once in a while. I don't think the treatment is the cause of that feeling. Some of my friends in here, when they talk about my treatment, they irritate me. I don't like to talk about it to anybody. Last night a friend of mine was talking

about it.   He was describing me to another friend of mine and he
said I liked to be pushed around, I like to have somebody to look after
me, to see that I do the things I should do, comb my hair and things
like that.   I didn't like it.   So, I don't know ... This morning I
started typing one of my lessons and I made a lot of mistakes with
the typewriter.   I didn't finish my lessons.   I used to feel like this
a long, long time ago, not just yesterday.

> *Harold's behavior during the forepart of this session demonstrates his am-
> bivalent attitude toward the writer and the therapy.   On the one hand, to hide
> the disappointment caused him by his correct anticipation that treatment was
> drawing rapidly to a close, he took occasion indirectly to chastise the writer
> and to minimize the therapeutic benefits.   On the other hand, like all patients,
> he fought tigerishly against surrendering completely the neurotic so-called
> 'secondary gain' which had until now provided him with reasonable protec-
> tion and excuse for his behavior.   Finally, he grudgingly admits the value
> of the therapeutic efforts and presses urgently for its continuation.*

L: 'Is this the first time you have felt like that since we began this work?'
No.   The last time was Sunday night; but before that I just used
to go outside and walk by myself, not talk to anybody.   When somebody would say something to me I'd just say "sorry" and keep
on going.   No; this isn't the first time.   I want to get away from
everything.
L: 'What do you want to get away from now?'
I don't know.   I want to get this treatment over with fast, as fast
as possible.
L: 'Why?'
Well, I don't know.   I'm coming over here and it is doing me real
good.   My eyes are a hundred percent better, more efficient.   They
feel heavy and strong.
*L: 'Have you ever considered the possibility that you would really
rather remain as you are, as you were before you undertook this work?'*
That may be so.   Sometimes it feels almost like going into something worse, knowing all this about myself.   And a few friends of
mine say to me that you are young, and you may do the wrong thing,
you haven't got enough experience, you may be hurting me instead of
helping me.   But I think you are all right, Doc.   These friends,
when they say something about my eyes I jump up and tell them I
don't want to talk about it.   They think the treatment is getting on

my nerves. It's hard for me to explain it. I think I've said everything. When I think back now I imagine some of the things were
wrong, that I must have created them in my imagination. Maybe I
don't remember what I was doing when I was ten, or twelve, or five.
It's all strange, probably because I don't know anything about it.
I don't even know what I'm saying now. I just like to get away from
everything and not even listen to any noise, just listen to the birds fly-
ing by and have everything nice and quiet with a little bit of sunshine.

L: '*Harold, do you remember when we were speaking some time ago of
resistance?*'

Maybe that's it . . .

L: '*You are sure you know what that means?*'

I—I think—it means—a force—which creates a—feeling to—cover
something up, to hide something, keeps you from—telling, holds you
—back, separates me—us—from—what we want to find out.

L: '*Now, Harold, I want to get back to the problem of why you stole?*'

Why did I steal?

Well; I can't tell you the reasons. I don't know. When I was
twelve, when I used to hang out with that gang of kids, we stole
everything that wasn't nailed down. I went to school, to St. A———'s
School, and several of these fellows were in the same class with me and
they lived in the same neighborhood. So I got into this gang. We
were all the same age, most of us the same size too. I wasn't smart;
but when it came to seeing things about stealing, to planning things
out and so on, I could do better than they could. We used to divide
ourselves into three groups and we'd separate, here one section and
there one section and so forth, and we'd steal everything that wasn't
nailed down. Then we'd bring the stuff to the clubhouse and if it
was anything good we'd split it up. I guess I thought I was a pretty
smart kid, not afraid of anything or anybody. I didn't have very
many companions before I started going with this gang. They all
seemed like swell, very swell fellows to me. There was another
fellow named Billie—I don't know whether he or I was the leader—
and most of the other kids looked up to us. When they'd steal
something they'd show it to him or to me and we'd get together and
decide what to do with it . . . batteries and car tires and everything
like that. I guess I took a delight in having all these kids come to
me and treat me like I was a father . . .

L: 'What does that suggest to you, Harold?'

It would suggest—that because of my—relations at home with—my father and my mother, I would naturally look for something like that to—balance off my feelings.

L: 'You're beginning to see why you stole. Now carry your line of reasoning a little further.'

Well, I used to feel that I wanted to be with the gang because I wasn't wanted at home by my father and mother.

L: 'Why should you feel that you weren't wanted by your mother?'

Well, because she was paying too much attention to my father. My father would work hard so when he came home he would be angry. He'd say that his back hurt and he'd tell my mother about it, and my mother, right away she would treat him like *I* wanted to be treated. I wanted her to pat me on the head too. Like the fellow was telling me last night; I wanted somebody to see that I do the things I ought to do . . . wash myself, comb my hair and things like that. I began to look into that yesterday after he said it to me. I tried to reason it out. It's true. I always wanted my mother to . . . Maybe that's the reason I like Perry. That's a good one! He makes me wash myself more than two or three times a day. He sees that I keep clean, that I don't sit around in dust and dirt and things like that. My mother used to see that I kept clean but sometimes she used to—well—she—when she'd tell me to do something she didn't mean to tell *me* that because she wanted me to do it. For instance, sometimes she'd tell me to brush my teeth for the reason they were dirty. I guess she saw my teeth were dirty and she'd make me brush them; but she'd make anybody brush their teeth when they were dirty; not just like they were *my* teeth. She would treat my sisters and myself about the same when it came to something like that, keeping clean. When she said something to me like that it wasn't emphasized for me as a particular individual.

L: 'And you, of course, wanted to be treated individually and specially.'

I find that's true, very true.

L: 'So that now Perry is, for all practical purposes, playing the role that your mother played. And he is very well suited to that role, isn't he?'

I guess he is. If my hair isn't combed . . . He notices everything and he tells me about it and keeps on telling me and telling me about it until I correct it. These other fellows, Carlson and Dobriski, they

seem to me . . . If something is wrong with me, my hair all mussed up
or my face dirty, they wouldn't tell me about it. When I find out
about it I get sore for their not telling me. Maybe they want me to
become a bum like they are?
   L: '*So Perry is, in reality, a substitute for your mother?*'
   Yes . . .
   L: '*Then that is the real reason why you feel the way you do and that
you don't want relations with him?*'
   Yes! That's it! That's it!
   L: '*Are you sure you understand it?*'
   I do. I get along with Perry. I like him a lot. Some of my
friends don't like him. I tell them I can take care of myself; I know
what I'm doing; but when I tell them that they only get madder. I
guess I feel sorry for Perry. He hasn't any friends, only me. Now,
after what we just said, I know it's more than just feeling sorry for
him. At first I didn't talk to him, but I did like him. Sometimes
when my hair isn't combed he tells me it looks like a mop. "If you
had a wooden leg they could use you for a mop." When I don't
shave for two or three days he won't talk to me. "If you don't shave
you look like a bum."
   I guess Carlson is right. I want somebody to run after me, brush
my hair and tell me what to do. Well, he said I was easily led. If I
see him I'm going to ask him what he means by that. I guess he
means that anybody could be friends with me easy. But he's wrong:
I really dislike to talk to people. When I'm talking with Perry or
Carlson or Dobriski and they start talking about me I don't like to
talk about myself so I switch it away. I don't like to talk about myself even with Dobriski . . .
   L: '*Do you recognize the fact that you actually dislike Dobriski? Has
it ever occurred to you?*'
   O—I—I don't . . . He's o.k. He's—a good kid. He's supposed
to be my—best friend, but I dislike him because he hangs around with
people I dislike . . .
   L: '*Is that the only reason?*'
   I used to like him a lot. I used to like him very much. He used
to be just like a brother to me. I guess when he went away from the
cell-block where we were living and started to hang around with
somebody else I started to dislike him then. I talk to him but when

I do I get mad right away and I want to fight him. I threatened him a lot of times already but it finally winds up that it doesn't do any good. I never had a friend like he was to me at first. In the sunlight when I look at him his eyes are in a funny position. That's a reason why I dislike him. He's got a chin like my father too. Inside the building he's got nice soft eyes but outside in the sunlight they look hard to me, cruel. I used to like him a lot, more than anybody else; but he is different from me. He picks on a lot of different people, the wrong kind of people, for friends. I know he dislikes Perry.

L: *'Do you think perhaps you dislike him for that?'*

Well, sometimes he appears to me just like my father. That's the real reason, I guess. Sometimes he acts to me like my father. He curses Perry out when he is with me, calls him all kinds of names. He never does it in front of Perry though, and one thing I will say: he talks very nicely about Perry in front of anybody else. He wants me to do everything he enjoys doing. He has real wide shoulders, big arms and hands, big bones in his arms. Sometimes when he picks up his pants and sticks his chest way out he reminds me of my father. Every time I talk to him we get in an argument. Dobriski reminds me of my father in his attitude on people that have a knowledge on some subject too. He rationalizes his own lack of knowledge and he says they probably don't have any idea of real life. It used to make me laugh. I know it just serves his inferiority feelings. I don't like those friends of his. Sometimes he talks to me in Polish too, just like my father.

Just last Sunday—you know—when the sun's rays were coming in and moving and jumping around, I was sitting at the table and I didn't know what happened. I didn't talk with anybody. I felt like throwing my plate straight up in the air. Then, in here, when we talked about it—my memory—what I was trying to hide—you know . . . I didn't speak to Perry for three days and even when he wanted to talk to me I wanted to walk away. That's the same way I treated my mother at home sometimes. My mother would call me and call me, and I used to turn away and run. I used to treat my mother like that. Then when I came home she'd give me a beating. When I came home maybe a week later she'd feel sorry and I'd feel rested and better.

Carlson, he doesn't dislike Perry very much: he likes Perry but he don't like the idea of my associating with him. But I don't care what people think. I don't worry about it. I don't have to report to anyone, especially any inmate. They're all small-minded. They probably think—if they have the choice between the good and bad—they all probably think the worst. Dobriski and I used to live in the same cell-block for years. We hung around together and were closer than brothers. O, we'd argue and we'd almost come to blows, but we'd always get back again and be friends.

L: '*But as Perry has more and more played the role of a mother to you, so Dobriski has more and more taken on the role of your father. Is that right?*'

Yes; I'm sure that's right. A long, long time ago we were playing down at the end of the yard and another friend of Dobriski's said something. We were rolling those balls and it was in the winter. Well, this fellow said something about my eyes. "What the hell is the matter with you? You're not too damned blind to see that, are you?" I got sore. I felt like hitting him with the ball but I threw it on the ground and walked away. Dobriski said he didn't hear it but I know he's a liar. And that reminded me of my father too, because one time I got into a fight with somebody about my eyes and my father hit me. I told Dobriski to get rid of him but for three months he kept hanging around with the fellow. He used to eat at the same table with us next to Dobriski. So I told Dobriski to get him off our table, to do anything to get rid of him, and it lasted like that for a few months. That was the first time I realized that there was something about him I disliked. I avoid him sometimes like I avoided my father. My father hit me one time when I was going to fight with somebody. I was only about sixteen and this guy was a man around forty-five. He was drunk and he said something about me in Polish. I started cursing him out and I was going to hit him. My father was there and he hit me from the back, hit me in the right ear. Then everything really started going bad with my father. I didn't want to talk to him at all. I always remember that and this incident with Dobriski reminded me of it again. They both seem to be about the same, Dobriski and my father.

You know . . . ripping up that match-box, now I know why. You see, I went outside and wanted to take a rest and I saw Dobriski with two other guys I dislike. These two fellows called him over and talked to him. So I called him a stooge and he got sore and I walked away. I was thinking about my father all the time. So I guess I was ripping the match-box just to take out on something how bad I was feeling . . .

THE FORTY-FIFTH HOUR

From what I am trying to understand about myself, why I've committed a lot of crimes, I think I was trying to prove to myself that I was more—superior than I was; that I was trying to prove my superiority. It's like myself are really two people and I try to prove to the other person that I'm more superior than he is. I would take a lot of risks and unnecessary chances, even when I went swimming or stealing, to prove myself superior to what I really was.

L: 'Let's return to the question of your stealing activities, Harold. Why did you take articles that didn't belong to you?'

Perhaps because I wanted to possess it . . .

L: 'And why did you want to possess it?'

Well—I—I—ever since I can remember—because—these things— my mother . . . Well, because ever since I can remember I wanted to possess—my—mother—more than anyone else . . .

L: 'Way back in your childhood you became definitely convinced that you could never surpass your father and possess your mother. How, then, did you possess things after that? By stealing, by taking, as substitutes, things forbidden to you. Does this explain to you why you went alone when you broke into a house? Can you understand the symbolism?'

It symbolizes—walking through a door—having an intercourse. Now I see . . . I—I couldn't have anyone else go with me. That was one way to—possess—my mother . . . Now I see. I can see—all these things—what they mean. And it is right.

L: 'Obviously you couldn't get things merely by asking for them. There was only one way for you to possess your mother, which is in many respects a perfectly normal childhood desire. In that stage of a child's life, the child is jealous of the father, so jealous that he actually wants to get him out of the way, even to kill him. We call that the 'Oedipus fixation.' Have you ever heard of that before?'

Yes. You told me a long time ago. It means the love of a son for his mother and dislike for his father.

L: 'Do you know the story of Oedipus?'

He is supposed to have been a Greek who killed his father and married his mother . . .

L: *'And he didn't know it at the time, just as you didn't know it until now. So you remained in that stage, at that level, instead of developing out of it as other children do.'*

Yes. My father was making money. He was bringing it home to my mother. He gave her things. I couldn't.

L: *'I wonder if this explains to you why you had intercourse with your sister?'*

My sister—is close to my mother. I always had a sort of feeling that she—that she—was my mother. I—I understand. I can see it all now. It's like a picture. I can see everything. It's—it's—it's all true: it's not hard to understand. I remember way back how I used to dislike my father even when I was a baby. I didn't like him. He always used to—lay with my mother all the time—and—even—when my sister was born—one reason why—I stuck my finger in her eye—was because I didn't like her because my mother would—take care of her too much. She had my cradle. I guess she was taking my place there when I got too big for the cradle. I thought I should still have it. I don't think I felt like that when the younger sister was born; but I could hear my mother crying when she was giving birth to her. I could hear her in the next room. I could hear my father talking to her. I was thinking that my father—was the cause of her being hurted. I was about ten years old then. I don't know what happened. I was in the room all by myself and it was dark and my mother was crying and I could hear my father talking to her and I know I was afraid of my father then. If he'd say something to my mother I didn't like and holler at her I resented it. I remember thinking about all that when I heard my mother crying in the next room.

I didn't have very much to do with him even when I was young. It always used to be my mother, even before my sister was born. I always thought that my mother liked me most as between my sister and myself: because my father thought more of my sister than of me I always thought my mother liked me better than my sister. My sister got more lickings from my mother than I did. When my mother gave me money to get out of the house when my father was home and she wanted me out of the house, why, I used to think that she thought more of me even then. But she never used to holler at me or scold me as much as she did my sisters. My oldest sister, she doesn't look like my mother; she has different hair and eyes and a different face.

L: 'Is that why you always wanted her to look more like your mother?'

Yes. I always liked to picture her as being quiet, never saying much, and weighing a little more than she does. I always wanted to picture her like my mother.

L: 'Did you ever steal from your sister?'

I guess I stole lipstick and things like that from her when I was about seventeen. She used to be fighting mad at me because she knew I did it.

L: 'Why did you steal lipstick from her?'

I used to hide it from her just for pleasure, just to hide it. When I went with girls I used to take their rings and hairpins and handker-chiefs. O, I'd collect everything, rings, necklaces, and when I got home I'd let my sister take anything she wanted. I gave her most of it, and now I understand why.

L: 'Why did you take these things from the girls?'

I didn't especially want them bad; but they—they had no great value for me—but now I see. I took them for the same reason I stole. O, yes; now I see. I was—my mother . . . I see it now.

There was a funny thing I remember now. I took a girl's handker-chief. Her name was Amy. She looked more like my mother than anyone else I ever knew. She was five or six months older than I was and she treated me just like a little baby; so I took her handkerchief and she got mad at me. I told her I'd never give it back to her. I took all the cigarettes out of my cigarette case and put the handker-chief in the case and dropped it in the river. I don't know why I threw that case away. It was a good case. It might have been for the same reason that . . . I remember I folded the handkerchief up and put it in the case and closed it, then I dropped it in the river. Throwing it in the river might mean that I wanted the handkerchief and the case to stay together for all time, so that nobody would ever disturb it; locked up in the cigarette case and at the bottom of the river so nobody would ever touch it again, especially not even my father.

L: 'Harold, when did you last sleep with your mother?'

The—the last time—I remember was when one of my sisters was about six or eight. That was about five or six years ago. My sisters used to sleep together and when my father and mother had an argument my mother would sleep with one of them and the other one would sleep with my father. I always slept in a bed all by myself. I remember sleeping with my mother but I don't remember when it was. O—I—one time when we lived on S———— Street . . . When we moved there I was about eleven or twelve and this was about when I was fourteen. My father used to go to work about six in the morning and I know I used to sleep on a bed my mother didn't want me to sleep on. It was a small bed. I thought it was alright but my mother used to pick me up and carry me over to her bed. Her bed was softer.

I never touched my mother. I—I was—afraid to touch her when she was in bed. I knew somehow that it was—forbidden. I never touched her. I was afraid to . . . When my father went to work early my mother would take me in her bed and I'd stay there until maybe eight o'clock, until it was time to get up and go to school.

My mother always gave me money; any time I wanted money she'd give it to me. I used to try different methods to get it from her. Sometimes I'd walk up and down, up and down, when she was trying to read, just to get her nervous: so finally she'd ask me why I was walking up and down and I'd tell her that I had nothing to do, and then she'd give me the money to get rid of me. Other times I'd put my arms around her quickly and kiss her and tell her how young and beautiful she looked. That was the more effective way. She'd always give me money when I did that.

It used to feel strange, sort of tingly, creepy-like when I lay in the same bed with my mother. If my mother awakened me when she picked me up and carried me to her bed, if I was really tired I'd fall asleep again. Sometimes I'd be asleep and I'd know my mother was there even in my sleep and I'd be afraid to touch her even if I wanted to. But it felt so—strange. I always felt I had no right to be there; that it was something I had no right to do. When I'd move or something my mother would say, "Lay still and don't move around so much!" When my sister and I were real young—I was about eight then—my father would go to work and sometimes in the morning we'd wake up and come in my mother's bed and we'd hit her with

pillows and she'd make believe she was mad.   But I was always
afraid, though.   I don't know what was the matter . . . .

I used to talk to my mother in any way I wanted to but I could
never say anything like that to my father.   My sister was just the
opposite: she could say anything to my father but not to my mother.
I could curse at my mother.   When she wanted me to do something
sometimes I'd say, "Hell, I'll do it some other time."   But I always
got along swell with her and we never had any trouble.   My mother
didn't like me to hang out with this gang I was running with.   One
reason she gave me money was to get rid of me and keep me away from
these kids.   She was always mad when I went in swimming.   I'd
go in swimming and my hair'd be wet when I got home and she'd raise
hell.   She'd tell me not to go swimming in three languages, but
finally it got so that she couldn't keep me out and I didn't listen to
her so she'd sigh and say, "Well, go ahead and don't bother me."

Well, so the reason I stole I see now comes from the fact that I never
got out of that Oedipus fixation stage, out of the stage where I wanted
my mother . . . And that's true.   I can see it all now, everything I did,
what it all means . . . When I wanted to steal something I'd hesitate
a while and then I'd tell myself not to be a coward, to go ahead and
do it.   A lot of times I'd have to force myself to do things.   I even
came close to killing my own father, but when I realized I couldn't fill
his shoes . . . Why didn't I come out of this stage, then?   Maybe I
would have lost that complex about my mother naturally if that
other fellow hadn't said anything.

L: 'In other words, Harold, you hurt that other fellow, in a sense, for
hinting at the truth.'

I guess I didn't want him to say anything like that.

My father is in the hospital now.   I don't know what's the matter
with him.   I sort of feel sorry for him.   This is the first time I ever
felt sorry for him.   Maybe that's because I understand myself
better now, understand that it isn't because of my father that I've
been doing these things, but because of the—memory deep down in
me from that—incident—I saw when I was a little baby.   Before
this, when he was sick—and he was real sick at times—I used to wish
he was dead, wish that he would die or go away.

L: 'Harold, as you said; you now feel sorry for your father because you
are beginning to understand these things.   The question now is, are you

*going to be able to pass the stage of mere understanding and go on to real
action? What are your relations with your father going to be after this?*
O, I'll never hurt him. ˙I'll be good to him and treat him decently.
I won't avoid him or anything—because I know—I should have
known a long time ago these things. My life, my whole life, is
changing. Yes. I put aside a lot of plans about stealing. That
Dobriski and I, we made a lot of plans what we were going to do when
we got outside, stealing mostly. But since a couple weeks ago I put
everything like that aside. I honestly did think I stole to get away
from home, get away from my father. My father I guess is a hard
man to get along with. Now I know what it was, why I couldn't
get along with him. Sometimes he used to talk to me decently and
when I think back on that I'm sorry about the whole thing, really
sorry.

L: *'Do you know what's wrong with your father?'*
He fractured his leg . . .
L: *'Have you written about it?'*
No. I have never said a word about him in my letters home. I
only got this letter yesterday. In all of the letters I've written home
I never said a word about him. When my mother mentioned him I
never liked to read about it. He's getting older now. He worked
hard for us. I remember when I was at my aunt's place I used to
think that my two sisters, my mother and myself, we could have a
nice little farm out there some day. I never included my father in
these plans. I know now why I didn't . . .

THE FORTY-SIXTH HOUR

L: *'Harold; have you been thinking about the things we've been discussing?'*
Yes. I've been thinking about it, and I was also thinking how it
really does connect. I know they do connect because sometimes I
can't think of anything right in this room and when I am four or five
hours by myself sometimes it will just come to me and I can refer to
it, associate it with something we said here. Everything we said is
true. I know something has happened to my eyes. I don't know
what it is but they never looked before like they look now. The
lenses are contracted and I can read small print now and they wink
about half as much as they did before. But the most important thing

is what's happened to me. Now that I know all these things I feel like a different person. I get along better with people now and I understand why I do things and I don't anymore act without thinking. There's lots of chance to get messed up in here, and now that I know why I want to do something I can keep myself from doing it. Before I would just do it and not think of why or what was going to happen. But about my eyes . . . A lot of specialists, doctors who treat nothing except diseases of the eye, they all said that the nerves are all good, that there is no reason my eyes were like that. My mother always thought it was due to the measles. Will measles have that effect on people's eyes?

L: '*Yes; measles can have an effect on the eyes; it may make them more sensitive to light. But it is very doubtful that such was the complete situation in your case. As a matter of fact, we know that your eyes were winking before you had the measles: therefore your winking certainly could not have been due to it. The measles, though, might well have reenforced the original condition. You had this traumatic, that is, shocklike. incident in your early life, and that appears to be the original cause of your winking. Now when you got the measles, this condition was undoubtedly aggravated. You see, physicians tell us that many diseases follow this process: the disease effects what is called the 'area of least resistance' in your body. Suppose, for instance, that a germ enters your body, and there already is a weakness (let us say) in your kidneys. It's quite likely, then, that this germ will settle in your kidney because its natural powers of resistance are already weakened. Now in your case it's perfectly possible that the measles may have affected your eyes, because your eyes were already weakened.*'

But now, within the last few months and especially the last few weeks, they wink much less. Before I could never keep them open at all for more than a second or so. They wink much less and I can see a lot better . . .

Doc, I wonder if you would please go through the whole thing, like a summary of the whole business?

L: '*If you wish.*

'*It all goes back to that morning. Now the night before; I think we can say with assurance that the night before was a Saturday night, and that evening you went to the moving pictures with your mother and your father. You were between six and eight months old. You were in your mother's arm, half-sitting, half-lying, and your father was sitting on the other side. You were looking across your mother and saw your father. The theatre was dark except for the lights coming from the projecting booth. Now on the screen you saw the face and figure of a dog or a wolf (probably a dog, probably Rin-tin-tin who was popular around that time), so that the face of the dog became closely associated with the light from the projecting room. You could see the light shining, as it were, directly on the dog. You were frightened by the dog, by what you saw, and you may or may not have been crying—whether you were or were not is unimportant: you were afraid.*

'Now the following morning you awaken early. Your mother is lying on the right side of her bed; your cradle is near her. You look across—the same way as you looked across from your mother's arms the evening before—and you see your father. You see him, and it looks as if he is hurting your mother. As a matter of fact he is lying on her. His face is hard; his eyes are hard; but your mother's eyes are tender and she looks as if she is being hurt. As your father withdraws, you see his penis. It looks to you like a strange, vicious animal. It looks like an instrument that can hurt, for you immediately apprehend that it is this which is hurting your mother. And you were afraid of it because you dimly knew that seeing your father and mother in that position was something you weren't supposed to see: and the reason you knew you weren't supposed to see it was because your mother pushed your father off and pointed to you, and he stopped what he was doing and removed himself. And then you were afraid of it because you thought it was going to hurt you.

'Now your mother gets out of bed. She comes over to your cradle and takes you out and into the other room, to the breakfast table. Your father comes in. At the breakfast table you look at your father; and immediately the shock of what just happened and the shock of the events of the night before, become associated directly with him. You look at him and you are afraid of him, of him and of his penis. Everything he does reminds you of these things that have happened. There is an awful amount of fear there. As a child, you feel it, and you start to cry. And as you start to cry it seems to you as if the whole room is getting black. All these events have served to remind you (since with a child so young all time is condensed and there are no sharp lines to divide time) of the night before, at the moving picture, where the blackness was pierced by the light

from the projecting room. Now you seem to see it coming from your father's eyes. His face seems all 'cut-up' just like the face of the dog you saw in the movie.

'Your mother placates you and calms you. But immediately you are completely alienated from your father, afraid of him. He reminds you of the things that caused you discomfort, fear, terror. And the fear of his penis, which seemed to you to be a threatening, dangerous and brutal weapon, thrusts you even more upon your mother, whom you believed it had hurt.

'So you closed your eyes. You ran away from it. The winking has come from the association of all this fear with the event you had witnessed. As we have seen, one way of running away from something is to close your eyes to it. Because for you the whole thing centered in your eyes. The eyes were the guilty organs. They were guilty of having seen that which they were forbidden to see. Now the fear of your father's penis— and all it meant—followed you through all your life. You have always felt afraid and inadequate and aggressive toward your father because your weapon was not as big or as powerful as your father's. So you later played with knives and guns: you stole money to buy guns. You were trying to convince yourself that you had a penis; trying to prove yourself as good as your father. And all the while the original dependence upon your mother became re-enforced as it became increasingly evident that you could never accept your father's relations with your mother, or reconcile yourself to him in view of your fear of him.

'Now every male child—or at any rate most male children—go through a period of such 'castration fears,' fears of losing the penis. You were afraid your father would steal this thing from you, would take it away. Your father actually threatened to have his dog bite it off.'

Yes; it was my father's dog. It would only listen to him . . .

L: *'And remember: when you saw your father that morning, he reminded you of the dog in the show the night before.*

'All your life you have been haunted by these castration fears and anxieties. That's one reason why you masturbated frequently. It was a very good way of convincing yourself from time to time that you were still manly, you still had a penis. And always it was closely associated with your eyes. It always has been. You even thought later on that when people looked at your eyes they could tell that you had been masturbating. So that's really why you closed your eyes: to shut out that first sight, that first knowledge. You had a deep feeling of guilt and you were afraid . . .

so you hid your eyes. All through your life this relationship—your father's eyes and his penis to your eyes and your fear of his penis—has been following you.'

Yes—yes. I can see it all. I can see it all now. That's why I took those knives and that pen knife from him.

I always thought I couldn't get along with my father, talk to him in a sensible way. When I'd say anything to him he'd always be right and I'd always be wrong. I always thought that was one way to keep apart, one reason we didn't talk together much; but I see now I had reasons to show him that I was as good as he was. He was stronger than me, so I was afraid of him. He'd tell me I was wrong so I wouldn't say anything to him.

L: 'And you were always afraid he'd have you castrated.'

O, yes. Maybe two years ago they were going to sterilize all convicts, people said. I laughed it off in front of everybody but I thought about it and thought about it. I never told anyone but I was afraid, so afraid. As a matter of fact, that idea has been in the back of my head for as long as I can remember . . .

My mother was always good to me. I always could talk to my mother. When my father threatened to sic the dog on me to bite my penis off my mother comforted me and said the dog wouldn't do it. She called the dog over, and when the dog had its paws on my lap I was afraid of him. Later on I started petting him myself . . .

L: 'To a child, things of that sort are very serious, crucial. It had, in your case, plenty of background as well. The soil was well prepared. First there was that very traumatic incident accompanied by the fear of your father's organ; then the deep fixation on your mother; then the castration fears. As a result, all your life you've felt inadequate, castrated. You could never do anything, never get anywhere.'

Even when I was growing up, from the time I was fourteen, I remember I always used to think in the back of my mind that the other fellows were better than me at driving a car, or swimming, or making some pretty girls, or in school. I was really a bright kid in school though, the best of all the boys in most of my classes. And swimming—I could swim and drive a car pretty well but . . . As a matter of fact, when I had intercourse with a girl I never liked to look at or touch her genitals, because they made me think of a castrated man, or made me think about not having genitals myself . . .

And then that—accident . . . I see I did it to get rid of my father somehow without really having to get rid of *him*. The whole thing fits. I'm sorry about that. I wish . . .

L: '*And the stealing?*'

The stealing? It—I—it was because I—wanted my mother and that was . . . I wasn't allowed to have her. So I stole things. I went into houses alone because I—didn't—want anybody else to—have her . . .

Yes. It's all right now. I even *feel* it now.

L: '*Now that you understand these things, Harold, we shall have to have a period of re-education before we are finished. We want to accomplish a complete change in your attitude toward yourself and the rest of the world. The eyes will take care of themselves. They are unimportant compared with the complete overhauling of your personality and life. There is nothing more to fear now.*'

I can see everything as it went by . . . All the years. All the things changed, the symbols changed and that's all; but what they stood for was still there. I used to be so afraid of his big arms and hands, afraid he'd beat me with them, so I went through many things. I can see now how it—all—made steps, all along, all the ways up . . .

Here Harold was placed in a deep hynotic sleep. Under hypnosis, he was requested to review the entire case and demonstrate his understanding of it. He was also asked to review the writer's summary and his own remarks as they occurred in the final hour. Finally, his comprehension was re-enforced by suggestion . . .

AUTHOR'S NOTE

Some months after the case had been closed, and after painstaking investigation, it was discovered that—significantly enough—the stabbing incident ended not in the death but in the complete and rather uneventful recovery of the victim. This, of course, resolved the writer's conflict as expressed on page 195. Harold, however, was allowed for some weeks to remain convinced that he had "killed" his antagonist; and only after the parricidal motive had again been fully discussed with him was this disclosure made.

It is a curious psychological phenomenon that Harold so readily and unquestioningly accepted the guilt for his abortive attempt to utilize a primitive mechanism to resolve his basic conflict.

SUMMARY

I

Through hypnoanalysis we have been able to obtain meaningful insights into the psychogenesis of the criminal psychopathic state. For the first time, we have been privileged to penetrate beneath the armor which persons of such classification present to the world, and to view in all their sinister automaticity the operationism of the responsible mechanisms. With but little effort we can reconstruct the peculiar constellation of events which formed the attitudes that influenced Harold's later behavior. We have observed the introjective process at work as it split off from the environment and absorbed all those singular and crucial events which later crystallized into habits of response and particular ways of viewing the setting against which subsequent behavior was enacted. The case of Harold supports the tentative speculations regarding the precipitation of psychopathy which have already been advanced in this volume. It testifies to the dynamic centralism of such motivants as the unresolved Oedipus situation or castration anxiety. In a word, it verifies the major but until now unproven hypotheses of the traditional psychoanalytic view of this entity.

The prepotency of hypnoanalysis could have been demonstrated with no greater forcefulness than it has been through its success with psychopathic personality, a condition which has resisted other investigative and therapeutic techniques. It is quite likely that the resistant nature of this disorder derives from the fact that it engulfs the *whole* personality, somewhat in the manner of a psychosis, from the very earliest age, and that one of its peculiar symptoms is an inability to come into rapport with anyone. At any rate, it wanted an instrument capable of making a frontal as well as a flanking assault upon the organism. It needed a technique of sufficiently active incisiveness to plunge into the farthest reaches of awareness and extract from therein, *in toto*, the historic scenes that were too painful to be faced without preparation.

If these sentences about hypnoanalysis ring with a note of confidence that seems unjustified with only a single case in evidence, the reader is reminded that the technique herein offered was utilized in other instances of psychopathic personality and a miscellany of other diagnositic entities. *In each case of psychopathy, essentially the same dynamisms were exposed as in Harold's case.* Of a series of six (including Harold's) the only discoverable differences were in the *dramatis personae* and—in all the others—a lack of the particular optic defect. One of the remaining five showed a biological anomaly; the other four were free of physical taint. Again, two of the six were products of the orphanage, one was brought up in a foster home and the others, like Harold, were reared by their own parents. In every case, not only were the precipitating events patently similar, but the broad outlines of individual history resolved into the unmistakable pattern shown by Harold's case. And, finally, each of the six cases has demonstrated by subsequent behavior and all those other signs on which a clinical evaluation of therapeutic success is based, the persistence at least to the time of this writing of the benefits of treatment.

The hypnoanalytic technique has been refined continually through direct employment either in an investigative or therapeutic way in a variety of cases. During the past five years, in addition to the six psychopaths already mentioned, the following variants were also studied: one male hysterical somnambulist, one sexually frigid woman, one feebleminded psychotic boy, two male anxiety neurotics, one male bronchial asthmatic, three male homosexuals, one male alcoholic, and one male kleptomaniac. None of the analyses exceeded four months and all of the subjects (with the exception of the frigid woman who was forced to abandon treatment) are today better off in every way for having gone through with it. Each case served as a crucible wherein our instrument of research and treatment was further shaped and hardened, enhancing particularly those aspects of the art of its application which cannot ever be communicated by the written word.

In strict fairness to psychoanalysis as an explanatory way of approach to the personality, it must be said that nothing new in the way of interpretation of behavior results from hypnoanalysis: that it tends rather to verify and substantiate the insights into behavior-dynamics which the psychoanalytic approach affords. For example, in the case where it was employed with an hysterical somnambulist, it exposed the primitive phantasy basic to the hysterical reaction and dissected out its components of latent homosexuality, sadism and castration-anxiety composed pre-Oedipally and transformed into the somnambulistic symptom. Apart from the unique concatenation observed with this patient, nothing appeared which either was not already known about hysteria or could not have become known from a psychoanalysis. The method of hypnoanalysis, however, made these items known more rapidly, provided more adequately for complete abreaction and so for a 'cure' for the condition. Furthermore, the 'fresh' insights into hysterical somnambulism which are claimed as regards symptom-formation and symptom-function were achieved by hypnoanalysis, it is true, but were the result of psychoanalytical regard and stemmed from propositions basic to psychoanalysis.

In short, hypnoanalysis is a radically abbreviated method for the investigation of the personality and the treatment of psychogenic disorders and aberrations of behavior.

So far there has been no direct mention of the curative value of hypnoanalysis. 'Cured' in an analytical sense carries a somewhat different meaning than 'cured' in a medical and lay sense: it implies rather than an amelioration of symptom or a disappearance of disease the accomplishment of an essential personality change which is the outcome of the redistribution of psychological energy formerly exploited by the pathological condition. In some cases symptoms do disappear entirely, and the medical sense of 'cure' can be used. The hysterical patient, for instance, has had no recurrence of the somnambulistic episodes since hypnoanalysis: the alcoholic patient is no more a slave to the bottle: the asthmatic no longer experiences intense attacks accompanied by 'death-threat' and panic. In other cases, what is accomplished is the cultivation of an ability on the part of the patient to *live with* his condition (so to speak), to accept it, even to "make the best of it." Such was the outcome with two of the three homosexuals who were studied and treated hypnoanalytically. In yet other conditions—in our series the remaining homosexual, the two anxiety neurotics and psychopaths—what is done appears as an alteration, permanent and deep-seated, of the patient's style of life.

In the case reviewed, the patient was 'cured' in the sense of alteration of style of life, and imbued with a real ability to live with his particular occular symptom. The alteration was based on what some psychologists call 'insight,' on a real understanding of the past and a reorientation of attitudes and aims. Harold today sees better, feels better, behaves better. Individuals who know him and work with him comment on his radically altered pattern of behavior. Gone is that sneering sullenness, that arrogant aggression, that Storm-Trooper mentality, that disregard for the rights and feelings of others. He knows that he was a psychopath: he knows why he was a psycho-path: he knows that he needs to be a psychopath no more. . . .

II

We have had in this volume a striking illustration of the truth of William A. White's remark that behind every criminal deed lies a secret. But more important, we have glimpsed the utter futility, the sheer waste, of confining individuals in barred and turretted zoos for humans without attempting to recover such secrets. Harold's case makes a mockery of current penological pretense. It points the finger of ridicule at the sterile corridors of modern prisons, the gleaming shops and factories, the bright young social workers, the custodial hierarchy—in brief, the whole hollow structure of rehabilitation that is based upon expediency, untested hypotheses, unwarranted conclusions from a pseudo-scientific empiricism.

Harold plundered and almost killed in response to those ungovernable needs which came flaring up from the deepest, remotest shafts of his being. Had he not undertaken analysis, all the trade-training, all the attentions of penal personnel would have been wasted on him; and like every other psychopath who leaves prison he would have been released again to the community as the same predatory beast who entered—with this exception: that his conflicts would have been driven more deeply and his hostility aggravated by a system that flatters itself that it is doing other than substituting psychological for physical brutality.

In spite of the self-flattery in which criminologists, penologists and the assorted professional and warder complement of the modern prison indulge, we are not today treating criminals; and, what is worse, in only a few isolated instances are we even learning anything about them. In all its bald essence, what we are actually doing today is removing a wrong-doer from the community; and while he is in a place of detention we are submitting him unmercifully to the unrequiting ministrations of an expensive officialdom. But beyond the half-hearted employment of a "shot-gun" technique which fires its charge in all directions at once, *we do nothing fundamental about crime or the criminal.*

There are two approaches to crime, each as important and vital as the other: one from the side of the community, one from the side of the specialist in behavior. Criminal acts are not so simple as our legal code or our sensation-mongering newspapers would have us believe. Crime is behavior which is motivated by prime forces that are not only social but intra-individual. It is precipitated by sociological situations, perhaps, but it is an individual expression that arises from the secret motives or wishes that lie buried deep within the personality.

The need is for an extension to the very limits of the type of activity which has been demonstrated in Harold's case; for such processing not only often changes the criminal into a useful citizen (always assuming that society will permit him to be an integral part of it when he is released), but it also teaches us lessons about crime that we can use with our and other people's children. . . .

BIBLIOGRAPHY

(N.B. Those references which are marked with an asterisk will be found helpful and instructive in those cases where a reader wishes additional background in psychoanalysis, hypnosis, psychopathy or criminology.)

ABRAHAM, K. *Selected Papers on Psychoanalysis.* Hogarth Press: London, 1927.
ADLER, A. *Studie über die Minderwertigkeit von Organen.* Bergman: Muenchen, 1907.
ALEXANDER, F. *Psychoanalysis of the Total Personality.* Hogarth Press: London, 1927.
*ALEXANDER, F. AND HEALY, W. *The Roots of Crime.* Alfred A. Knopf: New York, 1935.
*BARNES, H. E. AND TEETERS, N. K. *New Horizons in Criminology.* Prentice-Hall: New York, 1943.
BAUDOIN, C. *Suggestion and Autosuggestion.* Allen & Unwin: London, 1920.
*BRAMWELL, J. M. *Hypnotism, Its History, Practice and Theory.* Moring: London, 1906.
BREUER, J. AND FREUD, S. *Studies in Hysteria.* Nerv. & Ment. Dis. Pub. Co.: New York, 1936.
BRILL, A. A. *Psychoanalysis: Its Theories and Practical Application.* W. B. Saunders: Philadelphia, 1913.
*CANNON, W. B. *The Wisdom of the Body.* W. W. Norton: New York, 1932.
CANNON, W. B. Organization for physiological homeostasis. *Physiol. Rev.,* 9, 1929.
CASON, H. (ed.) *Summaries of Literature on Constitutional Psychopathy.* (5 vols. mimeo.) Springfield, Mo., 1942.
*CLECKLEY, H. *The Mask of Sanity.* C. V. Mosby: St. Louis, 1941.
ERICKSON, M. H. AND KUBIE, L. S. The successful treatment of a case of acute hysterical depression by a return under hypnosis to a critical phase of childhood. *Psychoanal. Quart.,* 10, 1941, 583.
FENICHEL, O. *Clinical Psychoanalysis.* W. W. Norton: New York, 1934.
FERENCZI, S. The role of transference in hypnosis and suggestion. *Contributions to Psychoanalysis.* R. G. Badger: Boston, 1916.
FERENCZI, S. *Theory and Technique of Psychoanalysis.* Hogarth Press: London, 1926.
FREUD, A. *The Ego and the Mechanisms of Defense.* Hogarth Press: London, 1937.
FREUD, S. *Collected Papers.* (4 vols.) Hogarth Press: London, 1924–25.
*FREUD, S. *The Interpretation of Dreams.* Allen & Unwin: London, 1915.
FREUD, S. *Beyond the Pleasure Principle.* Hogarth Press: London, 1922.
FREUD, S. *The Ego and the Id.* Hogarth Press: London, 1928.
*FREUD, S. *New Introductory Lectures on Psychoanalysis.* Hogarth Press, London, 1933.
*FREUD, S. *A General Introduction to Psychoanalysis.* Liveright: New York, 1935.
FREUD, S. *The Problem of Anxiety.* W. W. Norton: New York, 1936.
FRIEDLANDER, J. W. AND SARBIN, T. R. The depth of hypnosis. *J. Abnorm. & Soc Psychol.,* 33, 1938, 453.

FORSYTHE, D. *The Technique of Psychoanalysis.* Kegan Paul: London, 1933.
GLUECK, B. Psychological motive in criminal action. *J. Crim. Psychopathol.*, **2**, 1940, 21.
*GLUECK, S. AND GLUECK, E. T. *Five-Hundred Criminal Careers.* Alfred A. Knopf: New York, 1930.
HEALY, W., BRONNER, A. AND BOWERS, A. *The Structure and Meaning of Psychoanalysis.* Alfred A. Knopf: New York, 1930.
HENDERSON, D. K. *Psychopathic States.* W. W. Norton: New York, 1939.
HENDRICKS, I. *Facts and Theories of Psychoanalysis.* Alfred A. Knopf: New York, 1939.
HITLER, A. *Mein Kampf.* Reynal & Hitchcock: New York, 1940.
*HORNEY, K. *New Ways in Psychoanalysis.* W. W. Norton: New York, 1939.
HULL, C. L. *Hypnosis and Suggestibility: An Experimental Approach.* Appleton-Century: New York, 1933.
JANET, P. *The Major Symptoms of Hysteria.* Macmillan: New York, 1920.
JANET, P. *Psychological Healing.* Macmillan: New York, 1925.
JELLIFFE, S. E. *Sketches in Psychosomatic Medicine.* Nerv. & Ment. Dis. Pub. Co.: New York, 1939.
JONES, E. *Treatment of the Neuroses.* Wm. Wood: Baltimore, 1920.
JONES, E. *Psychoanalysis.* Cope & Smith: New York, 1929.
JUNG, C. G. *Two Essays on Analytic Psychology.* Bailliere, Tindall & Cox: London, 1928.
JUNG, C. G. *The Integration of the Personality.* Farrar & Rinehart: New York, 1939.
*KAHN, E. *Psychopathic Personalities.* Yale Univ. Press: New Haven, 1931.
KARPMAN, B. *The Individual Criminal.* Nerv. & Ment. Dis. Pub. Co.: Washington, D. C., 1935.
KOCH, I. L. *Die psychopathischen Minderwertigkeiten.* Maier: Ravensburg, 1893.
KUBIE, L. *Practical Aspects of Psychoanalysis.* W. W. Norton: New York, 1936.
*LICHTENBERGER, H. *The Third Reich.* Greystone Press: New York, 1937.
LINDNER, R. M. Homeostasis as an explanatory concept in psychopathic personality. *Proceedings of the 72nd Annual Congress of Correction of the American Prison Association*, New York, 1942.
LINDNER, R. M. Experimental studies in constitutional psychopathic inferiority. *J. Crim. Psychopathol.*, **4**, 1942, 1943, 252, 484.
LINDNER, R. M. Hypnoanalysis in a case of hysterical somnambulism. (mss. in press), *Psychoanal. Rev.*, 1944.
LORAND, S. *Psychoanalysis Today: Its Scope and Function.* Covici, Friede: New York, 1933.
MAUGHS, S. A concept of psychopathy and psychopathic personality: its evolution and historical development. *J. Crim. Psychopathol.*, **2**, 1941, 329.
*MUMFORD, L. *The Culture of Cities.* Harcourt, Brace: New York, 1938.
ORR, D. W. Is there a homeostatic instinct? *Psychoanal. Quart.*, **11**, 1942, 332.
PARTRIDGE, G. E. Current conceptions of psychopathic personality. *Amer. J. Psychiat.*, **10**, 1930, 53.
PLATONOW, K. I. On the objective proof of the experimental age regression. *J. Exper. Psychol.*, **10**, 1933, 190.

ROSANOFF, A. J. ET AL. The etiology of child behavior difficulties, etc. *Psychiat. Monog.* # 1, 1941.

SCHNEIDER, K. Die psychopathischen Persönlichkeiten. *Aschaffenburgs Handb. d Psychiat.*, 2 aufl., Leipzig, 1928.

SCHILDER, P. *Introduction to a Psychoanalytic Psychiatry.* Nerv. & Ment. Dis Pub Co.: New York, 1928.

SILVERMAN, D. Clinical and electroencephalographic studies on criminal psychopaths. *Arch. Neurol. Psychiat.*, 50, 1943, 18.

STEKEL, W. *Conditions of Nervous Anxiety and their Treatment.* Dodd, Mead: New York, 1923.

STEKEL, W. *Technique of Analytical Psychotherapy.* W. W. Norton: New York, 1940.

*WARNER, W. L. AND LUNT, P. S. *The Social Life of a Modern Community.* Yale Univ. Press: New York, 1941.

*WOHLGEMUTH, A. *A Critical Examination of Psychoanalysis.* Allen & Unwin: London, 1923.

INDEX

For the convenience of the reader, this index has been prepared to serve a dual purpose. The page references and listings in italics refer to the case history and the hypnoanalytical portions of the study. Those listings and page references in regular type refer to the remainder of the volume.